A Mighty Fleet and the King's Power

A Mighty Fleet and the King's Power

The Isle of Man

AD 400 to 1265

Tim Clarkson

First published in Great Britain in 2023 by
John Donald, an imprint of Birlinn Ltd

West Newington House
10 Newington Road
Edinburgh
EH9 1QS

www.birlinn.co.uk

ISBN: 978 1 910900 80 2

British Library Cataloguing-in-Publication Data
A catalogue record for this book is available on request from the British Library

Typeset by Initial Typesetting Services, Edinburgh
Printed and bound in Britain by Clays Ltd, Elcograf S.p.A.

CONTENTS

LIST OF PLATES

LIST OF MAPS

GENEALOGICAL TABLES

The Crovan dynasty, c.1079 to 1265

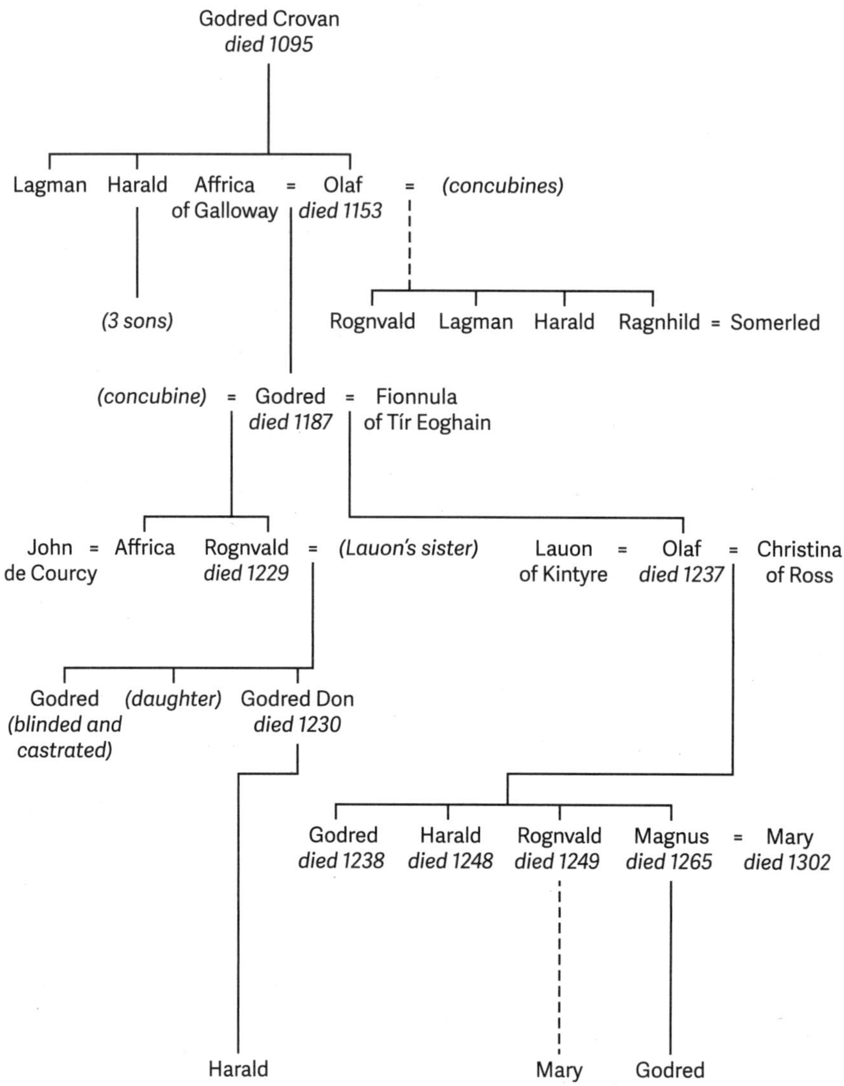

--- *uncertain descent*

The ancestry of Merfyn Frych and Rhodri Mawr

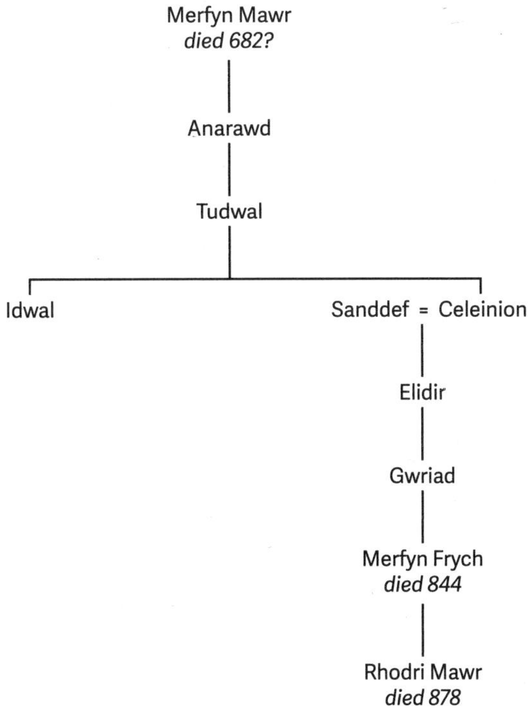

Britain, Ireland and the Isle of Man
N
W
E
S
Shetland
Orkney
Western Isles
Caithness
Hebrides
Moray
ALBA
(Scotland)
Iona
Argyll
Fife
Firth of Forth
North
Sea
Glasgow
Edinburgh
Lothian
STRATHCLYDE
Firth of Clyde
North Channel
Antrim
Galloway
Solway Firth
Ulster
NORTHUMBRIA
Man
Ireland
Irish
Sea
York
Connacht
Dublin
Chester
Anglesey
Gwynedd
England
Leinster
Powys
EAST
ANGLIA
Waterford
Munster
St George's
Channel
Wales
MERCIA
Dyfed
Gwent
ESSEX
WESSEX
London
KENT
SUSSEX
Cornwall
English Channel
0
50
100 km
0
50 miles

1

INTRODUCTION

This book is about a small island in the Irish Sea that has its own identity, its own language and its own remarkable story. *Ellan Vannin*, the Isle of Man, is best known to the inhabitants of the larger countries that surround it as a holiday destination, accessible by aeroplane or ferry from Britain and Ireland or from other, more distant countries. Few people outside Man are likely to know much of its history, although a larger number are no doubt aware of the Tourist Trophy or 'TT' motorcycle races for which it is rightly famed. Many will recognise the distinctive Three Legs emblem that appears on the Manx flag and in various contexts around the island. Anyone who has visited as holidaymaker or motorcycle enthusiast will know that Man has its own government and, while being British in many ways, is not part of the United Kingdom. Indeed, at one time it had its own kings and was the chief centre of power in an extensive maritime kingdom stretching northward to the Hebrides. The last of those kings died nearly eight centuries ago. The dynasty to which he belonged had ruled for some 200 years, having been founded by a Viking warlord called Godred Crovan in the last quarter of the eleventh century. Godred's fame has long since turned him into a mighty figure of legend, an ancestral hero who will one day return to protect the Manx people. He is one of many individuals who have played significant roles in the story of the Isle of Man since it first appeared in historical records 2,000 years ago. This book aims to tell one of the early parts of that story, from the fifth century to the thirteenth.

Objectives and scope

The written history of Britian and Ireland in medieval times, in so far as it has been preserved in contemporary texts, is essentially a tale of kings and kingdoms. There is, of course, much more to any region's history than the recorded deeds of its rulers, but these are the people whom medieval writers in Britain and Ireland tended to focus upon. Other high-status groups, such as the landowning nobility and senior clergy, likewise received similar attention because of their close connection with royalty. Groups at the opposite end of the social hierarchy are glimpsed only rarely, their stories largely left untold unless modern archaeology reveals something of how they lived. From the contemporary texts we thus glean little about the folk who were landless, poor or unfree. This book, being primarily a study of political history, necessarily concentrates on people of royal or noble stock. It looks at the various ways in which they interacted with one another in both the secular and ecclesiastical spheres. In so doing, it strives to reconstruct a narrative history of the Isle of Man in a period for which contemporary information is lacking. The dearth of source material means that the account is often fragmented, with many large gaps that only a measure of informed speculation by the modern historian can repair.

This book is a study of history, not of archaeology. Some archaeological information is utilised, especially in those instances where it sheds light on the historical narrative, but there is here no detailed account of sites and artefacts. Manx archaeology is a big subject with an ever-growing specialist literature and an enthusiastic community of experts, students and interested observers. Archaeological finds from around the island can be encountered at first hand in places such as the Manx Museum in Douglas, or – in the case of early medieval Christian sculpture – at local churches and churchyards. References to the relevant archaeological literature can be found in the chapter endnotes at the end of this book, which serve as signposts to the bibliography.

Chronology and terminology

The main narrative of this book encompasses a period of roughly 850 years, from the end of Roman rule in Britain around AD 410 to the death of the last king of the Crovan dynasty in 1265. To this timespan is added a short prologue at the beginning and an epilogue at the end. In broad chronological terms, the book's main focus is the early medieval period or Early Middle Ages – an era commonly seen as encompassing the period 400 to 1100 – together with a further 160 years to accommodate the Manx royal dynasty founded by Godred Crovan. The narrative therefore includes much of the period known as the Central Middle Ages, spanning four centuries from 900 to 1300.[1] A substantial portion of the book inevitably deals with the Viking Age, the chronological limits of which – in Britain, at least – are usually defined by two significant events: the Norse raid on Lindisfarne in 793 and the Battle of Stamford Bridge in 1066. Historians nevertheless recognise that many of the characteristics of 'Viking-type' activity continued well beyond the eleventh century in the Irish Sea region and in the maritime zones lying off the northern and western coasts of Scotland. Moreover, in all of these areas – which include the Isle of Man together with the archipelagos of Orkney, Shetland and the Hebrides – political connections with Scandinavia were maintained well into the 1200s. Here, unlike in the rest of Britain, the Viking Age lingered on, long after the conventional landmark date of 1066. Some historians of medieval Scotland, seeking a chronological label for this extended timeframe, speak of the 'Long Viking Age'. Others, including many archaeologists, prefer 'Late Norse', and this is the term adopted in the following chapters.[2]

The main geographical focus of this book is the Isle of Man (or Mann). Of these two spellings the first is here preferred, for no particular reason beyond the author's personal choice. The ways in which some other names of places or peoples are used in the narrative may, however, require explanation, especially for readers who are unfamiliar with early medieval history. The term 'Britons', for example, had a much more specific meaning a thousand years ago than it does today. To writers of the period after c.400 and before c.1200 it denoted a specific group of people: the 'native' inhabitants of Britain in areas south of what is now the Central Belt of Scotland between the firths of Forth and Clyde. The term did not encompass more recent arrivals, such as the English, nor the people living north of the Forth–Clyde line despite their being no less indigenous than their southern neighbours. These northerners, whose lands included the far island groups of Orkney and Shetland, were known in Late Roman texts as *Picti*, 'Picts', despite having been regarded by earlier classical writers as *Britanni*, 'Britons'. Another group, the Scots, originated in what are now the coastlands and islands of Argyll and the Hebridean region. According to their own foundation legends, their ancestors were immigrants from Ireland. Their name, recorded by Roman writers in the Latin form *Scotti*, perhaps originally meant something like 'Gaelic speakers'.[3] This brings us onto the subject of languages and to the ones spoken in the period and area under study here. Gaelic is a Celtic language spoken today in Ireland, Scotland and the Isle of Man. Each of these countries uses its own variant of what was once a single Gaelic or 'Goidelic' language. A different Celtic language, known to modern scholars as Brittonic or Brythonic, was spoken by the Britons. It, too, survives today in three regional forms: Welsh, Cornish and Breton. A form of

Brittonic was also spoken by the Picts before their adoption of Gaelic c.900, their replacing of one language for another having probably begun in the eighth century. Linguistic change in Pictland went hand in hand with political developments that saw Picts and Scots eventually merge together as one people ruled by a single royal dynasty and inhabiting a new, unified kingdom. The latter, known as Alba, was the precursor of the great medieval kingdom of Scotland. Alba's birth coincided with the emergence of a unified kingdom of England from a number of smaller kingdoms ruled by early English ('Anglo-Saxon') dynasties. The English spoke a Germanic language that had been brought to parts of eastern and southern Britain in Late Roman and Post-Roman times by migrants from Germany, Denmark and adjacent North Sea coastlands. More is said of the early English in the third and fourth chapters of this book. Their early kingdoms in Britain were mostly founded in the sixth century and were already well established when another Germanic-speaking group appeared at the end of the eighth century. This new wave of incomers is known collectively as 'Vikings'. The origin and meaning of this term are matters of debate but in a broad sense it refers to people of Scandinavian heritage who engaged in seafaring activity – raiding, trading or colonising – in foreign lands. The Vikings who sailed to Britain and Ireland originated mostly in Norway and Denmark, although some doubtless came from Sweden and from other lands around the Baltic and North Seas. Many of the early raids can be attributed to Norwegians, a people who in a medieval context are often referred to as 'Norse'. Raids by Norsemen began in the 790s and continued with increasing frequency into the early 800s. By the middle of the ninth century, the range of their activity had broadened from raiding to include trade and colonisation. Their language – Old Norse – was spoken in many parts of Ireland and Britain after they eventually settled down to become farmers, merchants and landowners. Among the various Viking groups in the seaways between Britain and Ireland were a number of individuals whose stories are closely connected with Manx history. These figures take key roles in this book's unfolding narrative.

The chronological structure of this book means that there are no chapters dealing with particular themes. The main narrative simply moves forward through time, from the last phase of Roman rule in Britain to the end of the Late Norse period. It begins in the second chapter where, after a preamble describing the Manx landscape and summarising the history of human settlement on the island, it moves through the Iron Age to consider the question of whether the Romans ever set foot on Man. Chapter 3 marks the beginning of the early medieval period, around the time when Roman rule in Britain effectively ceased. It looks at the founding of kingdoms on both sides of the Irish Sea and at the role of Man as a contested territory between ambitious warrior-kings in Ireland and Britain. This chapter also considers the beginnings of Manx Christianity in the fifth and sixth centuries, looking at traditions surrounding the island's early saints. In the fourth chapter, the narrative moves into the seventh century and to the heyday of Northumbria, the most northerly kingdom of the Anglo-Saxons or early English. Northumbrian contacts with Man are noted, as is Northumbria's influence on Manx culture. The chapter ends in the middle of the eighth century, not long before the Northumbrians first began to experience Viking raids. Chapter 5 takes the narrative into the ninth century, shifting the focus to the Welsh kingdom of Gwynedd. Our spotlight falls on a royal dynasty that ruled Gwynedd from the early 800s and which is regarded by some historians as having Manx origins. To what extent this is the correct interpretation of the data is one of the questions examined here.

The Vikings make their presence felt in Chapter 6, which discusses the first phase of their attacks on Britain and Ireland, the period of colonisation that followed and the political upheavals that accompanied it. We here see Man as one of a number of areas colonised in the final quarter of the ninth century, a generation or so later than Ireland or the Northern Isles of Orkney and Shetland. Indeed, the main phase of Viking settlement on Man appears to have been a secondary colonisation by people from older Norse settlements in Ireland and elsewhere. The book's seventh chapter then takes us from the late tenth century to the late eleventh, a period in which Man was caught up in a long-running contest for mastery of the Irish Sea region. The main protagonists were warlords of mixed Norse-Gaelic heritage together with ambitious kings from various Irish, Scottish, English and Scandinavian lands. In Chapter 8 we come face to face with the renowned Godred Crovan, founder of a royal dynasty that would rule Man for the next 200 years. We then follow the story of Godred's heirs and descendants into the twelfth century, as far as c.1150. It was around this time that the mighty Hebridean warlord Somerled began to emerge and, in Chapter 9, we see him in conflict with fellow Norse-Gaels in 'The Isles' (Man and the Hebrides). The same chapter and the next continue to tell the story of the Crovan kings of Man, with Chapter 10 bringing us to the last of them. His passing in 1265 paved the way for the Treaty of Perth, drawn up in the following year, which ended the period of Scandinavian authority in Man. The final chapter serves as both epilogue and overview, giving first a summary of Manx history from 1266 onwards before considering what the period c.400 to 1265 has bequeathed to the island as well as the ways in which this legacy is presented today.

A note on names

Many personal names used in the medieval period can be written in different ways, often with alternative spellings that make the variant forms of a particular name seem barely similar. Modern authors are faced with a choice as to which form of a name they wish to adopt in their writings. Many prefer spellings that reflect the name's origin in a medieval language such as Old Norse or Old Irish. Others instead prefer a modernised form of the name, usually coined in the author's own language. In this book, I have tended to use a mixture of modern and medieval spellings based on my own preferences.

Here are some examples of my preferred name forms, with variants shown in square brackets:

Godred/Guthfrith (English) [*Gofraid* (Irish Gaelic); *Guðrøðr* (Old Norse)]

Olaf (English) [*Amlaib* (Irish Gaelic); *Olafr* (Old Norse)]

Rognvald (Old Norse) [*Ragnall* (Irish Gaelic); *Reginald* (English)]

Sihtric (English) [*Sitriuc* (Irish Gaelic); *Sigtryggr* (Old Norse)]

Máel Coluim (Scottish Gaelic) [*Malcolm* (English); *Melkolmr* (Old Norse)][4]

The sources

Information on early Manx history is patchy and often unreliable. The various fragments of data do not provide sufficient material for a coherent, continuous, detailed narrative. Any attempt at reconstructing such a narrative for the period covered by this book is therefore a daunting task. Some observers might regard it as a fruitless endeavour. Others might recommend starting the exercise in the mid-eleventh century, when information does at least begin to become more plentiful, while acknowledging by way of a disclaimer that the preceding 600 years are largely blank. I myself feel that an attempt to include these earlier centuries is worth making, not least to put the spotlight on a place that is all too often seen as playing a peripheral role in the pre-Viking history of Britain and Ireland. Moreover, when the sources are examined closely, the story of Man from c.400 to c.1000 does begin to look less peripheral, less like a tale from the outer margins. In the following chapters we will see that Man was indeed connected to important political events throughout the entire early medieval period and that its rulers played active roles in international affairs. This will come as no surprise to readers who already know something of the island's Viking Age history, or to those who have heard of Godred Crovan and the royal dynasty that he founded in the late eleventh century. What may be less widely recognised is that Man's significance pre-dates the era of the Crovan kings and can be traced as far back as the 500s.

What, then, are the sources of information for pre-Viking Man? As far as the period from AD 400 to 1000 is concerned, it is certainly true that we have no documents of Manx origin and must rely instead on texts from elsewhere. These were produced by writers whose main focus was on happenings in their own lands and to whom Man was one among several offshore territories in the seaways between Britain and Ireland. One important group of sources is a collection of chronicles known collectively as the Irish annals. These take the form of year-by-year entries recording events of significance to contemporary observers, especially to religious communities at major monasteries in Ireland or in other parts of the Gaelic-speaking world. The annalists, being members of such communities, reflected in their writings the concerns and interests of abbots and bishops whom they served. Two chronicles in particular have supplied useful information for this book, namely the *Annals of Tigernach* (hereafter *AT*) and the *Annals of Ulster* (hereafter *AU*). Although preserved in fairly late manuscripts, respectively of the fourteenth and fifteenth centuries, they incorporate much material that is considerably older. Both are generally regarded as reliable sources, with the important caveat that their testimony should not be accepted as historical fact without some degree of scrutiny. Similarities in many of their year entries show that their respective compilers drew information from a similar set of source texts. One of these was a chronicle written on Iona, the tiny Hebridean island where the Irish saint Columba had founded a monastery in the middle of the sixth century. The original 'Iona Chronicle' has not survived, but it appears to have provided *AT* and *AU* with plenty of data relating to northern Britain in the period up to c.750. Other Irish chronicles, such as the *Annals of Clonmacnoise* and the *Fragmentary Annals of Ireland* – both of which survive in manuscripts no older than the seventeenth century – tend to be treated with more caution and scepticism.[5] Had the Iona Chronicle survived, it would have been one of the most important relics of early medieval Scotland. Its absence means that our main Scottish source for events in the first millennium AD is the *Chronicle of the Kings of Alba*, compiled in the tenth to twelfth centuries and now preserved in a manuscript of the fourteenth. This provides useful background material on northern Britain but sheds little light on Manx history. Other Scottish chronicles, such as one produced at Melrose Abbey in the thirteenth century, likewise give useful information on the early medieval period in general. So, too, do the Scottish historians John of Fordun and Walter Bower, respectively writing in the fourteenth and fifteenth centuries.[6]

Turning south, our survey of the primary literature reaches Wales and the chronicle known as *Annales Cambriae* or 'Welsh Annals' (hereafter *AC*). The oldest copy is a tenth-century compilation transcribed into a twelfth-century manuscript, while continuations in other manuscripts take the sequence of year entries as far as the thirteenth century. Despite proximity to, and intervisibility with, the North Welsh island of Anglesey, the Isle of Man receives only two mentions in *AC*, the first relating to a battle in 584, the second to an earthquake 100 years later.[7] From England comes a far more substantial set of year entries: the *Anglo-Saxon Chronicle* (hereafter *ASC*). This was begun in the late 800s in Wessex, the kingdom of the West Saxons, by scribes attached to the royal court at Winchester. Unlike the Welsh Annals and most of the Irish chronicles, *ASC* was written in a vernacular language – Old English – rather than in Latin. During the tenth and eleventh centuries, the Winchester scribes continued to update their text with new entries. Copies were made of the original chronicle and these were distributed to English monasteries to be separately maintained and updated, resulting in the different versions of *ASC* that survive today.[8] Although the chronological sequence of year entries in *ASC* was retrospectively pushed back through the centuries to pre-Roman times, Manx history makes no appearance until AD 1000. *ASC* is nevertheless a useful source for our present purpose, providing data for a broad historical backdrop from which significant individuals with Manx connections occasionally emerge. The same can be said of a number of later English chronicles written in Latin during the twelfth, thirteenth and fourteenth centuries. Their authors were contemporary with developments in the volatile political relationships between England, Ireland, Scotland and Norway that frequently affected the Isle of Man.[9]

For the earlier period covered by this book, the most reliable English source is Bede's *Historia Ecclesiastica Gentis Anglorum* ('Ecclesiastical History of the English People'), hereafter *HE*. Bede, who died in 735, was a Northumbrian monk and an author of various works on historical and religious subjects. Although his writings were guided by a belief that the course of human history represented the unending revelation of God's Will, Bede recognised the value of citing and verifying his sources. This brings him closer than many of his peers to our modern idea of what a historian should be. Yet, like all medieval writers, he worked to a personal agenda based on his own social, cultural and religious affiliations and cannot always be trusted to give a balanced account.[10]

One of the genres in which Bede wrote was hagiography, essentially biographical information on saints. The typical hagiographical text in Western Europe during the medieval period was the *vita* or 'life', usually written in Latin. This told the story of a particular holy man or woman, recounting various miraculous events that confirmed the individual's eligibility for sainthood. All such texts were based on early *vitae* of the fourth and fifth centuries, mostly of Continental origin, that essentially provided templates for later hagiographers. Bede himself wrote two *vitae* of the seventh-century Northumbrian saint Cuthbert, one of them in verse format. Other well-known *vitae* from Britain and Ireland include those of St Patrick, St Brigid and St Columba. A larger number of similar works are less well known, often because they deal with saints who today seem very obscure. In some cases, these saints are almost unheard of beyond the districts around the churches dedicated to them. One saint whose present-day fame is confined to a fairly limited area is Machutus or Maughold, patron of Kirk Maughold on the east coast of Man. Outside the island few people are likely to be aware of him. He is said to have lived in the fifth century, but little is known of him beyond what we are told in an Irish *vita* of St Patrick written in the late seventh century. Another early saint associated with Man is a certain Germanus who, according to a twelfth-century hagiographer, established a bishopric at Peel on the site of the present-day St German's Cathedral. I discuss Germanus and Machutus in more detail in Chapter 3. Here it is sufficient to note that neither of them is attested in any reliable source. Indeed, hagiographical works are notoriously unreliable as sources of authentic historical data. This is largely because they were not meant to be regarded as factual biographies. Their purpose was rather to demonstrate the sanctity of their subjects and to show why these individuals were deserving of sainthood. The usual form of demonstration was a series of episodes describing miracles performed by, or attributable to, the saint in question. Miracles did not even require the saint to be alive and could be attributed to him or her posthumously. A dead saint could be called upon to answer a prayer, or might appear as a spectre foretelling a particular outcome such as the result of a major battle. As well as describing various miracles, a *vita* was commonly used as a vehicle for reinforcing claims to land or status by the principal centres of a saint's 'cult'. Rivalry between different cults, or a clash of their ambitions, can sometimes be seen quite clearly in hagiographical writings. An example is the long-running contest between Armagh and Iona, the former being the centre of St Patrick's cult while the latter performed a similar role within the cult of St Columba. Both centres claimed ecclesiastical authority over the whole of Ireland and each produced hagiography to publicise and justify its claim. Armed with an understanding of the medieval hagiographer's *modus operandi*, the modern historian is well equipped to identify nuggets of genuine history among the various miraculous episodes. These nuggets need not even relate to the era in which the saint actually lived but might instead say something useful about the hagiographer's own time.[11]

The sagas

Looking beyond the 'Insular' sources – those written in Britain and Ireland – we turn to texts of Scandinavian origin. Of these, the most problematic yet potentially the most useful are the Norse sagas, a group of texts composed in Iceland in the twelfth and thirteenth centuries but depicting people and events of the Viking Age. They present historical information not in a series of year-by-year notices and summaries, as in the chronicles mentioned above, but as a storyline. Many of them contain dramatic episodes that would not seem out of place in fictional tales. Such elements have created scepticism among historians, some of whom are wary of using the sagas as sources for Viking-Age history. Others take a different view, preferring to see the saga writers as weaving their narratives around a core of authentic historical data.[12] Although produced in Iceland, many of the sagas describe events that took place in other areas colonised by Vikings. Hence, the settlements and seaways around the coasts of Ireland and northern Britain inevitably receive a great deal of attention. This is the case with sagas that focus on the kings of Norway such as those in the collection known as *Heimskringla*, and even with a work such as *Landnámabók* ('Book of Settlements'), which is primarily concerned with Iceland itself. It is, of course, especially true in the case of *Orkneyinga saga* (also known as *Jarls' saga*), an account of the powerful earls of Orkney. Moreover, a number of sagas specifically mention the Isle of Man and the 'Kingdom of the Isles', a polity in which Man held special status as a seat of royal power. *Orkneyinga saga* is one example. Another is *Hákonar saga Hákonarsonar* which describes the long and eventful reign of the thirteenth-century Norwegian king Hakon Hakonarson.[13] While all of these texts do contain embellished and possibly fictionalised episodes, it seems overly sceptical to dismiss them outright from serious historical study. A more objective approach is to treat them with appropriate caution by refusing to accept everything they say at face value while seeking to identify and discard the storytelling elements.[14] We should also keep in mind that similar caveats are no less applicable to those sources that we might otherwise consider reliable and authentic, such as Bede and the Irish chronicles. Indeed, it would be hard to deny that the sagas offer a rich vein of historical information that is worth extracting. In many instances, the information may have been passed more or less intact through several generations of Norse-speaking families in various parts of the Viking world. Today, thanks to the efforts of specialist scholars, we are able to use the sagas alongside other medieval texts as unique and valuable source-materials.

The Manx Chronicle

A medieval manuscript now held in the British Library contains the only chronicle for which a Manx origin seems certain. The manuscript itself is small – measuring only 30cm by 20cm – and contains thirteen separate texts bound together as a single volume. It was once part of a large collection of works assembled by the English antiquary Sir Robert Cotton (1571–1631) and is one of the fortunate survivors of a devastating fire that destroyed or damaged part of the collection in 1731. Among the thirteen texts is the one known today as *Chronica Regum Manniae et Insularum* ('Chronicles of the Kings of Man and the Isles'), commonly cited by historians as the Manx Chronicle.[15] Appended to this is a list of the bishops of Man and the Isles from c.1060 to 1376 and a description of the boundaries of Rushen Abbey, the principal Manx monastery in the Late Norse period. The Cotton copy of the Manx Chronicle was written in the thirteenth century by five scribes who are distinguishable from one another by their handwriting. We can probably assume that they were members of a religious order and that they were monks rather than nuns. One of them, almost certainly a monk at Rushen Abbey, wrote the majority of the year entries.[16] The other four added a few entries at the end. At the beginning, a preliminary series of entries runs from 1016 to 1063 and has little direct relevance for Manx history, dealing instead with events in England, Scotland, Norway and Denmark. The earliest piece of information with specific relevance to Man appears in the entry for 1066 and refers to Godred Crovan's involvement in the Battle of Stamford Bridge. The entry in question is misplaced at 1047, a type of error that occurs elsewhere in the Chronicle until it reaches the middle of the twelfth century. The final entry refers to 1316 and represents the sole contribution of the fifth scribe. Historians think that the original version of the Chronicle may have been written for Magnus Olafsson, the last king of Man, who reigned from 1254 to 1265, and that Magnus himself may have commissioned it.[17] We should note that the title *Chronicles of the Kings of Man and the Isles* does not appear in the original manuscript but is a modern borrowing from the opening phrase or 'rubric', which reads 'Here begin the Chronicles of the kings of Man and the Isles, of their bishops, and of some of the kings of England, Scotland and Norway'. On the question of reliability, the consensus of opinion tends towards the positive, with present-day historians accepting that the Manx Chronicle is a useful source, notwithstanding the usual caveats that apply to any medieval text.[18]

It is also generally accepted that the Chronicle was not the only document produced on Man in the Middle Ages, even if most of the others are now lost. The monastic archive at Rushen Abbey, for instance, must at one time have possessed texts relating to the Crovan kings who were its secular patrons. These kings usually resided on Man and some of them were buried at Rushen. The abbey surely possessed copies, if not the original texts, of royal documents such as charters, especially those recording gifts of land to the abbot. Around twenty charters associated with the Manx kings are identifiable today, whether complete or incomplete or known only as brief summaries. Some survive as copies in cartularies compiled at monasteries in England. A cartulary is a volume containing transcriptions of charters that usually relate to the rights, privileges and landholdings of a religious house. Medieval charters preserved in their original form rather than as copies are, of course, quite rare. From the Isle of Man only one original charter has survived from the period up to 1265 – a document relating to tolls on ships, issued by the last of the Norse kings.[19] Another type of secular source, one that might have provided data for the Manx Chronicle, is the royal saga. Indeed, it is possible or even likely that at least one of the kings of Man was the subject of a work similar to the aforementioned *Hákonar saga*, composed in honour of King Hakon of Norway.[20]

If such a text existed, it would surely have been known to the Rushen monks and would have been one of the Manx Chronicle's source texts. A document that was certainly used in this way was the Chronicle of Melrose, a Scottish work whose input has been detected in its Manx counterpart via information relating to events outside Man.[21]

The main scribe of the Manx Chronicle was no different from his peers in other lands by letting his own personal interests, opinions and allegiances colour his writing. He seems to have held an unfavourable view of the Norman takeover of England, remarking that Duke William of Normandy, otherwise known as William the Conqueror, 'kept the English to perpetual subjection'. His opinion of Edward the Confessor, whose death paved the way for William's invasion in 1066, was rather more positive. So, too, was his treatment of one particular branch of the royal house of Man over another, both branches being engaged in a ferocious contest for kingship in the thirteenth century.[22]

A number of editions, translations and facsimile reproductions of the Manx Chronicle are available today, in printed and electronic formats. Modern technology has made this important document widely accessible via online versions such as the one at the Manx Note Book website. This reproduces an edition by the Norwegian historian Peter Andreas Munch (1810–63), originally published in 1860 and revised fourteen years later by the Manx clergyman Alexander Goss who also added an English translation. The Munch/Goss edition was the standard text for more than a hundred years, until George Broderick published his own edition and translation in 1973.[23]

'A Mighty Fleet and the King's Power'

The title of this book combines two major themes that run through the narrative: naval resources and royal authority. It also reflects my own longstanding interest in the military aspects of medieval kingship. The wording is not mine but comes from a single line of verse in the *Manx Traditionary Ballad*, a poem composed c.1500 in the Manx Gaelic language. Otherwise known as the *Manannan Ballad*, the poem tells the story of the Isle of Man from ancient times, highlighting famous figures such as the legendary hero Manannán mac Lir and the renowned 'King Gorree' (Godred Crovan). One verse tells of Gorree's arrival on Manx shores, locating his landing place at the mouth of the Lhen River on the northern coast:

Lesh e Lhuingys hrean as Pooar y Ree
As ghow eh Thalloo ee y Laane
Shen y chied er ec row rieau ee
Dy ve ny Ree er yn Ellan.

With a mighty fleet and the king's power
He landed at the Lhen.
He was the first whose fate it ever was
To be a king in the Island.[24]

Modern scholarship

Manx history from the fifth to thirteenth centuries is not a subject with which many people outside the island can claim to be familiar. It is, in fact, a neglected topic within medieval studies, an oft-ignored appendage to the much larger histories of medieval Britain and Ireland.[25] There are, perhaps, logical reasons as to why this is the case. One is the simple matter of geography. Thus, while Man occupies a central position between Britain and Ireland, it yet remains oddly peripheral to both. It is at once a place easily visible from their shores yet also a separate entity, a land unto itself. Another reason is one that we have already encountered: the lack of contemporary sources. Early Manx history is easily overlooked when, even at first glance, we see its many gaps. These are most apparent in the fifth to ninth centuries, a period stretching from the end of Roman rule in Britain to the beginning of Scandinavian settlement. In our modern era, some writers dealing with Manx history from ancient times to the present day choose to skip over the period 400 to 800, using a sentence or two to acknowledge the lack of information before moving swiftly on to the comparatively better-documented Viking Age. Yet even the story of the Vikings on Man is itself incomplete. It incorporates plenty of archaeological evidence but lacks a coherent narrative until the second half of the eleventh century. By then, the Viking Age in much of the rest of Europe was almost over. Little wonder, then, that Manx history has traditionally been seen as commencing in 1079 with Godred Crovan's arrival on the island. This pivotal figure, the renowned King Gorree or 'Orry' of Manx legend, founded a royal dynasty that would rule for the next 200 years. On the history of Godred and his descendants we have fairly reliable, detailed information, chiefly via the Manx Chronicle but also from other more or less contemporary texts of Irish, Scottish, English and Scandinavian origin. Unfortunately, the sequence of year entries in the Chronicle does not reach backwards into the first millennium. If we seek insights into what was happening *before* Godred's time, we must rummage patiently for small fragments of data that may shed a little light. Not all historians regard this kind of endeavour as worthwhile, yet some do. The following brief survey will show how the early and pre-Viking periods on Man have been addressed by a selection of writers in the nineteenth, twentieth and twenty-first centuries.

Arthur William Moore (1853–1909), the foremost Manx historian of the Victorian era, dealt with the time before the Crovan dynasty in the first volume of his *History of the Isle of Man* (published in 1900). He covered the fifth to eighth centuries in a chapter entitled 'The Celtic Period', saying much about the transition from paganism to Christianity and the activities of saints such as Patrick and Maughold. He had less to say about the island's secular history during this period, describing it as 'an absolute blank'.[26] In Moore's opinion, there exists 'no trustworthy record of any event whatever before the incursions of the Northmen'. In a single paragraph of nineteen lines and an accompanying footnote of similar length, he moved swiftly through the alleged Manx connections of one sixth-century Irish king and two seventh-century English kings, soon reaching the end of his 'Celtic Period' chapter. He then turned his attention to the Vikings, discussing what he called the 'First Scandinavian Period' which he defined as the years 798 to 1079. Here, he stepped onto slightly firmer ground, finding several allusions to Man in the Icelandic sagas and thus building up a picture of Viking raids and settlements on the island in the ninth and tenth centuries. For his next chapter, under the heading 'The Second Scandinavian Period', he was treading a much more solid path, telling his readers about Godred Crovan and drawing on the Manx Chronicle. This chapter brought his narrative down to 1266 and to the reign of Magnus Olafsson, last king of the Crovan dynasty. Moore's scholarly reputation, richly deserved, makes the first volume of his *magnum opus* an essential starting point for anyone wishing to delve into early Manx history.

The high quality of Moore's work means that his predecessors in Manx historical studies cannot, in fairness, be compared to him. Their contributions were nevertheless important in their own time and are part of a long tradition of scholarly writing that led ultimately to Moore. We can therefore view William Sacheverell's *An Account of the Isle of Man* and George Waldron's *The History and Description of the Isle of Man*, respectively published in 1702 and 1726, in the context of eighteenth-century antiquarianism rather than for their value as textbooks. More akin to Moore, in terms of quality of research, was Joseph Train whose *Historical and Statistical Account of Man* was published in Douglas in 1845. While Moore was a Manxman by birth and ancestry, Train (1779–1852) was a Scotsman, born in Ayrshire. From humble beginnings as a weaver's apprentice and with almost no education he became an excise officer, a self-taught antiquary and a respected author. His writings on the folklore and antiquities of Scotland attracted the attention of Sir Walter Scott who consulted Train on these subjects while gathering material for his own novels. In 1817, after learning that Train was interested in acquiring a copy of Waldron's *Description of Man*, Scott suggested that Train himself should write a new history of the island. Train agreed to take on the project but was unable to get down to it until the late 1820s. Living in Scotland meant that he had to rely on information supplied by contacts on Man, although he did manage to visit the island in 1836. Inspired by a series of 'statistical accounts' that effectively recorded the geography, antiquities and economy of different parts of Scotland, Train applied a similar approach to his study of Man.[27] His reconstruction of the island's early history is commendable, although he had a tendency to use sources that would not now be considered reliable. One of these was Raphael Holinshed's *Chronicles of England, Scotland and Ireland*, published in the late sixteenth century. Although this had provided William Shakespeare with plenty of exciting material for *King Lear* and other plays, it unfortunately contains large amounts of imaginative pseudo-history that add little to knowledge of past events. The second chapter of Train's book, covering the sixth to early tenth centuries AD, is peppered with material invented by Holinshed and thus offers a fictionalised historical narrative. Moore, by contrast, was happy to accept that reliable source material simply did not exist and that the entire pre-Norse period of Manx history should be dealt with briefly and swiftly. Train's view of Godred Crovan was also not the one adopted by Moore. While the latter correctly equated Godred with the renowned King Gorree of Manx legend, Train instead saw them as separate individuals.[28]

Moore's *History of the Isle of Man* appeared at the dawn of the twentieth century and set a high standard for everything that has been published since. It has remained an important work on the subject for more than a hundred years and will, no doubt, continue to retain iconic status for a long time to come. The twentieth century bore witness to a number of other monographs on Manx history, each with its own way of dealing with the Late Norse era but essentially adopting Moore's minimalist approach to the preceding period. In a short book aimed at younger readers and published in 1949, the prolific educational author Clement Wallace Airne described the time from c.450 to c.800 on Man as 'apparently devoid of history'.[29] By this, he meant the secular aspect of history relating to kings and kingdoms, for he was able to write several pages on early Manx Christianity. In 1975, in the third edition of his excellent history of the Isle of Man, Robert Kinvig was of the opinion that 'although there is a great lack of ordinary records for the period between 450 and 800 it is clear that much of importance was taking place'.[30] Like Airne, Kinvig was here alluding to the dearth of information on secular history, having already found enough material on Early Christian archaeology to fill a twelve-page chapter. He thus presented the pre-Norse period on Man through the lens of religious history, concentrating on early ecclesiastical sites, carved stone monuments and traditions of missionary saints. Moving forward into the 800s and the Viking Age, both Airne and Kinvig were able to say a little more about secular affairs up to the arrival of Godred Crovan in 1079. With Godred, as we have seen, the historical data starts to become more plentiful. Neither Airne nor Kinvig, like Moore before them, saw much to be gained by hunting for scraps in the faint hope of reconstructing a coherent narrative of the time before the Vikings.

In the twenty-first century we find that Moore's *History* is being superseded by a new, multi-volume work. This comprises a series of edited volumes, each a collection of papers, all issued under the umbrella title 'A New History of the Isle of Man'. Published by Liverpool University Press, the series has so far (as at Summer 2022) seen three of its five scheduled volumes appear, namely the first, third and fifth.[31] Of these, the third deals with the period 1000 to 1406 and thus overlaps with the second half of this book. The fifth volume, the last, deals with the modern era from 1830 onwards, while the first introduces the natural landscape of Man. Still to be published are volumes 2 and 4, the former dealing with the prehistoric and early medieval periods up to the end of the first millennium AD, the latter with the period 1405 to 1830. The quality of scholarship in the New History is impressive. In the third volume, an essential resource for the medieval period on Man, papers by specialists in disciplines such as archaeology, philology and numismatics sit alongside others written by historians. Although essentially a collection of academic essays, it is intended for both the general and the academic reader. Its preface states that its authors have used 'the critical approaches to sources required by twenty-first century scholarship' and this is certainly true, yet the contents nevertheless appear more accessible to a broader audience than the hefty weight of the paperback edition suggests.[32] The first six chapters of Volume 3 cover the eleventh to thirteenth centuries, overlapping not only with the second half of this book but also with

R. Andrew McDonald's *The Sea Kings: The Late Norse Kingdoms of Man and the Isles, c.1066–1275*. Published in 2019, McDonald's book runs to some 400 pages and includes a comprehensive study of the Crovan dynasty from foundation to demise. Again, the thickness of the tome should not discourage the general reader from delving into it, especially as the story of the Crovan kings is at times reminiscent of a swashbuckling saga of piracy and intrigue. The as-yet-unpublished second volume of the New History will include coverage of the main part of the Viking Age, from the end of the eighth century to the start of the eleventh. This period of roughly 300 years is, as far as Man is concerned, poorly documented in the contemporary sources. A comprehensive modern study of this frequently neglected topic will therefore be welcomed.

Moving away from literary sources, the archaeological data relating to Man in the early medieval and Late Norse periods is substantial. Much of it relates to the Vikings and has been analysed by specialist scholars. A number of key sites have been excavated, the finds being described in detailed reports such as those produced by the Manx Archaeological Survey in the twentieth century. Analysis of the data has been distilled for presentation to a wider audience via illustrated booklets and online commentaries. The focus varies from island-wide to local, an example of the latter being Sandra Kerrison's concise guide to the Viking-Age archaeology of Jurby.[33] Anyone who accesses the archaeological data soon discovers that Man possesses an internationally renowned collection of Early Christian and Viking-Age sculptured stones. Of these, a large percentage are shaped slabs carved with crosses, often accompanied by inscriptions and finely worked designs. Information on these monuments is easy to access in various formats and – at certain churchyards around the island – on display boards erected alongside local sculptural collections. As far as printed information on the sculpture is concerned, the pioneering work is Philip Kermode's *Manx Crosses*, published in 1907, comprising a descriptive catalogue of the monuments. This was re-issued, with a new introduction, in 1994. More recently, a separate study with the same title has been written by Sir David Wilson, discussing the different phases and styles of sculpture from modern archaeological and art-historical perspectives.[34] Another recent work is a short booklet by Sara Goodwins, with colour photographs of selected monuments, providing a concise introduction to the subject. Publications on local collections of sculpture are also available, a fine example being Mike Clague's guide to the Kirk Michael stones. Comprehensive 'biographies' of individual monuments, such as Dirk Steinforth's study of Thorvald's Cross at Kirk Andreas, get to the heart of questions about what these unique relics are trying to tell us.[35]

Modern administrative divisions

In this book I often refer to places on the Isle of Man in association with the parishes to which they belong. The parish is an important element in the island's hierarchy of administrative divisions, sitting immediately beneath the 'sheading' but above the 'treen' and the 'quarterland'. There are six sheadings, five of which contain three parishes each while the sixth contains only two. The sheadings are listed below, with their constituent parishes in brackets.

Glenfaba (Patrick, German, Marown)
Michael (Jurby, Michael, Ballaugh)
Ayre (Bride, Andreas, Lezayre)
Garff (Maughold, Lonan)
Middle (Onchan, Braddan, Santan)
Rushen (Malew, Rushen, Arbory)

The Isle of Man: sheadings and parishes

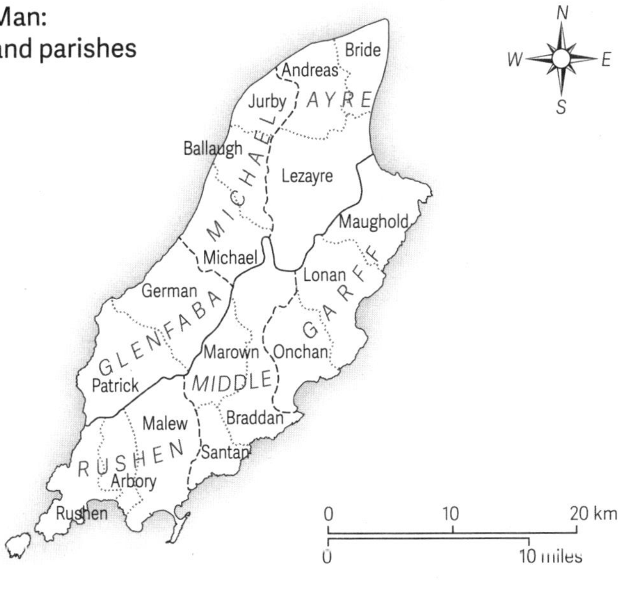

2

MANANNÁN'S ISLE

The Isle of Man lies in the middle of the Irish Sea. It is longer than it is wide, slightly tilted on a north-east to south-west axis and has a shape that has been described as a 'lozenge'. From its highest point on the summit of Snaefell the coasts of England, Ireland, Scotland and Wales are all visible in fair weather. Likewise, Man's distinctive outline can be seen from the surrounding lands. Viewed from a distance, it has the appearance of a single mountain rising from the sea. It is not particularly large, being some 45 km (33 miles) long and no more than 16 km (12 miles) wide, with an area of 571 km^2 (220 square miles). Nevertheless, its location has long made it a place of significance, especially in the context of maritime communication. Not without reason did a poet in medieval Wales refer to the Irish Sea as *Môr Manaw*, 'The Sea of Man'.[1] A glance at a map clearly shows Man's central position in the seaways but does not really indicate just how close the island lies to the neighbouring larger land masses. This proximity is best appreciated by standing on the summit of Snaefell on a clear day and gazing around in all directions. To the north, the coast of Scotland lies a mere 29 km (18 miles) away, with Burrow Head on the southern tip of the Machars peninsula in Galloway the nearest visible point. Looking west, the distinctive profile of the Mountains of Mourne reminds us that Ireland is only 60 km (37 miles) from Manx shores. The distance eastward to England is slightly less, with St Bees Head on the Cumbrian coast being the closest point. On the southern horizon lies the Welsh island of Anglesey, separated from Man by barely 80 km (50 miles) of water, and beyond Anglesey in the far distance the high peaks of Snowdonia can be discerned. Travellers journeying by ship from Manx ports to places in Britain or Ireland lose sight of land only for a short time if the weather stays fair. Vessels from Man seeking to exit the Irish Sea southward eventually pass through the narrows of St George's Channel between south-east Ireland and south-west Wales. Closer to Man is the Irish Sea's northern exit, the North Channel, giving access to the Hebridean Isles. Although generally quite shallow, the Irish Sea is prone to strong currents and frequent bouts of inclement weather. Around Man the tides and currents are particularly strong, as experienced sailors know only too well. Fierce storms rage across the island in winter. Even in summer, the coastline can quickly vanish from sight beneath a dense shroud of fog.

Turning to the physical geography of Man, we find that the island has two areas of upland separated by a central valley. The northern uplands contain the towering mass of Snaefell, rising to a height of 620 metres (2,034 feet). Beyond them lies a large coastal plain. Other, smaller areas of low-lying land lie below the southern uplands and at each end of the central valley around the towns of Douglas and Peel.[2] The soils of Man are fertile, especially those in the limestone area of the south-east and on the northern plain. This fertility can be measured by the fact that the island currently produces more than enough grain to sustain its 84,000 inhabitants. As well as being conducive to cultivation, the Manx landscape today supports livestock farming on a scale large enough to yield surpluses of beef and lamb for export.[3] In addition to the mainland of Man there are three smaller islands lying close by. The largest of these lies off the south-west coast and is known as the Calf of Man. The other two are St Patrick's Isle beside Peel and St Michael's Isle near Ronaldsway, both of which are now connected to the mainland by causeways. Unsurprisingly for a small island there are no great rivers, the longest being the Sulby River running northward for 18 km (11 miles) from Snaefell to meet the sea at Ramsey. More unexpected, perhaps, is the small number of good natural harbours. Indeed, the shores of Man can often seem inhospitable to boats seeking safe moorings, with sheer cliffs and perilous rocks being more common than sheltered havens. There are, however, a number of long, sandy beaches suitable for berthing the lighter type of vessel common in early times.

North and South

One aspect of Man's physical geography that permeates into its political history is a north–south divide or, more accurately, a division between the north-eastern and south-western halves of the island. The line of division is not the central valley running east–west but the watershed running along the top of the northern and southern uplands. This divide is reflected in the historical sources – the Manx Chronicle being an example – where distinctions are sometimes observed between 'Northside' and 'Southside' in matters of political allegiance. Specific instances from early history will be encountered in due course but, in the meantime, we may note that the island's present-day administrative boundaries still recognise a line of demarcation between North Man and South Man. It is likely that the notion of a north–south divide is considerably older than the boundaries – most of which were created in the Middle Ages – and that its origins lie deep in prehistory.[4]

Man is rich in natural resources, and these have been exploited by human communities for thousands of years. The first people are assumed to have arrived c.6500 BC during the Middle Stone Age or 'Mesolithic' period. By then, Man had been an island for some two thousand years, its connection to the surrounding land masses having been lost when the basin of what was to become the Irish Sea was flooded by melting ice at the end of the last Ice Age. The first settlers arrived in small vessels such as logboats and lived in temporary dwellings, moving from place to place around the island.[5] They used implements of flint or bone and lived by fishing, hunting and foraging. By 4000 BC, in the Neolithic Period or New Stone Age, the islanders gave up the nomadic existence of their ancestors to adopt a more settled lifestyle. Dwellings evolved from tent-like shelters to permanent homes built of turf, timber and stone. Hunting and foraging gave way to farming, with crops being cultivated and animals such as pigs, sheep and goats being husbanded. By then, most of the island's ancient woodland had been cleared, leaving only patches of forest in the deeper glens. Agriculture would have seen a north–side divide, with the light soils of northern Man being suited to a different range of crops from the heavier soils of the south. Cultivation would not have been possible in hilly areas, where the terrain was largely unproductive heath, but even here the soil provided grasses and other moorland plants for sheep and goats to graze upon. The sheep nurtured by the ancient islanders for meat and fleeces were no doubt similar to present-day small breeds such as the Manx Loaghtan.[6]

It was in Neolithic times that the people of Man first began to erect imposing monuments constructed from huge standing stones ('megaliths'). King Orry's Grave, associated in legend with the historical ruler Godred Crovan, is one such site, being a chambered tomb constructed between 4,000 and 5,000 years ago. Towards the end of the Neolithic Period, around 2000 BC, a distinctive and unique society flourished on Man. First identified following archaeological excavations on the site of the island's airport, the so-called 'Ronaldsway' culture is associated with pottery and tools produced in a style that evolved on the island rather than being imported from the surrounding lands. Its uniqueness is exemplified by a type of stone axe for which there is no precise parallel anywhere else.[7]

The end of the Neolithic saw flint tools and other stone implements being superseded by objects made from bronze. Boats became larger and sturdier, enabling the early Manx to engage in trade with coastal communities in Ireland and Britain.[8] Copper provides about 90 per cent of the metal used in bronzemaking, the rest being tin. Although tin is not found on Man, the island has substantial copper deposits and it is no surprise to find archaeological evidence for the making of bronze objects.[9] Tin came from Cornwall, the only area in Britain or Ireland where it is present in large quantities, either directly or – perhaps more likely – via intermediate trading contacts. Making something out of bronze was a time-consuming craft requiring specialist skills. Bronze objects were therefore expensive and only people of wealth and status could acquire them. Being rare and precious, a bronze implement or ornament was a suitable item to place in the grave of a revered family member, hence the discovery of such objects in Bronze Age burials on Man. In a burial mound at Port y Shee, in the parish of Braddan, a fine bronze razor was interred with the deceased. The latter had been cremated, with the ashes placed in an urn, a practice that marked a distinct change from the Stone Age custom of crouched burial. There were other changes in Manx society around this time. Dwellings became larger, typified by the 'roundhouse' which, as the name implies, was a circular building with a hearth in the centre. Constructed of stone or timber and roofed with turf or thatch, the roundhouse could accommodate a large family group together with domesticated livestock. Settlements of roundhouses, like small villages for one or more extended families, have been found in several locations on Man.[10]

Another innovation attributed to the Bronze Age is the fortified hilltop, whether sited on coastal headlands ('promontory forts') or on elevated inland sites ('hillforts'). Man has some thirty examples, all but two being of the coastal type. The larger of the two hillforts lies in the southern part of the island where the lofty summit of South Barrule, rising to a height of 483 metres (1,585 feet) is crowned by a double rampart. Traces of more than seventy stone-built circular huts have been found in the enclosed area, a considerable number that implies the presence of a populous community. Material from a hearth in one of the huts on South Barrule yielded a date in the sixth century BC, around the end of the Bronze Age and the beginning of the Iron Age. In the north, at Cronk Sumark, a much smaller hillfort sits on the rocky summit of a hill rising above what was once an extensive wetland.[11] The summit, with an extensive view over the surrounding lands, had strategic value and was clearly worth protecting, hence a pair of earth ramparts can be seen further down the slope. Such a site differs from the typical coastal promontory fort in lacking the natural defences provided by sea and cliff. Coastal forts needed artificial defences such as ramparts only on their landward sides.

Occupation phases at both Cronk Sumark and the larger hillfort on South Barrule are thought to have spanned the period of transition between the Bronze Age and the Iron Age. The latter is usually seen as beginning in the sixth to eighth centuries BC in Britain and Ireland where it is associated with the arrival of Celtic culture.[12] Iron ore is plentiful on Man and was processed by islanders from the early centuries BC onwards. They smelted it for the casting of tools and other objects in moulds, examples of which have been found by archaeologists.[13]

The Iron Age population continued to live in circular houses but, in some cases, these were considerably bigger than those of the Bronze Age. At Ballakaighen near Castletown, an archaeological excavation in the 1940s identified two substantial roundhouses that had been occupied in the first or second century AD. The larger measured almost 90 feet in diameter and had been roofed with a dome of thatch supported by hefty wooden posts. Other posts formed the outer wall against which a bank of earth had been piled. The residents of both houses had evidently been people of high status, members of the local landowning aristocracy.[14] Barely a mile away, a coastal fort at Close ny Chollagh yielded evidence of an Iron Age occupation phase that ended in the first century AD. Excavations in the 1950s identified four circular dwellings nestling snugly within a large hollow mound. Additional protection for the inhabitants was provided by the sea, by a natural gully and by a massive rampart of stone. The roundhouses here were quite large, one of them having a diameter of almost 7 metres. Their walls were remarkably well constructed using limestone that had been quarried in the locality. Each house was equipped with a hearth in the centre of the floor and a system of covered drains. The site seems to have been used as a permanent residence by only a dozen people but perhaps served as a stronghold and refuge for a much larger group when needed.[15] Some connection with their neighbours at nearby Ballakaighen seems probable, especially as the two large roundhouses there had no defences of their own. The fort at Close ny Chollagh was seemingly abandoned in the first century AD before being re-used approximately 800 years later by Vikings who erected a 'longhouse' of Scandinavian type.

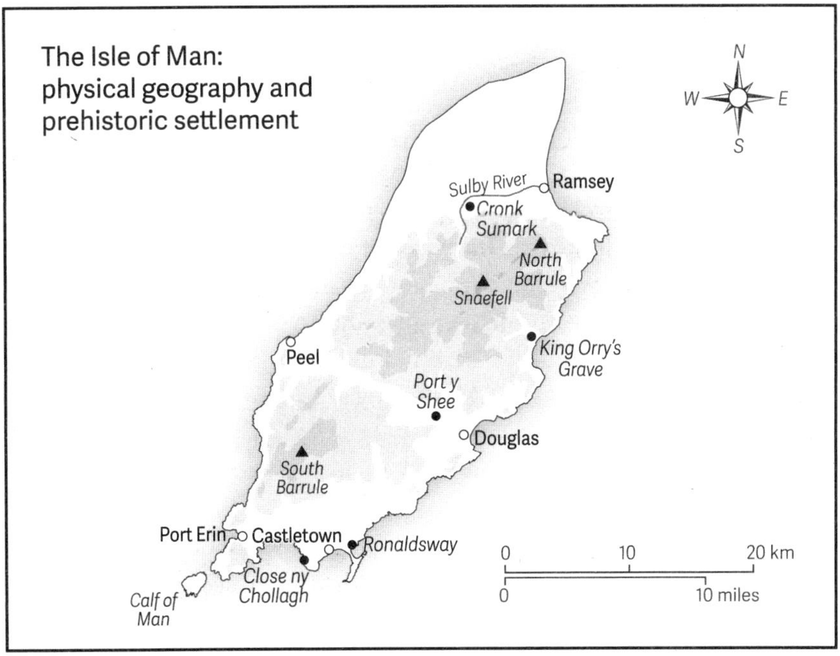

Being Celtic

The traditional, popular view of ancient Celtic culture sees it as originating in Continental Europe sometime around 500 BC. From there, it was supposedly brought to Britain and Ireland by a mass migration of people who belonged to an ethnic group known today as 'Celts'.[16] This view has been supplanted by a more nuanced scenario in which the migration was not of people but of language and culture. However, there is no agreement as to where and when Celtic speech or Celtic cultural traits first began. One theory locates the origin centre in Central Europe, another puts it in Gaul (modern France) while a third identifies the Atlantic seaboard (Spain, France, Ireland and Britain). The chronological aspect is also debated, with competing theories proposing an origin date ranging from the third to the first millennia BC. Amid all the uncertainty the key point shared by all sides in the debate is that the term 'Celtic' should be seen as a linguistic and cultural label rather than as an ethnic one.[17]

Rome and Man

The Roman conquest of Britain began in AD 43 with a full-scale invasion from Gaul (present-day France). After crossing the English Channel, Roman forces undertook a series of military campaigns that overwhelmed the native inhabitants. Within forty years, a Roman army was marching northward into what are now the Scottish Highlands. After several attempts to subdue this region, Rome eventually consolidated the northern frontier of her empire along a line drawn between the River Tyne and the Solway Firth. During the reign of the emperor Hadrian (AD 117–38) this frontier became an imposing element in the landscape when a massive stone barrier was built along it. Twenty years later, the frontier was briefly pushed northwards to a new line drawn between the firths of Forth and Clyde. This was marked by a rampart of turf, the Antonine Wall, abandoned within ten years of completion. Thereafter, excepting a couple of abortive attempts to conquer the further lands, Hadrian's Wall remained the Roman Empire's northernmost frontier for the next 300 years.

Since the time of the original conquest, Roman geographers had mapped the coasts of Britain and Ireland and the seaways in between. They were aware of various isles, large and small, in the Irish Sea and in Hebridean waters further north. Some isles were seen as more significant than others. We know, for instance, that Roman forces attacked Anglesey in AD 60 and again in 77, eventually annexing it to the Empire. They took these actions because Anglesey, which they called *Mona*, was being used as a refuge and stronghold by native Britons who refused to surrender.[18] What we do not know is whether Man was similarly targeted by Rome's military might. While it is certainly true that we have no record of any such campaign, this does not necessarily mean that none took place. A Roman assault on Man might simply have been omitted from the few contemporary accounts that have survived. Needless to say, it is highly unlikely that the island would have been ignored. The Romans would have seen it from the coast of northern Britain and also from Anglesey, as well as passing it during naval patrols and other voyages in the Irish Sea. One suggestion is that Man might be the island of *Mona*, described by the Roman general Julius Caesar (died 54 BC) as lying between Britain and Ireland.[19] This is generally regarded as an unlikely identification, for *Mona* was the Roman name for Anglesey which is almost certainly the place Caesar had in mind. A more certain reference to Man appeared some seventy years after Caesar's death when Pliny the Elder, writing in AD 23, mentioned *Mona* and *Monapia* as separate islands off the coast of Britain. There is no doubt that *Monapia* is Man. It is thought to be a Roman rendering of a native name such as *Manavia*, the first syllable being short in both names and hence sounding similar.

Around a hundred years after Pliny, the Greek geographer Ptolemy referred to the islands *Mona* and *Monaoeda*, the latter being a variant name for Man.[20] There is then a gap of nearly 300 years until the next reference, by the historian Orosius in the early fifth century. In his best-known work, *Seven Books of History Against the Pagans*, Orosius describes Man as being near Ireland, adding that it is 'fair-sized and has a fertile soil' and that it is inhabited *a Scottorum gentibus*, 'by Gaelic-speaking (or Irish) people'. Although most of the surviving manuscripts of the *Seven Books* give the name of Man as *Mevania*, the oldest gives *Evania* and this is likely to be the correct form used by Orosius himself.[21] The erroneous form *Mevania* looks like a scribe's attempt to reconcile *Evania* with a name containing initial M-, like *Monapia*/*Manavia*, when making a copy of the original text. However, the incorrect form stuck and was picked up by other scribes writing more copies. It also appears in the works of subsequent authors who used those same copies as source material. With the exception of

Orosius' *Evania*, the Roman names for Man all share the prefix *Mon-/Man-* which is thought to be of pre-Roman origin. Philologists have suggested that this prefix, seen also in the Roman name of Anglesey, was originally *Mona* or *Mana*. It probably derives from a common Celtic word for 'hill' or 'mountain', a word that has since developed into Welsh *mynydd* and Gaelic *monadh*.[22] Caesar's *Mona* would then mean 'hilly island' or 'mountain island', an apt description for Anglesey which has the looming mass of Holyhead Mountain on its western side. In Man's case the mountain giving rise to the *Mon-/Man-* prefix would be Snaefell.

As stated previously, although there is no firm evidence that the Romans visited Man, it is hard to believe that they would have ignored it, given its nodal position in the Irish Sea. From their settlements on the western side of Britain they could see it as clearly as we can see it today.[23] Moreover, the Romans were actively involved in trade networks between Britain and Ireland, either directly using their own ships or indirectly as third-party recipients of Irish goods. Indeed, it is not unrealistic to imagine merchants and sailors, whether Romans or Romanised Britons, berthing their vessels in Manx harbours or on Manx beaches to conduct face-to-face business with local people. Manx seafarers likewise probably sailed to Britain, to engage in trade or – perhaps more likely, given Man's later association with piratical activity – to indulge in raiding. Yet we need not assume that relations between Manx and Roman were generally characterised by mutual hostility. If the Manx had posed a significant threat to Roman interests, their island would surely have been brought under the imperial yoke and forced to accept a permanent garrison. In the absence of archaeological evidence for such action, or indeed for any kind of Roman presence, we can assume that the imperial authorities in mainland Britain decided to leave Man unconquered. Just as they briefly contemplated the conquest of Ireland in the first century AD before shelving the idea, they may have considered the pros and cons of attaching Man to the Empire before deciding against it.

Manannán mac Lir

In Irish mythology, Manannán is a warrior god whose father Ler (*Lir* in the genitive) is a personification of the sea. Manannán, who appears also in Welsh mythology as Manawydan, is sometimes seen as an equivalent of the Roman sea god Neptune. He is depicted as a ruler of the Otherworld, his realm being known in Irish Gaelic texts by names such as *Emhain Ablach* ('Emain of the

Apple Trees') and *Tir Tairngire* ('Land of Promise').[24] He appears in a number of stories within the four main groups or 'cycles' of Irish mythology. In the Ulster Cycle, his wife becomes the lover of the legendary hero Cuchulainn, their affair ending when Manannán uses magic to make them forget one another. From the Cycles of the Kings comes a story of c.700 called *The Voyage of Bran* in which Manannán uses his powers of prophecy to foretell that the titular hero will be the ancestor of a famous warrior. The latter turns out to be a historical figure, Mongán mac Fíachnai, whose father Fiachnae mac Báetáin was an Irish king whom we shall meet again in Chapter 4. In the ninth-century Irish tale *Cormac's Glossary*, Manannán is portrayed as a great mariner and merchant who lived on Man. A later story, preserved in an Irish manuscript of c.1400, envisages four separate Manannáns, each with a different father. It reiterates the description of one of them, Manannán mac Lir, as a merchant and mariner, adding also that he was a druid. It describes one of his namesakes, Manannán mac Cirp, as ruling the medieval realm known to history as the Kingdom of Man and the Isles. In Manx folklore Manannán mac Lir is the first ruler of Man, wielding authority over the island from a mighty fortress on the summit of South Barrule. There, on Midsummer Eve each year, he received a sheaf of rushes by way of a tax on his subjects.[25] The antiquity of this tradition is uncertain, especially as it appears in no source older than the sixteenth century. Another Manx legend of doubtful provenance tells of Manannán mac Lir residing at Peel Castle, using his magical powers to create the illusion of a large force of defenders when the actual garrison consisted of only one soldier.[26] Perhaps the best-known Manx example of Manannán-related lore is the idea that the Isle of Man gets its name from him. This tradition is mirrored by another in which the name of the god is borrowed from the island's name, a more plausible scenario given the likelihood that the root word *Man-/Mon-* is undoubtedly ancient and must predate the Manannán lore. In this context we may note that one possible meaning of *Manannán* is 'little Manxman', the suffix *-an* frequently being used as a diminutive in Gaelic languages. Whatever his true origins, Manannán the sea god seems an appropriate personification of Man's long heritage of maritime connections.

Manx druidism

As mentioned above, the Romans launched two campaigns against Anglesey in the first century AD. Both were reported by the contemporary writer Cornelius

Tacitus, son-in-law of the renowned general Gnaeus Julius Agricola who led the second invasion. Although Tacitus did not specifically allude to Anglesey's rich deposits of copper, these may have been a significant factor in Rome's determination to conquer the island. Some modern commentators believe that another factor was druidism, supposedly a pre-Christian religion overseen by priests and sorcerers called 'druids'. The words of Tacitus himself are often cited in this context. In his account of the first Anglesey campaign, he described the native forces opposing the Romans as being accompanied by 'the druids, lifting their hands to heaven and pouring forth dreadful imprecations'.[27] The ensuing battle, a Roman victory, was followed by a destructive rampage in which the sacred groves of the natives were destroyed. These places, scorned by Tacitus as 'devoted to inhuman superstitions', were associated with sacrificial altars where people were ritually slain. Here, we may note that Tacitus does not imply that the druids were involved in these killings. Indeed, nothing in his description of religious rites on ancient Anglesey would have been unduly shocking to contemporary Roman eyes. Yet he nonetheless managed to conjure for his readers an image of extreme barbarity. What happened to the island's druids he does not say, but we can assume that many perished in the battle or in the ensuing destruction of sacred sites. At no point in his narrative does Tacitus suggest that the slaughter of druids was a key objective behind the Roman assault. He simply states that the island's defenders were aided by the presence of druids whose 'dreadful imprecations' initially terrified the Roman troops.

In our own era, much has been made of these references to druids on Anglesey. They have been interpreted as evidence that the island was a druidical headquarters in the first century AD, a refuge for druids from other parts of Britain fleeing the Roman advance. An extension of this theory sees Man as a similar offshore refuge, one that offered sanctuary to druids who managed to escape the slaughter on Anglesey.[28] Romantic though these ideas might be, they have no firm basis in historical or archaeological evidence. Neither Anglesey nor Man can be envisaged as major centres of druidism in pre-Roman times, or at any period thereafter, merely on the basis of what Tacitus says. Part of the reason for this scepticism is the absence in the archaeological record of any site that can be associated with the druids whom he mentions. What would such a place look like and how would we identify it as a venue for druidic activity rather than for some other purpose? Tacitus refers to sacred groves and altars on Anglesey. Even if these were identifiable archaeologically, we would have no reason to assume that they were exclusively connected with druids. Nor can we assume, as many people now seem to do, that druids routinely used prehistoric ceremonial sites such as stone circles and megaliths, or that they were members of a formal religious order. The simple truth is that we know very little about ancient druidism. Popular ideas about the role of druids in Iron Age Britain and Ireland are largely based on guesswork or wishful thinking, often from a modern neo-pagan perspective.[29] If druids were ever on Man their presence has not yet been found and recognised. Sacred rituals, some involving human sacrifice, were no doubt witnessed by the Manx population in pre-Christian times, but whether the individuals who oversaw these events should be called 'druids' is a moot point.

The end of Roman Britain

By the middle of the fourth century, the coasts of Roman Britain were under sustained assault by seaborne raiders from outside the Empire. In the western seaways, Irish pirates prowled in fleets of swift, hide-covered boats; down the eastern coast came Picts from the far north; from across the North Sea came marauding shiploads of Saxons, Angles, Jutes and Frisians. The raids placed a huge burden on the Roman military authorities. Many of the soldiers in Britain belonged to static garrisons in forts such as those along Hadrian's Wall. The few mobile units that did exist could barely hope to reach the site of a raid before the marauders sailed away with loot and captives. To make matters worse, Roman military units in Britain were frequently withdrawn to support defensive campaigns on the Continent, where key frontiers were continually under threat from Germanic and Asiatic peoples. The garrison of Britain was further depleted whenever an ambitious general, seeking to make himself emperor, led considerable numbers of soldiers over to Gaul. And still the raids continued. In 367, according to one Roman writer, the various pirate groups formed an alliance, a 'Barbarian Conspiracy'.[30] Together they planned a co-ordinated assault on Britain, intending to sweep aside the Roman garrisons and ravage the land. Their plan succeeded: Britain was overwhelmed and thrown into turmoil. Only a Roman counter-offensive from Gaul prevented further chaos. Nevertheless, a deadly blow had been struck and there was to be no lasting recovery.

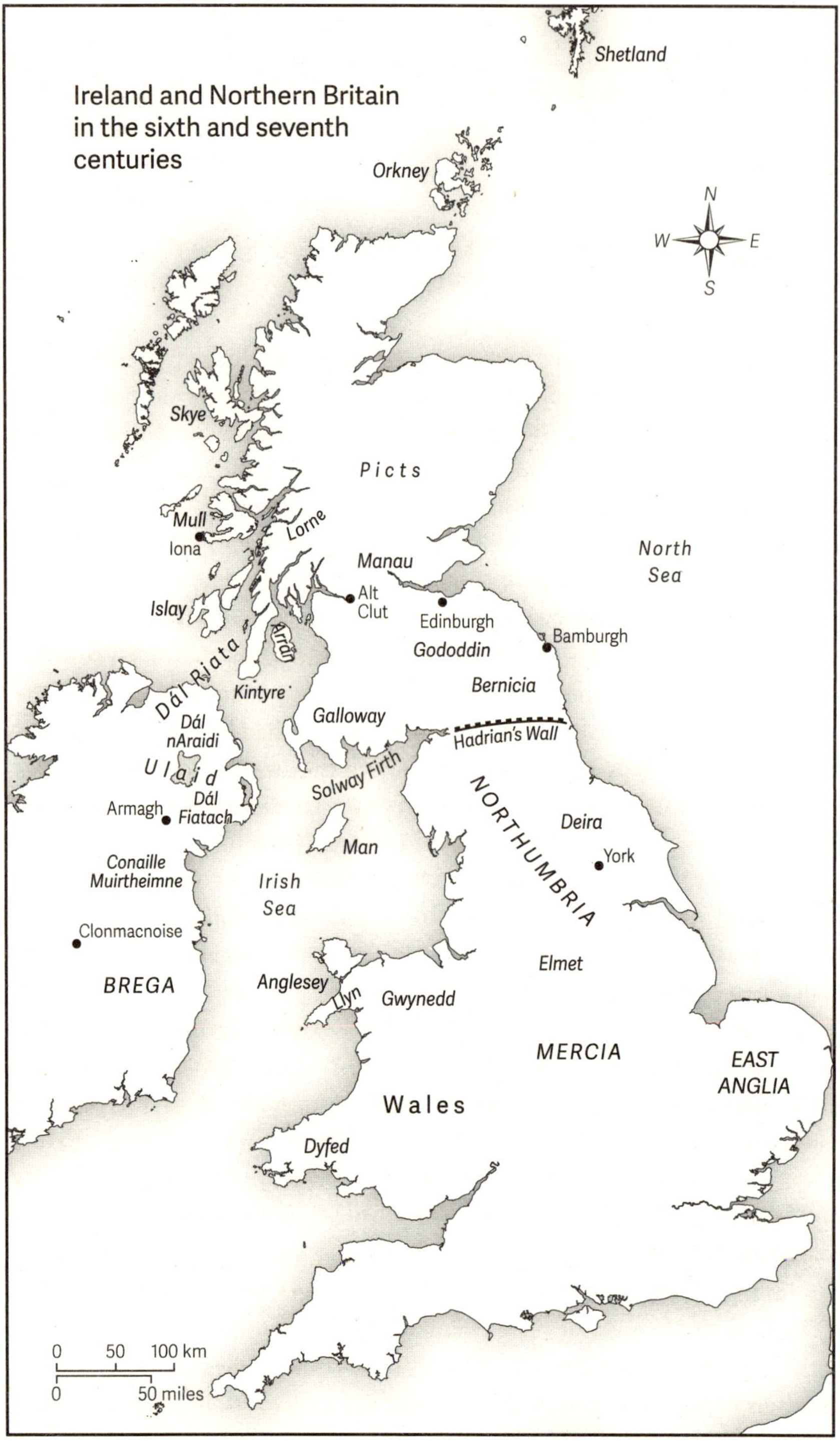
Ireland and Northern Britain in the sixth and seventh centuries
Shetland
Orkney
N
W
E
S
Skye
Picts
Mull
Iona
Lorne
Manau
North Sea
Islay
Alt Clut
Edinburgh
Bamburgh
Arran
Gododdin
Dál Riata
Kintyre
Bernicia
Dál nAraidi
Galloway
Hadrian's Wall
Ulaid
Solway Firth
Dál Fiatach
Armagh
NORTHUMBRIA
Deira
Man
York
Conaille Muirthemne
Irish Sea
Clonmacnoise
Elmet
BREGA
Anglesey
Llyn
Gwynedd
MERCIA
EAST ANGLIA
Wales
Dyfed
0 50 100 km
0 50 miles

3

GAELS AND BRITONS

Roman rule in Britain ceased in the early fifth century. How, why and precisely when it ended are questions that the contemporary sources do not answer. Modern historians traditionally pinpoint 410 as the year when Britain ceased to be part of the Western Roman Empire. In that year, the emperor Honorius wrote to the leaders of the Britons to say that he could no longer protect them and that they should organise their own defence. Honorius, who reigned from 393 to 423, was dealing with serious crises on the Continent and could not send reinforcements to outlying provinces. In Britain, meanwhile, the military situation had become critical. Raids by Irish, Pictish and Saxon pirates had caused much misery in the fourth century and showed no signs of abating in the fifth. By 410, substantial numbers of Roman troops had been withdrawn and those left behind were struggling to cope with the attacks. Yet Honorius was unable to help. Whether he was permanently withdrawing Roman authority from Britain or merely warning the inhabitants that he was temporarily suspending military aid is hard to say. It is possible that he and his successors intended to regain control of Britain as soon as the Continental problems settled down.[1] As things turned out, their authority was never to be restored. What happened instead was the total collapse of the Western Empire itself, the final act coming in 476 when the last emperor was overthrown. By then, the part of Britain formerly under Roman rule had effectively been independent for a couple of generations. Power had fallen into the hands of a Romanised native elite who, after initially attempting to retain a semblance of centralised control, had eventually divided the land into separate political entities. As the fifth century drew to a close, these entities evolved into small kingdoms whose rulers competed with one another for territory and status. The early medieval period, an era sometimes described as the 'Dark Ages', had begun.

There is no definitive map showing all of the kingdoms that emerged in what had once been Roman Britain. We know the names and approximate locations of some of them, but no amount of guesswork is going to fill the many blank spaces. We likewise know that the inhabitants of most kingdoms were native Britons, some of whom were more Romanised than others. By c.500, a number of these kingdoms had been taken over by a new elite whose language and cultural identity were quite different. The newcomers were the Anglo-Saxons, the early English, a people claiming descent from fifth-century immigrants – Angles, Saxons and Jutes – who had arrived in Britain from Germany, Denmark and the adjacent North Sea coastlands. The English spoke a Germanic language that was utterly unlike Brittonic, the Celtic language of the Britons. By c.550, English kings were ruling large swathes of southern and eastern Britain.[2] Sometimes they waged war against their British neighbours, sometimes against each other. Further north, on the other side of the now-redundant Hadrian's Wall, dwelt Britons who had not been under direct Roman rule except for brief periods of military occupation. These people, whom we can call the Northern Britons, had likewise formed their own small kingdoms and were engaging in predatory warfare. Beyond them lay the lands of the Picts, speakers of a language similar to Brittonic but with their own distinctive cultural identity. Like the Britons and the English, the Picts were divided into kingdoms whose rulers competed for territory and superiority.[3] As the fifth century ended and the sixth century began, another people emerged into the historical record: the Scots. Unlike the neighbouring Picts and Northern Britons, the Scots were Gaelic speakers like the Irish. They were destined to become deeply interwoven with the history of the Isle of Man.

Scottish origins

According to their own foundation legend, the Scots first came to Britain as colonists from Ireland. The legend asserts that they took over the Hebridean archipelago and the adjacent coastlands of what is now Argyll. Here they established a new kingdom, called Dál Riata, their first king being Fergus Mór ('Fergus the Great') whose reign commenced c.500. So says the legend.[4] It offers a plausible answer to the question of why Gaelic, the language of the Irish, came to be spoken in a part of north-west Britain in the sixth century. Moreover, the legend's narrative of a mass migration from Ireland has long been accepted as an authentic account of Scottish origins. Yet the fact that it is a legend is often overlooked, as is the possibility of alternative explanations for the presence of Gaelic speakers in a corner of northern Britain. One alternative sees the early Scots not as Irish immigrants but rather as a native group who switched from Brittonic to Gaelic speech because of proximity to – and close contact with – the Gaelic-speaking inhabitants of north-east Ireland.[5] Another alternative is that the actual sequence of events lies somewhere between this idea of 'gaelicised Britons' and the mass-migration scenario of the foundation legend. A gradual process of gaelicisation, involving small numbers of Irish settlers co-existing with native Brittonic speakers, might then be envisaged. The migration hypothesis would remain, but without the large-scale population movement implied by the legend. In this compromise scenario, groups of Gaelic speakers from Ireland settled in Argyll and the Hebrides for economic or social reasons, not ousting the native Britons but co-existing alongside them and eventually assimilating them. Intermarriage would no doubt have facilitated the switch from Brittonic to Gaelic in those families where the Irish element was dominant. A key stage in the process would have been the moment when a Gaelic-speaking royal dynasty took control, transferring its main centre of power from an ancestral seat in northern Ireland.

A movement of people from north-east Ireland to north-west Britain would not have been an isolated occurrence. Historical and archaeological evidence indicates the presence of Irish settlers in Wales in the fifth century.[6] Just as the foundation legend of Dál Riata tells of an Irish royal dynasty establishing a new kingdom in Britain, so a similar tradition in Irish lore claims that the Welsh kingdom of Dyfed was founded by an immigrant elite from the Deisi people of southern Ireland. Likewise, the Llyn or Lleyn Peninsula in North Wales is believed to take its name from the Laigin, a population group from Leinster who are said to have migrated to Wales in post-Roman times. It is a reasonable assumption that a similar and broadly contemporary phase of migration, spanning the fourth and fifth centuries, brought considerable numbers of Irish settlers to the Isle of Man.[7]

Turning back to the Scots, whatever their true origins, their kings emerged in the sixth century to become significant players in the politics of Britain and Ireland. It is useful to note that Dál Riata, their sprawling realm, was not really one kingdom but a regional hegemony encompassing various territories, each with its own royal family (in some cases, more than one).[8] In so far as it can be defined on a map, Dál Riata spanned the waters between Argyll and north-east Ireland to incorporate part of what is now County Antrim. On the Argyll side, the principal royal families were Cenél nGabráin ('Gabrán's Kindred') whose heartland was the long peninsula of Kintyre, Cenél Loairn (Loarn's Kindred') in Lorn and Mull, Cenél nÓengusa ('Óengus' Kindred') on Islay and Cenél Comgaill ('Comgall's Kindred') in Cowal and Bute. Violent competition for the overkingship of all Dál Riata became a dominant theme in relations between these *cenéla*, with Cenél nGabráin frequently coming out on top. Another theme was direct involvement in the politics of Ireland, especially in the north-east where the 'Irish' portion of Dál Riata became embroiled in regional wars. As we shall see below, the aggressive ambitions of one sixth-century northern Irish king impinged not only on Dál Riata but also on Man.

The name Scotti

The earliest evidence for the term 'Scot' comes from Roman writers. They identified the *Scotti* as one of the barbarian peoples who raided Roman Britain from the third to early fifth centuries. The meaning of *Scotti* is unknown, but it is thought to be a Latinised form of a word that the Romans applied to all Gaelic speakers regardless of where they lived.[9] In Roman eyes it may also have had connotations of piracy in the Irish Sea. Indeed, Latin *Scotti* might derive from a name that one or more groups of Gaelic-speaking raiders originally applied to themselves. One modern theory suggests that there may have been an Indo-European root word *skot*, from which a similar word in Primitive Irish was subsequently coined, and that these words had connotations with 'darkness', as does the ancient Greek word *skotos*.[10] The broad application of *Scotti* to include all speakers of Gaelic, whether in Ireland or Britain, remained in use throughout the early medieval period, in contemporary literature if not in everyday discourse. Not until the end of the period did its meaning narrow to become an ethnonym for the Gaelic-speaking inhabitants of northern Britain.

Early Christianity on Man

Christianity gained a firm foothold in Britain long before the end of the Roman period. By the early fourth century it had become so well established that the British churches were represented at an ecclesiastical council in Gaul by three of their own bishops.[11] After the end of Roman rule in the early fifth century, Christianity remained the preferred religion for many Britons in Romanised areas and began to spread further afield into 'barbarian' regions north of the old imperial frontier. It developed in Ireland during the same century, its expansion there being attributed to British missionaries such as Palladius and Patrick. The latter subsequently became a cult figure at the centre of a large body of hagiography which gave him most of the credit for leading the Irish away from paganism. Two hagiographical stories also claim that Patrick brought Christianity to Man. In one, preserved in the twelfth-century Irish text *Lebor Gabala Erenn* ('The Book of the Taking of Ireland', commonly known as 'The Book of Invasions'), Patrick defeated Manx paganism by slaying a trio of local gods. This is simply a hagiographical legend created to enhance Patrick's achievements by making him the evangelist of Man. Another twelfth-century source, a *vita* of Patrick written by the English monk Jocelin of Furness, says that the saint visited Man where 'by his miracles and preaching' he converted the inhabitants to Christianity and appointed a bishop to serve them. The appointee, Germanus, established his episcopal seat on St Patrick's Isle at Peel. He is a very obscure figure but is commemorated in the dedication of St German's Cathedral, the ruins of which stand on St Patrick's Isle today. According to Jocelin, the isle acquired its name because Patrick had lived there during his visit to Man. It is more likely that the name was bestowed long after Patrick's time by Christianised Norse settlers who had been exposed to the cult of Patrick in Ireland or in north-west England.[12]

The stories connecting Patrick and Man in *Lebor Gabala* and in Jocelin's *vita* can be set aside as hagiographical fiction. So, too, can the tale of an Ulster chieftain called Mac Cuill who is said to have incurred Patrick's wrath. This story appears in a seventh-century *vita* of Patrick by Muirchu, an Irish monk who supported a claim by the church of Armagh to be the premier church of Ireland. In one passage, Muirchu describes Mac Cuill confessing to Patrick that he had planned to kill him. The saint responded by ordering Mac Cuill to board a small boat and set out to sea. At the mercy of the elements, the exile was eventually cast ashore on *Euonia* – the Isle of Man. There he met two bishops, Conindrus and Rumilus, supposedly the first missionaries to bring Christianity to the Manx. Mac Cuill became their pupil and eventually succeeded them as bishop. Muirchu concludes the story with these words: *Hic est Maccuil di Mane, episcopus et antestes Arddae Huimnonn* ('This is Mac Cuill of Man, bishop and prelate of Ardd Huimnonn'). There is much to puzzle over in this story. Mac Cuill is otherwise unknown and seems to be a literary invention.[13] The bishops Conindrus and Rumilus are likewise unattested in other sources, unless they are the priests Cynan and Run associated in Welsh lore with a place called *Manan* (or *Mannia*). If the Welsh tradition is independent of Muirchu – and we cannot be sure that it is – we might feel more confident about the historicity of Conindrus/Cynan and Rumilus/Run and of their connection with Man. Their episcopal successor Mac Cuill has, unsurprisingly, been identified as St Maughold or Machutus, the alleged founder of the Manx monastery at Kirk Maughold. Muirchu himself does not allude to such a connection but may have left it up to his readers to join the dots, as subsequent writers have certainly done. The first to make the connection was Jocelin of Furness who included a version of the Mac Cuill legend in his own *vita* of Patrick. Jocelin stated that Mac Cuill, whom he called Magiul, was also known as Machaldus. He added that the stone coffin (sarcophagus) of Magiul/Machaldus lay in the cemetery at Kirk Maughold where, instead of bones, it contained a well of fresh water that healed ailments. Jocelin plainly had minimal information on the saint. In the sixteenth century, the Scottish historian Hector Boece tried to equate the patron of Maughold with Mac Caille, a fifth-century Irish bishop associated with the famed St Brigid of Kildare. There was no ancient tradition behind this, so we can disregard it as Boece's own invention. In fact, we are left wondering if Kirk Maughold preserves the name of a saint at all. It might instead preserve the name of a place, perhaps a well-known geographical feature in the locality.[14] Staying with the topic of names, we turn back to Muirchu's *vita* and to the place he calls Ardd Huimnonn. Here the Gaelic word *ardd* means 'high ground' in the sense of a headland or promontory. Huimnonn is more difficult to interpret but it is often assumed to refer to the Maughold district, solely on the assumption that Muirchu had some knowledge of Manx place-names that we no longer possess. A more sceptical view sees Muirchu's story of Mac Cuill as little more than an exercise in ecclesiastical fiction, one that contains nothing of value pertaining to the birth of Manx Christianity. Indeed, its main purpose was probably to offer pseudo-historical justification for a claim of ecclesiastical authority by the senior clergy of Armagh over the monastery at Maughold.

It is worth noting that a number of place-names on Man are associated with Patrick in local traditions of uncertain origin. These names probably reflect the arrival of Patrick's cult in the Norse period (late ninth century onwards). Jocelin's account of Patrick and Germanus might even be a borrowing from Manx folklore based on local explanations for the name of St Patrick's Isle at Peel.[15]. One such tradition says that Patrick founded the first church on Man at Ballakilpheric in the parish of Rushen. Here, on a hill known as Cronk y Dooney, stood a small chapel or 'keeill', now no longer visible. The Manx Gaelic word *dooney* occurs in three placenames on the island and derives from Irish *domnach* which has the dual meaning 'Sunday' and 'church'.[16] The second part of Ballakilpheric seems to derive from *Keeill Pheric*, 'Patrick's keeill', while the surrounding land was formerly known as Kirk Patrick, 'Patrick's Church' (*Kyrke Patryk* in 1511). The antiquity of these names is unknown, as is the date of the keeill. The early ecclesiastical term *domnach* may, however, suggest Early Christian activity. The same can be said of the other two *dooney* sites on Man (Knock y Doonee in Andreas parish and Rullic y Doonee in Malew) but at Ballakilpheric the Patrick connection is unlikely to pre-date the Norse period.

Another early saint associated with Man is Sanctan, the eponymous patron of Kirk Santan in the south of the island. Sanctan was a sixth-century bishop whose name appears in church dedications on both sides of the Irish Sea. In an Irish text of c.800 he is identified as a Briton without any mention of a Manx connection. He is said to have spent most of his ecclesiastical career in Ireland. The link with Man is first encountered in a Scottish document of the late thirteenth century which refers to *Ecclesia Sancti Santani* (St Sanctan's Church) on Man.[17] This dedication and the one at Kirksanton in present-day Cumbria are now assumed to have been bestowed by Christianised Norse settlers migrating east from their older colonies in Ireland, most likely in the tenth century, unless the Manx dedication was imported from the Cumbrian site via a subsequent phase of colonisation. There is no reason to believe that St Sanctan himself ever set foot on Man, although we should consider the possibility that a British cleric migrating to Ireland may have paused his journey on Manx shores.[18]

Early Christian archaeology on Man

Bereft of an authentic historical narrative for the beginnings of Manx Christianity, we turn instead to archaeology. Physical evidence of early Christian activity on Man is indeed available, some of it still visible in the modern landscape. Its best-known and most visually impressive form is the carved stone memorial, whether richly adorned with sculptural patterns or inscribed with a simple cross. The earliest Christian monuments on Man were erected in the sixth century. They represent the beginning of a sculptural phase that can be described as Early Manx, approximately spanning the pre-Viking period from c.500 to c.900.[19]

Most of the Early Manx memorials have been found in ancient cemeteries that are not associated with ecclesiastical sites such as churches or monasteries. The cemeteries, although usually small in area, often show evidence of having been used for hundreds of years, in some cases from the early medieval period through to relatively modern times. Approximately 180 such sites have been identified, many of them potentially dating back to the beginnings of Manx Christianity, but only a few have been subjected to archaeological excavation. The oldest Christian graves, where they can be dated with any measure of confidence, usually take the form of stone-lined 'cists'. Also known as 'lintel graves', cists are fairly common in Early Christian cemeteries in Britain and Ireland. They are characterised by slabs laid along the sides and ends, with flat stones laid on top to form a kind of lidded box. The typical orientation is west–east, conforming to Christian ritual, so that the head of the deceased lies at the western end.[20]

Many of the small Manx cemeteries contain rectangular structures known as keeills. These little stone buildings, comprising a single room, were long regarded as being contemporary with the earliest graves and memorials. They are thought to be old chapels where religious ceremonies such as burials were conducted by priests from a nearby church. The current view among archaeologists and historians is that, while some keeills might indeed belong to the Early Christian period (c.400 to c.800), others date from the Viking Age (c.800 to c.1100) or later. It is even possible that a majority of them do not pre-date the eleventh century.[21] Few of these sites have undergone a modern archaeological excavation, this being the only method of establishing a secure chronological context.

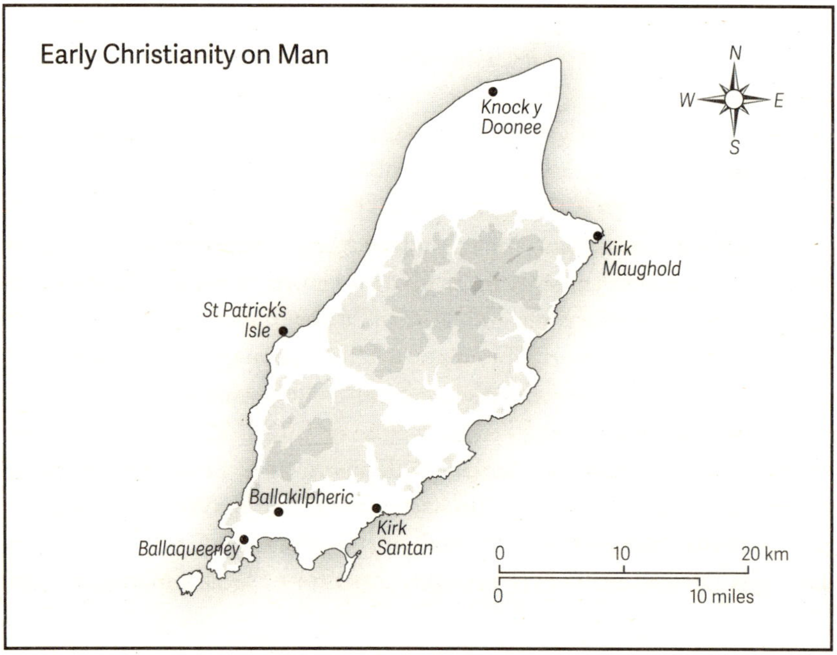

Early Christian inscriptions

In Roman Britain, inscriptions carved on stone monuments used the Latin alphabet. Later, after Roman rule had ended, Latin remained in use by Christianised Britons as the medium of inscriptions carved on memorial stones. Brittonic, the vernacular language of these people in everyday discourse, was not used in such commemorations. The situation was different in contemporary Ireland where a unique form of writing was devised. This used an alphabet of straight and oblique strokes incised above, across or below a single line. Known as ogham script, it appears on Irish monuments from the fourth to ninth centuries. The vast majority of Ireland's ogham stones, some 300-plus, are found in the south-west. Others are known from western Britain, predominantly in south-west Wales where more than forty have been identified. There is a close correlation between the Welsh ogham inscriptions and the kingdom of Dyfed which, in the early post-Roman period, received substantial Irish immigration. Dyfed was one of the kingdoms of the Britons by the middle of the sixth century, but its population included many people of Irish heritage, descendants of earlier settlers, who still spoke Gaelic.[22] On Man, eight ogham inscriptions have been identified, five of which are from the fifth to sixth centuries. Of the other three, one has been dated to the sixth to ninth centuries while two are considerably later and belong to the eleventh or twelfth centuries. Of the five early examples, one is accompanied by an equivalent inscription in Latin. This kind of bilingual commemoration also occurs in Wales and is an overtly Christian feature. Of the Welsh Latin ogham stones, one of the most famous is at Castell Dwyran in Carmarthenshire. It commemorates Voteporigis, an otherwise unknown individual formerly (but erroneously) identified as King Vortipor who ruled Dyfed in the sixth century.[23]

In addition to the ogham stones, another Manx monument with an Early Christian connection comes from the parish church of Santon. Discovered in the churchyard in the eighteenth century, it now stands inside the church. On one face it has an inscription in Latin: *Aviti monomenti*, 'the monument of Avitus'. Although the wording does not contain any religious phrases, a Christian connection is implied by the use of Latin – the language of the Church – and by close similarities with inscriptions found in Christian contexts in mainland Britain.[24] The style of lettering has enabled specialist scholars to date the inscription to the early sixth century. Of Avitus himself nothing is known, but he was evidently a person of local importance. The absence of a patronymic ('son of...') could indicate that he was a cleric, but might simply mean that he was a secular individual whose father's name was not added for some reason. The present-day church, dedicated to St Sanctan (or Sanctain), was built in 1774 but is traditionally believed to stand on the site of a keeill. If the tradition is correct, and if the keeill is of the earlier, pre-Viking type, we might imagine that the memorial stone was erected beside a small chapel. Perhaps Avitus was a priest who ministered to an embryonic Christian community in this part of Man?[25]

The aforementioned bilingual Latin ogham stone from Man was discovered in an old burial ground at Knock y Doonee in Andreas parish. The Latin inscription incorporates the words *hic iacit* ('here lies'), a formula seen on Early Christian memorials from the western side of mainland Britain:

> AMMECAT FILIUS ROCAT HIC IACIT ('Ammecatus, son of Rocatus, lies here')

The names of the deceased and his father are Latinised forms of Celtic names. These men presumably used a Celtic language – Gaelic or Brittonic – in their everyday speech. Unless either one or both of them was a cleric, they perhaps had little knowledge of Latin and relied on others for the accuracy of the inscription. The accompanying ogham, incised along one edge of the stone, is now incomplete but still partly legible. It repeats the name and patronymic in Gaelic:

> [e]b[i] catos m[a]qi roc[a]t[os]

The word *maqi* is related to present-day *mac*, meaning 'son of'. Its presence implies that Ammecatus/Ambicatos and his family were people of Irish origin, or that their community included people who spoke Gaelic.[26] Whoever commissioned the carving plainly intended that it should be seen and understood by local inhabitants. It is therefore a reasonable assumption that this part of Man had been colonised by Gaelic-speaking Irish settlers.

Another of the Manx ogham inscriptions is noteworthy for including what may be the name of an identifiable population group. The stone in question comes from Ballaqueeney at the southern end of the island. It has no Latin inscription, but the ogham reads as follows:

> BIVAIDONAS MAQI MUCOI CUNAVA[LI] ('Bivaidonas, a son of the tribe of Cunava[li]')

If the name *Cunava* is an ethnonym, it could refer to a fairly small group of people, such as an extended family, or to a much larger group, such as the inhabitants of a kingdom. One suggestion is that Cunava is a rendering of *Conaille*, possibly referring to Conaille Muirtheimne, a kingdom of north-east Ireland in what is now County Louth.[27]

A second stone from Ballaqueeney commemorates DOVAIDONA MAQI DROATA. The usual interpretation is that the deceased was 'Dovaidu son of Droata'. However, some observers prefer to see Droata not as a personal name but as the word 'druid', thus giving a wholly different meaning to the inscription. This stretches credulity somewhat, for the stone was discovered at a keeill site and thus has a Christian context. It would be strange indeed to find a druid – a pagan priest or mage – being mentioned on such a monument at a time when paganism was in retreat on both sides of the Irish Sea. We can probably disregard the notion of druids at Ballaqueeney, or anywhere else on Man, in the fifth or sixth century. It is far more likely that Dovaidu's father was simply a man whose name was Droata.[28]

In addition to the stones bearing inscriptions, we find a less elaborate type of Christian memorial: the grave marker incised with a simple cross but with no other form of carving. Such stones are often difficult to date, but some examples from Britain and Ireland appear to be from the sixth century. Dating is achievable only when the stone is associated with sites or artefacts that can be assigned to a specific period. Without a datable context, any cross-incised stone might be later, even much later, than the pre-Viking era. On Man this type of monument is known from a number of sites but only a handful, less than a dozen, can be assigned a date before 900 with any measure of confidence.[29]

So what do the early inscribed stones tell us about the population of Man in the fifth and sixth centuries? Perhaps the simplest answer is that the island appears to have been inhabited by Gaelic speakers and Brittonic speakers who lived in peaceful co-existence, a situation mirrored in parts of contemporary Wales. On their family memorials they respectively used the ogham script of Ireland and the Latin alphabet of Roman Britain. Had they not managed to co-exist, if their relations had been characterised by mutual hostility, there would have been no need for the parallel ogham and Latin inscription of the Knock y Doonee stone. In both Wales and Man there may have been fully bilingual families in which, because of intermarriage, both Gaelic and Brittonic were spoken. What these Early Christian stones on Man do not tell us is what language was spoken by the island's rulers. Who wielded authority in the period 400 to 600, the very time when Christianity was taking hold: a Gaelic-speaking elite or a Brittonic-speaking one? This is one of the most difficult questions in Manx history. To answer it we must go back to the literary sources in the hope of finding clues.

Báetán

The Irish province of Ulster takes its name from the Ulaid, a people of the early medieval period whose territory encompassed the eastern part of present-day County Down. One of the dominant groups among the Ulaid was the Dál Fiatach kindred whose chief centre of power lay at Dun Lethglaise in present-day Downpatrick. Dál Fiatach kings frequently claimed the overkingship of the Ulaid, although this claim to primacy was often challenged and counter-claimed by rival kindreds, most notably the Dál nAraidi or 'Cruithin' of present-day Antrim. One of the most ambitious and powerful Dál Fiatach kings was Báetán mac Cairill whose reign began c.572. According to later Irish tradition, Báetán not only held the overkingship of the Ulaid but also the high kingship of Ireland as well as superiority over parts of north-west Britain. The Irish poem *Clann Ollaman Uaisle Emna*, now lost but cited in other texts, listed a number of places under his authority. One of these was Man.[30] Another Irish text refers to Báetán waging a military campaign on Man and bringing it under his dominion. As he is clearly a potentially significant figure in early Manx history, he warrants a closer look.

Information on Báetán comes from various sources. Although collectively these fail to provide a coherent narrative of his career, they supply as much data as we can reasonably expect for an Irish king of the sixth century. The most reliable texts are the Irish annals which note Báetán's death in 581. Other sources are more controversial. *Berchan's Prophecy*, a long poem composed in Gaelic in the twelfth century, evidently refers to Báetán in its verses on various unnamed Scottish and Irish kings.[31] Although the *Prophecy* reports the activities of these rulers in a curiously allusive fashion, in many cases the identity of a particular individual can be deduced. Báetán is almost certainly the anonymous 'king from the north' whom the *Prophecy* depicts as holding sovereignty over all Ireland, winning three battles in northern Britain and fighting both Scots and English. An even later mention of Báetán comes from the *Book of Lecan*, an Irish compilation of the late fourteenth or early fifteenth century containing older texts of varying provenance. Among its contents is an account of Báetán's dealings with Áedán mac Gabráin, a king of Dál Riata, who is shown swearing an oath of submission to Báetán at Islandmagee on the Antrim coast. The same account is also the source for the military campaign mentioned above, in which Báetán is said to have subdued Man to his rule. It is worth quoting the relevant passage in full:

> And Man was cleared by him of foreigners, so that dominion over it has belonged to the Ulaid from that time forward; and in the second year after his death the Gaels abandoned Man.[32]

The lost poem *Clann Ollaman Uaisle Emna* includes Man among several territories from which Báetán exacted tribute as overlord, the others being Munster and Connacht in Ireland and the Hebridean isle of Skye. We know of this poem's existence only because it is quoted in medieval Irish genealogical texts.[33] Its testimony appears to support the claim in the *Book of Lecan* that Báetán conquered Man. However, in neither case is the source of information completely reliable, hence the information cannot be accepted at face value. There is, nevertheless, some reason to be optimistic that we are here seeing real events of the sixth century rather than retrospective pseudo-history concocted in later times. Our optimism comes from two entries in the Irish annals that lend support to the Lecan text:

> 577 – The first expedition of the Ulaid in Eubonia
> 578 – Return of the Ulaid from Eubonia.[34]

Like the name *Euonia* mentioned earlier in this chapter, *Eubonia* is a name for Man coined in literary Latin. What the Irish annalists seem to be describing here is a seaborne military campaign which began in 577 and ended in the following year. It involved action on Man by Ulaid forces at a time when their paramount king was Báetán mac Cairill. The annal entries appear to corroborate information from the later sources, namely that Báetán invaded and conquered Man. A plausible interpretation, combining all of the data, is that Báetán's Manx campaign comprised two separate expeditions mounted in consecutive years.[35] This is implied by the expedition of 577 being described as the 'first'. War fleets and armies in pre-Viking times usually campaigned on a seasonal basis, returning home for the winter and not mustering again until spring. Báetán's ships and soldiers presumably returned to Ireland after their first expedition to Man in 577 before mounting a second invasion in the following year's campaigning season. There is no record of a third expedition, nor do the annalists confirm that Báetán achieved his objectives. However, if we accept the testimony of the *Book of Lecan*, we can infer that the two-year campaign was successful, with Man being cleared of 'foreigners' and the Ulaid forces sailing home in 578. The assertion that the Ulaid ruled Man 'from that time forward' refers to a brief period between 578 and the date when the Gaels 'abandoned' the island. The latter event, occurring within two years of Báetán's death, seemingly marked the end of Ulaid dominion over Man. Since Báetán died in 581, the end can be dated to 582 or 583. It was surely connected to his demise. Nor need we be surprised that this period of Ulster overlordship turned out to be brief. Early medieval hegemony was usually personal and temporary, being imposed by a powerful king but rarely passing by default to his successors. The latter usually had to fight their own battles, subduing rivals at home and abroad, if they wished to pursue territorial ambitions beyond their core domains. This is how Báetán and other rulers rose to positions of superiority that allowed them to subjugate large territories, and why their hard-won personal hegemonies normally died with them. Báetán seems to have been the overlord of Man for just three or four years from his defeat of the 'foreigners' in 577–8 to his death in 581, after which the island ceased to be under Ulaid rule.

There is a hint in another Irish source that Báetán's invasion of Man was not the first by a Dál Fiatach king. A twelfth-century poem on the kings of Ulster has this to say of his father:

> Cairell reigned twenty-five years, ravaged Man and died in Arran.[36]

Unlike the annal entries that appear to corroborate the account of Báetán's Manx campaign in the *Book of Lecan*, this brief allusion to a raid by Cairell receives support from no other source. Nevertheless, it might be argued that these traditions of Dál Fiatach activity on Man support one another in some measure. Báetán's Manx campaign is generally accepted as historical. If the campaign attributed to his father is likewise seen as more than a later invention, we are probably seeing a determined effort to impose overlordship on Man by two generations of Dál Fiatach kings. Cairell ravaged Man but may have failed to conquer it before his death on the Isle of Arran in the Firth of Clyde. His son evidently fared better, even if his hold on Man turned out to be fairly brief.

Áedán mac Gabráin

Another Gaelic-speaking king who has been associated with warfare on Man in the sixth century is Áedán mac Gabráin of Dál Riata. The relevant source is the *Annals of Tigernach*, one of the main Irish chronicles, in its entry for the year 582:

> The battle of Manau (*Cath Manand*) in which the victor was Áedán mac Gabráin.[37]

Some modern observers, interpreting *Manau* as the Isle of Man, have proposed that the annal is reporting a battle fought on the island in the year after Báetán's death. This idea appears to be supported by the *Annals of Clonmacnoise*, a sixteenth-century Irish chronicle written in English, which states that 'Áedán, Gabrán's son, king of Scotland, fought a battle on the Isle of Man'. However, the associated year of 504 is clearly an error, for Áedán's reign did not commence until 70 years later. The Clonmacnoise annalist has simply made a duplicate of the entry in *AT* and misdated it, while giving the battle a Manx setting that is no more than an assumption. The setting was not given entirely without reason, for *Manau* was indeed one of the old names for Man. In the early-ninth-century Welsh chronicle *Historia Brittonum*, for example, *Manau* is explicitly equated with *Eubonia*, one of several latinised names for the island.[38] Nevertheless, a much better candidate exists for the *Manau* where Áedán won his victory in 582. Our attention turns to a region of mainland northern Britain known in medieval Welsh sources as Manau or 'Manau Gododdin'. The name *Gododdin* was borne by a post-Roman kingdom of the Northern Britons that existed in the area around Edinburgh until the mid-seventh century. By the 1500s, when the *Annals of Clonmacnoise* were being compiled, neither Gododdin nor Manau Gododdin were remembered outside the narrow confines of Welsh literature.[39] There is no doubt that Manau Gododdin is a much closer fit with the geography of Áedán's military career than the other Manau, the Isle of Man, which the Welsh called *Ynys Manaw* (*ynys* = 'island'). Áedán's campaigns, as far as can be discerned, seem generally to have been fought in mainland Britain, the only exception being a raid on Orkney. One of his victories was won against a people called Miathi, reported by Abbot Adomnán of Iona (died 704) in a hagiographical *vita* of St Columba. In Roman times the Miathi were known by the Latin name *Maeatae*. Their heartlands lay around the head of the Firth of Forth, extending westward along the Forth Valley, with

Stirling's imposing Castle Rock probably being their main centre of power in the sixth century.[40] A memory of this people lingers today in a couple of place-names in Central Scotland: Dumyat (earlier *Dun Myat*) and Myot Hill. The Miathi heartlands lay in the northern *Manau*, a name still surviving in place-names such as Slamannan ('Moor of Manau'), Dalmeny (formerly *Dunmanyn*, 'Fort of Manau') and Clackmannan ('Stone of Manau'). Áedán's victories over the Miathi and in *Manau* were almost certainly one and the same: a battle fought in northern Britain in 582. It seems rather less likely that he waged an otherwise unrecorded campaign on the Isle of Man.[41]

King Brendinus

The medieval Scottish historian John of Fordun, writing in the fourteenth century, wove a fanciful tale in which Áedán mac Gabráin sent two kinsmen – a son and a nephew – to join a campaign against the English king Ceawlin. The nephew, Brendinus, was described by Fordun as a king of the Isle of Man. The campaign ended in defeat at Fethanleag, a battle placed by Fordun in the fifteenth year of Áedán's reign.[42] Fethanleag also appears in the *Anglo-Saxon Chronicle* as the site of a battle fought in 584 by Ceawlin, a historical king of the West Saxons, against the Britons. The location, now lost, is thought to be in the vicinity of Stoke Lyne in Oxfordshire. The southern English context was no obstacle for Fordun, who simply borrowed the *ASC* entry for his own purposes. He gave the battle a Scottish dimension by adding Áedán mac Gabráin to the original protagonists. Ceawlin's main adversary in Fordun's version was 'Malgo, king of the Britons', whom we can identify as the sixth-century North Welsh ruler Maelgwn, king of Gwynedd. According to Fordun, Malgo sought military assistance from Áedán, who sent forces led by his son Griffin ('a distinguished knight') and nephew Brendinus, *regulus Euboniae* ('kinglet of Man'). In the ensuing battle, placed by Fordun south of Stainmore in the North Pennines, the Britons and their allies were vanquished and Áedán's son Griffin was slain. Fordun adds that Brendinus had a brother called Adelfius whose daughter married Philtanes, 'king of Ireland', to become the mother of three famous Irish saints: Fursey, Foillan and Ultán. This saintly trio, together with Ceawlin and Malgo/Maelgwn, are the only people in the entire sequence of events whose historical existence is not in doubt. Most of the rest appear to be characters invented by Fordun, with others being plucked from texts of dubious reliability. No earlier writer mentions the Manx king

Brendinus, a figure seemingly created by Fordun for this story. It is a measure of the dearth of information on sixth-century Man that the only 'native' ruler to whom we can give a name is a fictional character.

The Manx Britons

Who were Báetán's adversaries on Man, the 'foreigners' whom he expelled from the island? It is reasonable to assume that they were not fellow Gaels. No Gaelic speakers on the island, using the language that Báetán himself used in everyday discourse, would have been described as 'foreign' by an Irish chronicler. Báetán's enemies on Man plainly did not originate in Ireland, nor indeed in another Gaelic-speaking region such as Dál Riata. Moreover, the late sixth century is far too soon to identify them as Vikings, a group to whom Irish chroniclers frequently assigned the label *Gall*, 'foreigners'. The Viking Age lay more than 200 years in the future. Nor are Báetán's enemies on Man likely to have been English. The territorial expansion that brought English warrior kings to the western seaboard of northern Britain was achieved not in the sixth century but in the seventh. We can therefore identify the 'foreigners' whom Báetán expelled from Man as Britons.

We can go further, by suggesting that they were 'foreign' not only from an Irish perspective, but from a Manx perspective too. In other words, they were not native to Man. Although some Manx people spoke Brittonic in the sixth century, co-existing with fellow islanders who spoke Gaelic, they were not strangers on their own soil.[43] The 'foreign' Britons whom Báetán encountered on Man should therefore be seen as outsiders. Where did they come from? With no answer forthcoming from the Irish chronicles, we turn to their British counterpart, *Annales Cambriae*, the Welsh Annals. The oldest known version of *AC* was compiled in the tenth century but survives in a manuscript written some 200 years later. Its entries provide important information, despite generally being briefer and fewer than those in the Irish chronicles. It hardly needs repeating that neither the Welsh nor the Irish chronicles should be taken at face value. They must be handled with caution. In the main, however, *AC* is accepted by historians alongside Irish equivalents such as *AU* and *AT* as a fairly reliable source.[44] Under the year 584, the Welsh chronicle has *bellum contra Euboniam* ('a battle against Man'). A plausible context here is the end of the Ulaid 'dominion' over Man which, as we have seen, lasted from the late 570s to the early 580s. The year 584 is close enough to the date of the Ulaid withdrawal in 582 or 583 to suggest that we are seeing linked events relating to a change of overlordship from Irish to British. The brief period of Ulaid overlordship was achieved by the expulsion of enemies who were neither Gaels nor Manxmen but 'foreigners'. It may have been the return of these same foreigners that led to the battle in 584 *contra Euboniam*, 'against Man'. Given that our only source for this battle was written in Wales, in a Brittonic-speaking milieu, we can identify one set of protagonists as Britons. That they fought *contra* Man indicates that they were not already on the island but sailed there in a war fleet from another land. Where did they come from?

Looking out from the shores of Man, the closest neighbouring territory of the Britons in the sixth century was Galloway. The existence of one or more British kingdoms in this region is implied by the presence of high-status ecclesiastical and secular settlements. Of the ecclesiastical sites the best known is the monastery at Whithorn on the Machars peninsula, a feature visible from Man. Of the secular sites, the hilltop fortresses at Trusty's Hill and Mote of Mark were centres of sixth-century royal activity. Unfortunately, despite this impressive physical evidence, we know nothing about any Galwegian kingdoms in this period – neither names nor specific locations. Nor can any sixth-century North British kings identified in the sources be linked to Galloway with any measure of confidence.[45] In any case, the close proximity of Galloway does not necessarily mean that the Britons who waged war 'against Man' in 584 were Galwegians. We therefore turn south, to Wales, where a number of British kingdoms are known to have existed in the early medieval period. Of these, the nearest to Man was Gwynedd. Founded in the fifth century, Gwynedd appears to have originally comprised the island of Anglesey together with part of the adjacent mainland across the Menai Strait and a swathe of coastland eastwards as far as the River Conwy. The kingdom's name is thought to derive from Irish Gaelic, with either *Feni* 'Irish people' or *fian* 'warband' providing the root word.[46] That the name of a kingdom of the Britons should have a Gaelic origin is not unduly strange when we recall the evidence for Irish settlement in Wales in the late fourth to early fifth centuries. Medieval writers often latinised the name Gwynedd to *Venedotia* – a name that closely resembles *Feni* – hence the use of the adjective 'Venedotian' by modern historians. The kingdom nevertheless adopted a British rather than an Irish identity. Throughout the early medieval period, Venedotian kings often imposed superiority over other parts of Wales and sometimes further afield. One of them may have launched a campaign that led to the battle against the Isle of Man in 584. Possession of Anglesey would have given him easy access to Man via a sea voyage of only

50 miles. At the time of the *bellum contra Euboniam*, the king in question was Rhun ap Maelgwn, by then in the twilight years of a long reign (c.547 to c.586). It may have been Rhun who led, or sent, a war fleet to Man in 584. A hypothetical reconstruction of what was happening on Man in the late sixth century can therefore be presented. It offers a context for the Irish and Welsh chronicle entries by envisaging a struggle between kings of Ulster and Gwynedd for control of Man in an era when the island's population comprised Gaelic-speaking and Brittonic-speaking communities. In this scenario, the protagonists were the Dál Fiatach of Ulaid and the royal house of Gwynedd, led by their respective kings Báetán mac Cairill and Rhun ap Maelgwn. Hostilities erupted c.577 at a time when Man may have lain under Rhun's overlordship. An Ulaid expeditionary force, led by Báetán, invaded the island and succeeded in sending Rhun's subordinates ('foreigners') back home to Gwynedd. The native Manx then found themselves under Báetán's overlordship, which lasted until his death in 581. Within a couple of years of Báetán's passing, his successors lost control of Man and sailed home. A force from Gwynedd sailed to the island, winning a battle and imposing (or re-imposing) Rhun's dominion. In the aftermath it is likely that any Gaelic-speakers among the island's landowning elite would have been particularly vulnerable, especially if they had benefitted during the period of Ulaid overlordship. Some might even have been ousted from their estates in favour of other islanders – not necessarily Brittonic speakers – who had remained loyal to Gwynedd throughout the conflict.

Man and Rheged

The foregoing scenario is founded on an idea that Britons from Gwynedd were the 'foreigners' whom Báetán cleared from Man and also the warriors who fought a battle *contra* Man in 584. Alternative theories can, of course, be proposed. Outside Wales there were other groups of Britons living within easy reach of Man, any of whom might be identifiable as the 'foreigners' confronted by Báetán. The Galloway Britons have already been mentioned but there were also those in what are today the coastlands of Lancashire and Cumbria in north-west England. Although we do not know the names of any sixth-century kingdoms in these areas, we can assume that one or more such polities did exist and that their rulers may have had sufficient military capability to launch seaborne assaults on Man. Nevertheless, we have no hint that any Northern Britons were involved in the battle against Man in 584, nor do we know which of their kingdoms would have been likely to mount such a campaign. Contrary to a widespread assumption, there is no evidence that the nearest North British kingdom to Man was Rheged. The latter is mentioned in heroic poems attributed to Taliesin, a bard or court poet who served a sixth-century king of Rheged called Urien. The poems survive in texts written in Wales hundreds of years later and have been subjected to detailed scrutiny by specialist scholars.[47] Opinion on the poems is divided with regard to provenance and authenticity. Some experts suggest that several poems contain genuinely archaic elements indicating composition in the late sixth or early seventh century. Armed with such arguments, and with a handful of enigmatic place-names from the poems, many historians identify Rheged as a kingdom located on one or both sides of the Solway Firth. Notwithstanding its widespread popularity, this theory rests on extremely flimsy foundations that fail to withstand rigorous scrutiny. All that we really know about Rheged is that it lay somewhere in northern England or southern Scotland and that it was ruled in the second half of the sixth century by a famed warrior king called Urien. We cannot even be certain that *Rheged* was the name of Urien's kingdom rather than of a specific district or settlement within it. Whether Urien was still living and reigning at the time of the *bellum contra Euboniam* is uncertain but the poems that eulogise him do not mention a campaign on Man, nor indeed does any of the heroic poetry relating to North British kings.[48] Given the existence of later traditions connecting the rulers of Gwynedd with Man, a good case can be made for seeing the battle of 584 as part of a campaign by Rhun ap Maelgwn to impose (or re-impose) his overlordship on the island.

Into the seventh century

In his *Ecclesiastical History*, completed in 731, the Northumbrian monk Bede described the Isle of Man as a territory of the Britons. What he meant was that the island was, at that time, under British rule. He said nothing about the languages spoken there and may have assumed that most of the inhabitants were Brittonic speakers. We know from Bede's own writings that he was familiar with the works of the fifth-century historian Orosius. The latter, as we saw in Chapter 2, had regarded the inhabitants of Man as Gaelic speakers or, perhaps more specifically, as Irish. The seemingly opposing viewpoints of Orosius and Bede can be reconciled when we consider them alongside the chronicle entries relating to the 570s and 580s. Thus, when Orosius wrote his *Seven Books* in the early 400s, Man was presumably ruled by a Gaelic-speaking elite of Irish origin. In the late sixth century, according to the scenario I have put forward in this chapter, Irish kings from Ulster and British kings from Gwynedd competed for control of Man in a conflict that the Britons eventually won. By the early 700s, when Bede produced his *Ecclesiastical History*, Man was still under British rule.[49] As noted above, the picture that begins to emerge is of an island where the presence of Gaelic-speaking and Brittonic-speaking communities after c.500 encouraged ambitious kings on both sides of the Irish Sea to seek dominion over it. We can probably infer that the political situation had stabilised before the dawn of the seventh century. By c.600, then, the dominant group on Man was most likely a Brittonic-speaking elite whose leaders acknowledged the authority of Gwynedd's kings. Practical government of the island may have been delegated to a prince of the Venedotian royal family, ruling as a vassal of Gwynedd with a Latin title such as *regulus* ('under-king' or 'kinglet'). He and his descendants, while essentially creating a separate Manx dynasty, no doubt maintained their ancestral connection with North Wales.

Celtic Christianity

Early saints such as Patrick and Sanctan, whose careers were spent mostly in Ireland, are often seen as representing a 'Celtic' version of Christianity. So, too, are their peers who laboured across the sea in Britain. To modern eyes, the most iconic centre of what is nowadays described as the 'Celtic Church' was a monastery founded by the Irish saint Columba on the Hebridean isle of Iona in 563. To the English monk Bede, writing in the early 700s, Columba and his successors in the Iona abbacy were stubborn adherents of ecclesiastical customs that differed from those practised elsewhere in Western Christendom. Bede, like most of the English clergy, conformed to mainstream or 'Roman' customs. He regarded continued adherence to 'Celtic' practices at Iona and elsewhere as nothing short of an abomination. In his *Ecclesiastical History of the English People*, he highlighted two areas of concern that epitomised the dispute. One was the style of tonsure favoured by Celtic clergymen which differed from the 'tonsure of St Peter' – a fringe of hair around a shaved crown – worn by their orthodox Roman peers. The other issue, the more crucial of the two, was the method used by Iona and other Celtic religious houses to calculate which Sunday each year would be designated as Easter Sunday. By the mid-seventh century, the Easter disagreement had grown into a bitter stand-off between the Celtic and Roman sides, with neither willing to compromise. Matters came to a head in 664 during a synod convened at the northern English monastery of Whitby, the proceedings of which were summarised by Bede. At Whitby the Roman side triumphed, albeit only in so far as clerics in the English kingdoms were concerned. Southern Ireland had already fallen into line with Roman customs, but it would be another fifty years before Iona and her satellites in the north of Ireland followed suit. Among the clergy of Wales and Cornwall, and among the Northern Britons, conformity with orthodox practices came even later. Many centuries afterwards, when the Reformation paved the way for a Europe-wide adoption of Protestant beliefs, ancient accounts of the stubborn resistance of Celtic abbots to the diktats of Rome took on the guise of a heroic struggle against the Papacy. Furthermore, in the nineteenth century a romanticised view of the original dispute conjured an image of the typical Celtic monk as a clean-living, nature-loving liberal, untainted by – and bravely opposed to – the rigid rules of an authoritarian Roman Catholic Church. This image persists in many quarters today and, despite its modern origins, is frequently assumed to be historically accurate. Those for whom it holds a special appeal fail to recognise it as a post-medieval construct. Even Bede was fully aware that his contemporaries on Iona, whose opinions on Easter and the clerical tonsure he regarded as delusional, remained at all times loyal servants of the Church of Rome.[50]

4

NORTHUMBRIAN CONNECTIONS

During the late sixth century, around the time when kings such as Báetán mac Cairill were exercising their ambitions in the Irish Sea region, another royal dynasty was establishing itself as a significant military power. Its heartlands lay not on the western side of Britain but in the east, in Bernicia, a territory centred on what are today the coastal areas of Northumberland. Bernicia had once been a domain of the Northern Britons but, by c.550, its rulers were an English-speaking elite who had probably taken control by force. The apparent speed with which the population of Bernicia rejected its ancestral British identity in favour of a newfound 'Englishness' suggests that the dynastic change was not only accepted but welcomed.

The origins of Bernicia's English kings are shrouded in a haze of legend and pseudo history. Bede, himself an Englishman and a Bernician, identified the dynastic founder as a man called Ida. Bede reported a tradition that Ida had seized the great coastal fortress of Bamburgh in 547, making it his main centre of power. A hundred years after Bede's death in 735, the Welsh author of *Historia Brittonum* implied that Ida's chief adversary was Outigirn, a man with a Brittonic name who may have been Bernicia's last British king.[1] Whatever the truth behind these traditions, the eventual outcome was that Bernicia became the most northerly of the early English kingdoms. By the 570s, Ida's sons were waging war against neighbouring British kings, with mixed results. Before the end of the sixth century, Ida's grandson Æthelfrith was greatly expanding the boundaries of Bernicia at the expense of the Northern Britons. Æthelfrith rose to become a powerful warrior king on a par with Áedán mac Gabráin. In 603, these two mighty warlords clashed in battle, at an unidentified place called *Degsastan*, with Æthelfrith emerging as victor.

There is no record of Bernicia or any other English kingdom troubling the inhabitants of Man during the sixth century. In the early seventh, however, the island is said to have fallen under the authority of Edwin, Æthelfrith's rival and successor. Edwin was a prince of Deira, a kingdom roughly coterminous with the later county of Yorkshire. Deira, like Bernicia, had been taken over by an English-speaking elite who had established their own royal house. The inevitable rivalry between the Bernician and Deiran dynasties came to a head when Æthelfrith took control of Deira and expelled its crown prince Edwin. The latter fled into exile, seeking sanctuary with an English king in Mercia and with another in East Anglia. It was with East Anglian help that Edwin eventually mounted a successful challenge against Æthelfrith. The latter perished in a decisive battle in 617. Edwin then returned home to take up the Deiran kingship. After expelling Æthelfrith's family he seized control of Bernicia, effectively ruling the two northern English kingdoms as one, even as Æthelfrith had done. This unified realm became known as Northumbria, a name meaning 'the lands north of the Humber Estuary'.

Bede held a great admiration for Edwin, lauding him as a fine example of an English Christian monarch. He depicted Edwin as a mighty overking whose superiority was acknowledged in many parts of Britain. Although Bede may have been keen to magnify the dominance of Northumbria's seventh-century kings, there can be little doubt that it was frequently extensive.[2] We can therefore envisage Edwin's overlordship being recognised by a number of other rulers who, after pledging their allegiance to him, sent regular payments of tribute to his treasury. Edwin's paramount status was consolidated in 626 with a crushing victory over one of the southern English peoples, the West Saxons, in revenge for a failed assassination attempt instigated by their king. Edwin was still a pagan at the time but converted to Christianity in the following year, his baptism being performed by Paulinus, an Italian priest who had been appointed as the first bishop of York. In religious matters, Paulinus was a fervent advocate of the 'Roman' way of doing things. In this regard his views represented the mainstream of Western European Christianity. As we saw at the end of the previous chapter, a somewhat different set of religious customs had long been practised in the Celtic areas of Britain and in parts of Ireland. Here, despite recognising the authority of the Pope, many holy men and women followed practices that their 'Roman' peers regarded with disdain. Such differences weighed heavily on the mind of a man like Paulinus. To him, the process of converting the pagan English to Christianity was an opportunity to steer newly baptised kings like Edwin towards the Roman side and away from the maverick customs of the Celtic clergy. Moreover, a powerful English Christian ruler who nurtured wide territorial ambitions offered the prospect of invading the lands where those same recalcitrants dwelt. When Bede tells us that Edwin brought British territories under his rule, we can surely picture

Paulinus urging the king to root out the stubborn Celtic clerics who continued to reject Roman orthodoxy.[3]

According to Bede, Edwin's hegemony extended to Anglesey and Man. Bede grouped these two islands as an archipelago, describing them as *Mevanias Brettonum insulas quae inter Hiberniam et Britanniam sitae sunt*, 'the Mevanian islands of the Britons which are located between Ireland and Britain'.[4] Anglesey was part of the kingdom of Gwynedd so we should not be surprised to find Bede describing it as being under British rule. More interesting is his identification of Man as British, especially as his source for the mis-spelled name *Mevania* was a copy of Orosius' *Seven Books*. As we saw in Chapter 2, Orosius stated that Man (*Evania*) was inhabited by Gaelic-speaking people whom he may have assumed were of Irish stock. If Bede had understood Man to be wholly or partly under Irish rule, he would not have described it as British alongside Anglesey. Two possibilities thus arise. One is that Bede was telling his readers that Man as well as Anglesey lay in British hands during Edwin's reign in the early seventh century. The other is that Bede was describing the political reality in the time when he was writing, a hundred years after Edwin's death. Either way, his assigning of Man to the Britons rather than to the Irish does not preclude the continuing presence there of Gaelic speakers during Edwin's reign in the seventh century. Bede was perhaps alluding to the political situation I envisaged in Chapter 3, in which a period of British ascendancy on Man began in the late 500s after the demise of Báetán mac Cairill. If this ascendancy was imposed from Gwynedd, we can assume that the Venedotian kings were the Britons to whom Bede was referring. By the early 600s, a branch of this dynasty may have ruled Man as a subordinate royal kindred, wielding authority over a mixed population of Manx Britons and Manx Gaels. By c.630, the dynasty of Gwynedd was itself acknowledging an overlord in the person of Edwin of Northumbria. I suggest that Man, like Anglesey, was one of Gwynedd's satellite domains in the seventh century and that Bede knew this to be the case.

We can be fairly certain that Edwin was the first English king to claim dominion over Man. His interest in the island would have arisen from his broader interest in the affairs of western Britain, epitomised by his dealings with the kings of Gwynedd. He was an Englishman joining various Irish and British rulers competing for power in the seaways between Britain and Ireland.[5] His chief adversary among the Irish is likely to have been Fiachnae mac Báetáin, king of the Cruithin, a powerful figure in north-east Ireland like his father's namesake Báetán mac Cairill. Fiachnae, who appears in some sources with the mysterious epithet 'Lurgan', no doubt perceived Edwin's sovereignty in Man as a challenge to his own ambitions in the Irish Sea region.[6] Although no surviving source tells of conflict between these two kings, an old Irish tale – now lost – may have described a raid by Fiachnae on Edwin's territory. Only the title of this work is known today, preserved in a catalogue of stories compiled in the tenth century or earlier. The title is *Sluagad Fiachnae meic Baetain co Dun nGuaire i Saxanaib*, 'The hosting of Fiachnae mac Báetáin to Dun Guaire among the English'. This 'hosting' or raid is usually seen as an otherwise unrecorded attack on English territory, specifically the Bernician royal fortress of Bamburgh which had fallen under Edwin's control after the death of Æthelfrith in 617.

The word *dun* often means 'fort' and is a Gaelic equivalent of Brittonic *dinas* or *din*. To the Britons, Bamburgh was known as *Din Guayroi*, a name similar to *Dun Guaire* and often seen as its Irish equivalent.[7] However, the identification is by no means certain. If a seventh-century Irish king had brought his fleet over to Britain, landing there with his army before penetrating deep into English territory and attacking the chief citadel of Bernicia, we might have expected Bede or an Irish chronicler to mention it. No such campaign is reported in the *Ecclesiastical History* or in the *Annals of Ulster* or anywhere else. Even if Fiachnae possessed the logistical capacity to march his forces all the way over to Bamburgh on the shore of the North Sea, what would he have hoped to gain? There is no indication that Bamburgh was Edwin's primary residence. In any case, an Irish invasion of Northumbria in the seventh century would have been unprecedented. A brief notice in a contemporary chronicle is the very least we should expect.

I am therefore sceptical of the idea that an assault on Bamburgh lies behind the lost tale of Fiachnae's raid. For me, Dun Guaire remains unidentified. It was probably not Ráith Guaili, a fort (Gaelic: *rath*] attacked by Fiachnae in 623, despite the superficial similarity of the names. Ráith Guaili is more likely to be the place of this name in Munster, or perhaps Ráith Guala in present-day County Down, much closer to Fiachnae's core domains.[8] As for Dun Guaire, it was located *i Saxanaib,* 'among the English' – in other words, it lay in territory under English control – either at the time of Fiachnae's attack or when the catalogue of Irish tales was being compiled. This might mean no more than that it lay under an English king's overlordship and protection. Fiachnae's reign overlapped with both Æthelfrith's and Edwin's, but of these two only Edwin is depicted by Bede as flexing his ambitions in the Irish Sea region. I suggest that a plausible location for a clash between the respective ambitions of Edwin and

Fiachnae was the strategic island of Man. Both kings may have sought dominion over it. Was Dun Guaire a Manx site utilised by Edwin as a base for seaborne raids of his own?

Anglesey was a key domain of Gwynedd's kings and contained important places with which they were closely associated in the sixth and seventh centuries. A palace (Welsh: *llys*) stood at Aberffraw on the island's south-west coast and a royal burial ground lay at nearby Llangalwaladr. Edwin's dominion over Anglesey should mean that all of Gwynedd was subject to him. His opportunity to intervene in the kingdom may have come c.625 after its king, Cadfan, abdicated or died, especially if the succession fell into dispute. Edwin might then have used Anglesey as a stepping stone to Man if the latter needed to be taken by force. Later Welsh tradition claimed that Cadfan's son Cadwallon was besieged by Edwin's forces on Glannauc, the tiny isle of Priestholm off Anglesey's eastern coast, before escaping to exile in Ireland.[9] If this is historically accurate – and we have no compelling reason to doubt the tradition – we may wonder if the fugitive Cadwallon first sought refuge among fellow Britons on Man. Perhaps the Manx rulers offered him sanctuary, thereby arousing Edwin's wrath and precipitating an English assault on their island? Alternatively, Edwin may have conquered Man before Anglesey, using the former as a base for an invasion of Gwynedd. In such a scenario, the most likely springboard for an initial Manx campaign is the coast of what is now Lancashire. If this had already been annexed to Edwin's expanding hegemony, his forces would have had access to the Ribble estuary as a point of embarkation. Ships might then have been supplied by subordinate rulers in British territories west of the Pennine Hills.[10] Indeed, although Edwin's heartland of Deira lay in the east, his early conquest of Elmet, a British kingdom centred on what is now Leeds, foreshadowed the likely fate of kingdoms further west. It is not difficult to imagine the whole of Lancashire falling under his sway, even if we possess neither a record of the campaign nor a map of the political geography. We might even wonder if a conquest of Man is what first brought him into conflict with the rulers of Gwynedd, his takeover of one Mevanian island leading to a conflict that ultimately subdued the other to his overlordship.

The Tribal Hidage

Bede, writing a hundred years after the zenith of Edwin's reign, almost certainly never visited Man. Yet he knew that the island's size – or, more specifically, its economic worth – was equivalent to around 300 hides.[11] The hide was a unit of measurement employed by early English kings to assess the productivity of their domains. It represented the amount of land required to support the needs of a single household. In extent it nominally corresponded to 120 acres, but this was a somewhat arbitrary figure when the underlying basis for an assessment of 'hidage' was the value of a piece of land rather than its area. The source of Bede's hidage figure for Man is unknown but someone had evidently done the necessary calculation. Who? When? Why? These are questions that remain unanswered. As is so often the case in our journey through early Manx history, we are left to make informed guesses.

For Bede, the hidage figure gave his readers a rough idea of Man's agricultural productivity. In the same breath he also gave a figure for Anglesey: 960 hides. The two 'Mevanian' islands had clearly been measured according to an English system of land assessment. Was this done during Edwin's reign, by Northumbrian assessors, as part of a broader survey of all lands under his overlordship? Such surveys were no doubt useful when tribute payments expected from subordinate rulers were being estimated on behalf of an overlord. Alternatively, the hidage figures for Anglesey and Man might have originated in a separate exercise, a 'Mevanian' survey unrelated to any larger purpose. The fact that Bede gives both figures together could imply that they were similarly linked in his source. They may have been drawn up as a combined assessment for an English king who wielded authority over both islands. We know that Edwin had this authority. On the other hand, perhaps he commissioned a valuation of all the numerous territories under his dominion? This brings us to one of the key discussions around his reign, for some historians see it as the time when a document known as the *Tribal Hidage* was compiled. This enigmatic text (hereafter TH) survives in a number of manuscripts, the oldest of which was written in the eleventh century. There is as yet no agreement on the date or provenance of the original text.[12] TH is essentially a list of thirty-five peoples, the 'tribes' of the title (a creation of the late nineteenth century). Some tribes are identifiable but others are not, their names being too obscure. Alongside each name is a hidage figure ranging from 300 hides for the smaller groups to a huge 100,000 hides for the West Saxons. Although the true purpose of TH is unclear, it is often interpreted as a survey of subordinate peoples whose rulers were required to render tribute to an overking. The hidage figures are then seen as representing the wealth of each people's territory, a value corresponding to the amount of tribute they were expected to pay. The list is headed by Mercia, prompting a suggestion that TH was compiled for one of the powerful

Mercian kings of the seventh to ninth centuries. Other historians instead see it as a Northumbrian list of all the territories subject to Edwin, compiled when he was at the height of his power. This suggestion gains support from the omission of Deira and Bernicia, these being Edwin's core domains rather than lands he had conquered or placed under tribute.[13] It would be unsurprising to see Mercia, the realm of his nearest English neighbours, shown in a prominent position at the beginning of the list.

Among the unidentified peoples in TH are the *Westerne* ('Westerners'). One suggestion is that their lands lay on the western frontier of English territory, near today's Anglo–Welsh border, and that they might be the group elsewhere named as *Magonsaete* who lived in what is now Herefordshire. An alternative is that the 'Westerners' were simply any Britons who lived on the western fringe of Edwin's hegemony, here lumped together under one generic label.[14] Since no identifiable group in what is now Scotland appears in TH, the name *Westerne* arguably excludes the Northern Britons between the firths of Clyde and Solway. It might refer instead to Gwynedd, together with other lands that were under Venedotian rule when the list was compiled. The two Mevanian islands – Anglesey and Man – might therefore lie subsumed within the 7,000 hides of the 'Westerners'.[15]

Later Northumbrian kings

Edwin's reign ended in 633 when he was slain in a battle at Hatfield on the south-eastern frontier of his kingdom. His nemesis was Cadfan's son Cadwallon, the new king of Gwynedd. Bede's description of Cadwallon as a rebel indicates that he was one of Edwin's vassal rulers when the conflict began. Rebellion by a vassal not only marked the violent rejection of an overlord's authority but could also signal an attempt to take his place. This ambition seems to have been one of Cadwallon's motives in rising up and going to war. His decisive victory at Hatfield effectively made him the new paramount king of central Britain. With his Northumbrian rival gone, he rampaged through Deira and Bernicia on a year-long quest for plunder, leaving a trail of destruction and bloodshed that later prompted Bede to demonise him as a savage.

Edwin's fall ended the first period of English overlordship in Man, theoretically allowing the island's own rulers to assert their independence. Whether they accepted Cadwallon as their new Venedotian overlord is unknown, but it remains a strong possibility. Bede paints a portrait of

Cadwallon as a very powerful king who kept a circle of other kings – both British and English – as his vassals. Given the proximity of his family's Anglesey heartland to Man, it seems probable that the Manx fell under Cadwallon's sway and that their rulers pledged allegiance to him. Indeed, gaining (or regaining) control of Man and its naval resources may have been high on Cadwallon's list of objectives when he launched his rebellion against Edwin. As well as being an economic and strategic prize, the island undoubtedly possessed numerous ships that could be pressed into service as a war fleet. Edwin must have received Manx tribute payments and Cadwallon may have expected to divert those same revenues to his own coffers in Gwynedd. In an era when a king's quest for power and status trumped ethnic or cultural affiliations, it would have mattered little to Cadwallon whether the Manx tribute came from fellow Britons on the island or from Gaelic-speaking descendants of Irish settlers.

Cadwallon's period of supremacy turned out to be brief. Having triumphed at Hatfield in 633, he was defeated and slain in the following year in a battle further north, at a site near present-day Hexham. His adversary was the Bernician prince Oswald, a son of the mighty Æthelfrith. Exiled by Edwin after their father's death in 617, Oswald and his siblings had been fostered in Dál Riata among the Gaelic-speaking Scots. There they had been exposed to Christianity, albeit not the 'Roman' variety embraced by Edwin and Bishop Paulinus. The young Bernician exiles had instead been nurtured in the Celtic ways of the Columban Church via its principal monastery on Iona. Oswald had become a fervent devotee of Columba and believed that a vision of the saint had appeared to him prior to the battle against Cadwallon.[16] Spectral apparitions aside, the victory over Gwynedd's fierce warrior king was decisive. It propelled Oswald to the throne of Bernicia and brought Deira under his sway. It also gave him a fearsome military reputation that prompted neighbouring kings to pledge allegiance to him. In practical terms, their homage came with a package of obligations that included regular tribute payments to his treasury. Pledges of loyalty to a superior king could be sealed with an inter-dynastic marriage, such as the union between Oswald's younger brother Oswiu and a princess of Rheged within a year or two of Cadwallon's demise. Any king who refused to submit to Oswald faced the prospect of violent conquest, a fate that seems to have befallen the king of Gododdin – the British kingdom around Edinburgh – in 638.[17] Although the geographical extent of Oswald's overlordship is uncertain, we know from Bede that it was broadly similar to Edwin's. Oswald's authority should therefore have encompassed the Mevanian islands of Anglesey and Man. If, like Edwin, he held Gwynedd under his sway, then Anglesey would have been subject to him anyway. Likewise, if Man was still answerable to Gwynedd's kings, then it, too, was doubtless a part of Oswald's hegemony. In any case, Man's position in the northern part of the Irish Sea, within sight of what must have been English-controlled territory on the Cumbrian coast, surely made it a logical target for Oswald.[18] Whether he ever came to the island in person, to impose his authority or to receive homage from the Manx elites, is unknown. Nevertheless, it was during Oswald's reign that an Irish king is said to have launched an assault on Man. According to the twelfth-century poem *Clann Ollaman Uaisle Emna*, mentioned in the previous chapter, the Dál Fiatach ruler Dúnchad mac Fiachnai 'raged against Man'.[19] Assuming this attack really happened, it can be dated to Dúnchad's brief reign (c.637–44) and may have been an attempt to wrest Man away from the Northumbrian yoke.

Oswald, like many powerful and ambitious kings in this period, eventually met his death on a battlefield. He died in 642 at the hands of the Mercians whose pagan king Penda went on to dominate Northumbria for the next thirteen years. Penda's vassals included a king of Gwynedd called Cadafael, son of Cynfedw. Since neither Cadafael nor his father appear in the Venedotian royal genealogies, they presumably belonged to a family that did not usually compete for the kingship. Nevertheless, we should see Cadafael as a powerful ruler in his own right who gave allegiance to Penda because it was politically advantageous to do so, regardless of whether he feared the Mercian king. Cadafael withdrew this allegiance in 655, on the eve of Penda's great battle against Oswald's brother Oswiu. He simply led his army out of the Mercian king's camp and went home. This was not the action of a bold subordinate but rather a demonstration of independence by a man who was not afraid of the consequences. Cadafael may even have been an overking in his own right, like his predecessor Cadwallon, holding sway over a network of subordinate kings and using their forces to bolster his military strength. Just as we have suggested that Cadwallon may have wielded authority over Man, so we might imagine Cadafael doing so too.

The battle between Penda and Oswiu resulted in the former's defeat and death. His fall released his vassals from their obligations, leaving them free to forge new political relationships. With Penda gone, Oswiu found himself in a position of military superiority. Other kings stepped forward to pledge their allegiance to him. He initially exercised considerable control over the Mercians, until they rebelled and threw off the yoke. The Picts, too, were more or less under Oswiu's overlordship and some of their southern territories were under his direct rule. Of the few surviving kingdoms of the Northern Britons, at least one, the mysterious Rheged, may have been fully absorbed into Bernicia during Oswiu's reign (642–70).[20] Although we have no record of Oswiu's dealings with the Britons of Wales and Man, his hegemony was at least as wide-ranging as Oswald's. It no doubt extended to Gwynedd and included both Mevanian islands.

Allies and enemies

Oswiu's reign ended not in violence on the battlefield but, unusually for this period, with a peaceful death in his own home. He was succeeded by his son Ecgfrith, a belligerent figure whose reign was characterised by conflict. Ecgfrith waged war on, or beyond, all of his borders: south, north and west. He engaged in a bitter rivalry with his southern neighbours, the Mercians, whose new kings were the sons of Penda. Northward, beyond the Firth of Forth, Ecgfrith faced revolt from Pictish vassals and led more than one expedition against them. Westward, in the Irish Sea, he seems to have become embroiled in a struggle for power involving several competing groups. The latter were those whose rivalries in the region had been erupting periodically since the sixth century: Irish, Britons and – more recently – Northumbrian English. Although we lack a clear narrative of the contest in Ecgfrith's time, a number of entries in the Irish annals suggests a likely sequence of events. The first entry reports a battle in north-east Ireland in 682, at *Mag Line* (now Moylinney) in Antrim, in territory of the Cruithin:

> The battle of Ráith Mór Maigi Lini against the Britons, in which Cathassach son of Máel Dúin, king of the Cruithin, fell, and Ultán son of Dícuill.[21]

The protagonists were the Cruithnian king Cathassach and a force of Britons whose place of origin is not specified. Ráith Mór ('Great Fortress'), now Rathmore in County Antrim, was a key stronghold of the Cruithin. Several attempts to identify where the British warriors originated have been made. One theory sees them as invaders from Alt Clut, 'Clyde Rock' (now Dumbarton), the royal fortress of the last surviving realm of the Northern Britons, here waging war against Irish enemies of their king.[22] This is certainly possible, given the likelihood that the seaways between the Firth of Clyde and the Antrim coast would have been a bone of contention among various powers. Less plausible is a suggestion that the Britons at Ráith Mór were a roving band of mercenaries from the recently defunct kingdom of Rheged.[23] Such a scenario has been proposed because of a popular theory that Rheged included Galloway and other areas near the Solway Firth. The theory provides a backdrop for imagining Rheged's disaffected warband emigrating after the Northumbrian conquest of the Solway region and going to Ireland where they served as swords for hire. In truth, our total inability to locate Rheged deprives this scenario of any merit. Moreover, there is no precedent for it. The battles of Britain and Ireland in pre-Viking times did not, as far as we know, involve autonomous bands of stateless warriors fighting as mercenaries for foreign kings.

We should therefore look elsewhere for the identity of Cathassach's British foes. The likelihood is that they originated not as refugees from a recently conquered land but from a functioning political entity, a place with strong maritime links to the Irish Sea. The kingdom of Alt Clut is, as already noted, one possible candidate. However, it is not mentioned in the Irish chronicle entry, nor is its king named there among the protagonists. Such omissions are not conclusive, for not every Irish annal relating to the Clyde Britons mentions their royal fortress or one of their kings. Nevertheless, the fact that many annals do give this information makes its absence worthy of note. Nor was Alt Clut the only territory of the Britons in the late seventh century. Another was Gwynedd, still a powerful force at this time. An additional alternative is Man.[24]

We can be fairly certain that Man's rulers in the late seventh century were Britons and that they had a close connection with the dynasty of Gwynedd. If the Manx had their own king, he was either a Brittonic-speaking Manxman or a scion of the Venedotian royal house. He may have been subordinate to the king of Gwynedd, who in turn may have acknowledged the hegemony of Ecgfrith of Northumbria. Even as a vassal ruler, a king of Man would have had leeway to pursue his own military ventures if these broadly aligned with the policies of an overlord. Hostile contact between Man and north-east Ireland in the late seventh century is thus a possibility. A raid on Cruithnian territory by Manx Britons, leading to the battle at Ráith Mór, offers a plausible context for the chronicle entry of 682. The annalists' description of the battle is immediately followed by an additional piece of information: *iugulatio Muirmin inmano*. The context of these words is uncertain but their position at the end of an entry reporting a major battle suggests that the *iugulatio* ('slaughter') might be an associated event.

The name Muirmin is thought to be an Irish rendering of Mermin, an early form of the Welsh name Merfyn. Hence *iugulatio Muirmin* can be translated as 'Merfyn was slaughtered'. Merfyn's name identifies him as a Briton. His violent death may have come at the hands of the Cruithin. The word *inmano* is unintelligible and only makes sense when split into two as *in mano*, which in Latin can mean either 'in captivity' or 'in [a place called] Manau'.[25] There are two candidates for such a place: Manau in northern Britain and the Isle of Man. The former lies a considerable distance from Ireland and is an implausible setting for Merfyn's demise if his killers were Cruithin. The Isle of Man is a better candidate, not only because of its proximity to Antrim but also because of its connections – explored more fully in the next chapter – with men bearing the name Merfyn. We thus have good reason for thinking that the battle of Ráith Mór was linked to the subsequent slaying of Merfyn, a Briton, on the Isle of Man.[26] Was Merfyn a Manx king who, after attacking Cruithnian territory in 682, perished on Man in the following year? If so, his violent death may have been Cruithnian revenge for the slaying of Cathassach. Some historians identify this Merfyn as Merfyn Mawr, a figure named in a genealogy or 'pedigree' preserved in a medieval Welsh manuscript.[27] The epithet *Mawr* means 'great' and implies that its bearer was a ruler of renown. If Merfyn Mawr and his namesake 'Muirmin' who died *in Mano* really are one and the same, and if this individual led the Britons at the battle of Ráith Mór, we may be seeing a king of Man who flexed his military muscle in Ireland before perishing in a counter-offensive on home soil.

The next event to be considered is an assault on Irish territory by Northumbrian forces. This occurred two years after the battle of Ráith Mór and is the first recorded instance of an English invasion of Ireland. Although the Northumbrian army was sent by Ecgfrith, it was not led by him in person. He instead delegated command to Berht, a high-ranking Bernician nobleman. The target was Brega, heartland of the powerful Irish king Finsnechta Fledach. Berht's warriors landed in June 684 and went on a rampage of destruction that included the burning of churches and monasteries. The attack represented a challenge to Finsnechta's emergence as a potential threat to Ecgfrith's ambitions in the Irish Sea region.[28] It has been suggested that control of Man and its surrounding waters might have been one of the factors that prompted Ecgfrith to launch such an aggressive strike.[29] Another factor, according to the *Annals of Clonmacnoise*, was 'the alliance between the Irish and the Britons'. While the lateness of the source makes us wary of accepting such a statement at face value, it is possible that the annalists are here alluding to a real alliance between an Irish king – presumably Finsnechta – and a British counterpart. The latter can be located to one of three places around the Irish Sea where British rule still endured in the 680s: Gwynedd, the nearest British kingdom to Brega; Alt Clut, last kingdom of the Northern Britons; and the Isle of Man. If Finsnechta's ally was the ruler of Man, it is not difficult to see why this would have enraged Ecgfrith, who surely regarded Man as under his own authority or at least as a target of his ambitions. Whatever the true reasons behind the Northumbrian assault on Brega, Ecgfrith's objectives were seemingly achieved. His army and fleet returned with 60 Irish hostages, the human element in whatever treaty Berht imposed on Finsnechta.

With Finsnechta effectively neutralised, Ecgfrith was at liberty to consolidate his influence in the Irish Sea. As things turned out, his hegemony collapsed within a year of the attack on Brega. In May 685, during a decisive battle against the Picts, he was slain alongside a great many of his soldiers. The Northumbrian ascendancy that had dominated Britain for most of the seventh century died with him. In the wake of his death a new pattern of alliances and allegiances was formed. It left Ecgfrith's successors with a much-reduced role in the Irish Sea by handing the initiative back to the native peoples.[30] Within this new political environment the Britons of Gwynedd, Man and Alt Clut still had significant roles to play. One of these three groups became involved in the affairs of north-east Ireland in 697, fifteen years after the battle of Ráith Mór. This time, the entry in the Irish annals gives minimal information, telling us only that 'Britons and Ulstermen (Ulaid) wasted Mag Muirthemne'.[31] The latter was the heartland of Conaille Muirthemne, a Cruithin kingdom in what is today County Louth. Again, we have no clue as to where the British force originated, but Man can be considered a strong possibility. The same British power, or a different one, slew King Írgalach of Brega in 702, five years after the plundering of Mag Muirthemne. The scene of Írgalach's death was Ireland's Eye, a small isle north of Dublin.[32] Whether his British enemies came there as allies of a rival Irish king or as seaborne raiders pursuing their own objectives we cannot say. The setting suggests that this was a raid on Brega, perhaps a British version of Ecgfrith's assault eighteen years earlier. If the attackers were Manxmen, their outward voyage would have been completed within a day. The following year saw a battle between Britons and Ulstermen in the Ards peninsula on the north-east coast of Ireland. This signalled a breakdown of whatever relationship had forged the alliance against Brega in 697.[33] Here, on the plain of Cuilinn, the Ulstermen were victorious and a man referred to as 'Radgann's son, an enemy of God's churches' was slain. We can infer that Radgann's son was one of the British leaders. To be regarded by Irish chroniclers as an enemy of churches, his targets must have included religious sites. His father's name is not attested elsewhere and cannot be matched to any name in the royal genealogies of Gwynedd or Alt Clut. Is it possible that Radgann and his son were Manx Britons?

The final event in this sequence of chronicle entries comes in 709 when King Cellach of Leinster fought a battle against dynastic rivals, losing two of his sons in what seems to have been a heavy defeat. Among the casualties was a certain Luirg who fell alongside 'Cellach's Britons'. The latter have been seen as a force of mercenaries hired by Cellach, but this is not the only possible interpretation.[34] The Britons may have been sent by their own king to help Cellach and, as in earlier campaigns, it is possible that they came from Man. Luirg, an individual known only from this annal, has a name of Gaelic origin and may have been one of Cellach's Irish allies.

Taking a broad look at the chronicle record of British military activity in Ireland between 682 and 709, we may note that the geographical setting comprises a swathe of coastal territory running some 160 miles north to south.[35] The most northerly battle in the sequence lay 180 miles from Gwynedd but barely 50 miles from Man. Likewise, the southernmost battlefield lay approximately 100 miles from Man, yet twice as far from Alt Clut. On distance grounds alone, an expedition to either Ulster or Brega was a relatively straightforward option for a Manx fleet. There is little doubt that the rulers of Man could easily muster enough ships for such a venture, together with a sufficient number of warriors. I therefore support the idea that the Britons recorded as fighting in Ireland in the late seventh and early eighth centuries came not from Alt Clut or Gwynedd or the defunct kingdom of Rheged, but from the Isle of Man.[36]

A royal exile on Man

The second half of the eighth century was a time of dynastic uncertainty in Northumbria, with rival factions deposing kings and installing others on the throne. One king who found himself caught up in this turmoil was Osred who came to power in 789 after the previous king, his own uncle, had been assassinated. Osred's reign lasted barely a year before he himself was deposed in favour of a former king called Æthelred who had likewise been ousted a decade earlier. Taken captive by Æthelred's followers, Osred was released after being forced to accept the clerical tonsure of a monk. He was then exiled from the kingdom, making his way to the Isle of Man. There he remained for a couple of years until 792 when, with the help of loyal noblemen back home, he secretly returned to Northumbria. Hoping to regain the throne, he gathered a band of warriors, but these men abandoned him and he was betrayed to King Æthelred. Taken captive for a second time, Osred was eventually slain on the king's orders. He died on 14 September 792 and was buried at the Northumbrian monastery of Tynemouth on the shores of the North Sea.[37]

5

BISHOPS, MONKS AND KINGS

In Chapter 3, we encountered the traditional belief that a monastery was founded at Kirk Maughold by the eponymous saint Maughold or Machutus in the sixth century. The tradition can be traced back no earlier than the twelfth-century hagiographer Jocelin of Furness.[1] Nevertheless, a considerable number of sculptured stones from the site show that it played an important role in the story of early Christianity on Man, regardless of any uncertainty about its origins. The oldest known stones from Maughold were carved in the seventh to ninth centuries, between the Early Christian period (c.400 to c.600) and the first phase of Norse colonisation (late 800s). They bear witness to a thriving ecclesiastical settlement – a monastery with associated stone-carving workshops. Unfortunately, no written record of this settlement exists, nor is there any mention of a place called *Maughold* until long after the end of the Viking Age. As a place-name (rather than as the name of a saint) Maughold is first mentioned in a document of 1302, written at the English priory of St Bees on the coast of present-day Cumbria, which refers to *Kirkemaghald*.[2] The name is of Norse origin and means 'church of St Maughold'. It is likely to be far older than the early fourteenth century and may even have been coined by pagan Vikings during their raids on Man.

In Chapter 3 we also observed that the great monastery of Armagh in north-east Ireland sought to obtain spiritual authority over Man in the late seventh century, using a story about St Patrick's encounter with a pagan bandit called Mac Cuill to justify this claim. Just as Patrick was retrospectively adopted by Armagh as its holy patron, so Mac Cuill is almost certainly intended to be seen as Patrick's disciple and as Kirk Maughold's eponymous founder. In the story, Patrick confronts Mac Cuill before forcing him into exile upon the sea. While the story itself bears the hallmarks of ecclesiastical propaganda, it offers a fascinating glimpse of the relationship between Manx and Irish Christianity 200 years after Patrick's death.[3] More specifically, it looks like an attempt to show that the monastic brethren at seventh-century Maughold should be subservient to Armagh, because their founding saint had allegedly been subservient to Patrick.

The Maughold monastery occupied the site of the present-day parish church which sits in the south-west corner of an irregularly shaped churchyard. Archaeological excavation has been restricted by the churchyard's continued use as a burial ground in modern times, but some small-scale projects have been undertaken. An excavation in the early twentieth century found traces of what appeared to be the boundary of an ancient enclosure, delineated by a ditch and bank. This was located near the remains of a rectangular building known as the East Keeill, a structure tentatively identified as a monks' hut or 'cell' within the monastic enclosure. The ditch and bank seem to have run parallel to the churchyard's perimeter wall along its inner side, suggesting that the wall now encloses a slightly larger area than the original monastic precinct. It is hard to plot the likely course of the ditch and bank, which presumably mark an ancient boundary, but it may have followed the line of the present wall on the southern and eastern sides.[4] There are traces of three more keeills within the churchyard, all of them rectangular. These appear to have been built no earlier than the eleventh century: one of the trio has fragments of tenth-century sculpture in the fabric of its walls, while another was constructed on top of pre-Viking cist graves which its builders disregarded.[5]

The pre-Norse (Early Manx) sculptured stones at Maughold comprise a mixture of intact monuments and pieces of broken ones. A common form of monument at the site was the stone slab incised with a cross, the latter varying in design. One fragment of an early cross-slab was discovered in 1900 and has since been assigned to the seventh century.[6] The cross is in what we would now call the 'Maltese' style and is surrounded by a double ring. It was originally accompanied by a Chi-Rho – an Early Christian symbol – and the Greek letters Alpha and Omega, symbolising the concept of 'the beginning and the end'. A seventh-century date has been reached by comparison with similar carvings from the Hebrides which have been assigned to this period. Another of the Maughold slabs contains a Maltese cross within a double ring, with a marigold-shaped 'hexafoil' below, and is thought to have been carved c.650.[7] Other cross-slabs at Maughold contain inscriptions, usually in Latin. One inscription, commemorating a man called Branhui, appears on a slab fragment discovered in the churchyard in 1948 when a new grave was being dug. One face of the slab had been carved with a ring-headed cross, in the centre of which a rectangular panel contained the inscription IHS XPS BRANHUI HUC AQUA DIRIVAVIT, 'Jesus Saviour. Christ. Branhui brought water to this place'. The text, incised in a rounded 'uncial' script of the kind used in manuscripts of c.800, provides a fascinating glimpse of life at the monastery in pre-Norse times. Branhui's name is probably Brittonic, not Gaelic, but nothing more is known of him.[8] We can surmise that he was a member of the Maughold religious community, one who was skilled at water engineering. The work for which he was commemorated may have been an aqueduct of some sort, a structure perhaps associated with a stone-lined conduit discovered in the churchyard in modern times.

Also commemorated on a cross-slab at Maughold was a man of high ecclesiastical rank whose name appears in a Latin inscription. Carved quite roughly, the inscription runs in a circle around a marigold-shaped hexafoil and in parts is difficult to interpret. The current view among many specialist scholars is that the correct translation is '[In the name of] Christ, Irneit, holy priest, God's bishop in the island, and abbot'.[9] The status of the individual is generally accepted, for the word EPPS after his name seems certain to represent *episcopus*. the Latin word for 'bishop', while what appears to be the word ISUL should likewise be a rendering of Latin *insula*, 'island'. However, the name Irneit is obscure and occurs nowhere else. We cannot even be sure if it is Brittonic or Gaelic. We can nevertheless feel confident that this stone commemorates an early bishop of Man whose episcopal seat lay at Maughold. Below the hexafoil are two additional inscriptions, each running vertically alongside an incised cross, but these add little by way of context and merely say 'In the name of Christ' and 'An image of Christ's cross'. Dating the monument is no easy task, but a clue may be given by the hexafoil which possibly reproduces the design of a bishop's seal. A similar design, with an encircling inscription, occurs on a metalworking mould from Suffolk in what was once the kingdom of East Anglia. The East Anglian mould was used to cast the seal of an English bishop called Æthelwald who lived in the ninth century. It has been suggested that the design on Irneit's stone may be a representation of his own seal and, moreover, that he was Æthelwald's contemporary. Alternatively, the hexafoil need not be a seal at all and could simply be an example of ornamentation, in which case the ninth-century date becomes less firm and an earlier date of c.700, based on the lettering style, can be proposed.[10] Bishop Irneit, whatever his cultural origins and whenever he lived, was clearly an important figure in early Manx history. The word I[N]SUL[A]- on his memorial implies that his ecclesiastical authority encompassed the whole island, even though we have no record of such a bishopric in the historical sources, nor indeed any mention of bishops of Man before the eleventh century. Alongside his episcopal rank, Irneit seems to have held the abbacy at Maughold, overseeing the life and work of the monastery. Both the Brittonic- and Gaelic-speaking elements in the island's Christian population may have acknowledged his spiritual authority.

While the hexafoil on Bishop Irneit's memorial could perhaps indicate some sort of contact with, or influence from, the churches and clergy of East Anglia, a more overt English connection appears on another stone from Maughold. This upright slab is incised with a cross encircled by a double ring within which *Blagcmon* has been carved in Anglo-Saxon runes. Each arm of the cross contains a pattern of carved interlace forming three loops, known as a 'triquetra'. Blagcmon is an Old English personal name meaning 'Blackman' and was not uncommon.[11] In this instance, it probably belonged to an English monk who lived at the Maughold monastery. The stone is usually seen as one of a pair, the other being a fragment containing part of a ringed cross and a truncated runic inscription which translates as *-gmon*. This almost certainly repeated the name Blagcmon, prompting a suggestion that the two stones once marked the head and foot of a grave.[12] Assigning a specific date to such a burial is difficult, but the eighth century provides a plausible chronological context. This was when the Northumbrian monastery at Whithorn in Galloway was flourishing, its abbots enjoying the patronage of Northumbria's kings. Blagcmon might have been a Whithorn monk who spent his final years at Maughold during a phase of close contact between the two sites.

If a link with Whithorn seems likely, it was probably only one among a number of connections forged by the Maughold community in the pre-Norse period. Links with monasteries in Ireland, Pictland, the Hebrides and Wales seem to be reflected in sculptural influences on monuments from the site. Which of these areas played a major role in establishing the first ecclesiastical settlement at Maughold remains unclear. Based on the date-range of the oldest monuments, roughly 620 to 720, we might guess that the monastery was founded c.600. This would place its origins within a generation of the troubled period in which I envisage a conflict between Irish and British kings for control of Man. In Chapter 3, I suggested that the victors in this struggle were Britons from the royal dynasty of Gwynedd. If we seek to identify the secular patron who gave the original grant of land for a monastery to be built at Maughold, we need look no further than a king of Gwynedd in the late sixth or early seventh century.

Although Maughold was probably the most important early monastery on Man, it was not necessarily the only one. Hints of another have been found on St Patrick's Isle at Peel where archaeologists discovered a medieval cemetery containing graves from the sixth, seventh and eighth centuries. Traces of wooden buildings from the Iron Age have also been discovered, confirming the site as a settlement of considerable antiquity and supporting the case for it being the location of an early monastery. The iconic round tower, known locally as the Monks' Tower, is reminiscent of those erected as refuges at Irish monasteries in the Viking Age. It seems, however, to be of twelfth-century origin.[13]

Man and the Merfynion

In the mid-nineteenth century, a large granite cross-slab could be seen in a hedge running alongside a road near the village of Port e Vullen in Maughold parish. The stone had formerly been located in a keeill before being moved to the roadside. In 1894 it was transferred to a safer location in the churchyard at Kirk Maughold and now stands in the cross house. It is one of the most famous early medieval monuments on Man. Standing almost 1.8 metres high, it is carved on one side with a deeply incised ringed cross. Each of the four arms of the cross is decorated with a circular boss while a fifth boss sits at the centre. One of the rounded 'shoulders' of the slab bears a Latin inscription, carved in uncial letters: *crux guriat*, 'Guriat's Cross'. No clue as to Guriat's identity is given on the monument, but the name is Brittonic not Gaelic, being an early form of the Welsh name Gwriad.[14] The latter appears in a medieval Welsh genealogy or 'pedigree' showing the ancestry of Rhodri Mawr, 'Rhodri the Great', a ninth-century king of Gwynedd. Rhodri's predecessor on the throne of Gwynedd was his father Merfyn Frych ('Freckled Merfyn') whom he succeeded in 844. In the pedigree, Merfyn's father is Gwriad, son of Elidir. In 825, Merfyn founded Gwynedd's 'second dynasty' of kings, known in Welsh tradition as the Merfynion. The first dynasty, the Maelgyning, had ruled since the mid-sixth century. The Maelgyning were descended from their eponymous ancestor Maelgwn, a king whose son and successor Rhun we encountered in Chapter 3. Maelgwn himself was said to be a descendant of Cunedda, a mysterious and possibly legendary figure from northern Britain who supposedly migrated to Wales to expel Irish colonists sometime around AD 400. The last Maelgyning king of Gwynedd was Hywel ap Caradog, whose death in 825 enabled Merfyn Frych to establish a new dynasty of his own. Who, then, was Merfyn and where did he come from? Is there a connection between his father, Gwriad ab Elidir, and Guriat's Cross on the Isle of Man? To find answers to these questions we turn first to the medieval Welsh poem *Cyfoesi Myrddin a Gwenddydd ei*

Chwaer ('Myrddin's dialogue with his sister Gwenddydd'). This contains a prophecy about various Welsh and North British kings in which Merfyn Frych is described as *o dir Manaw*, 'of the land of Manau'. Specialist scholars have dated the oldest parts of the *Cyfoesi* to the tenth century, only a hundred years after Merfyn's death in 844.[15] The 'land of Manau' in this context is the Isle of Man. The other Manau, in what is now Scotland, lay 300 miles from Gwynedd and had ceased to be a territory of the Britons long before the ninth century. The *Cyfoesi* is therefore telling us that Merfyn came from Man, yet this is not his only link to the island in early Welsh literature. His great-grandmother was a lady called Celeinion whose own great-grandfather Merfyn Mawr, 'Merfyn the Great', is usually identified as the Merfyn ('Muirmin') slain *in mano* ('on Man') in 682.[16] In Chapter 4, I suggested that Merfyn Mawr was a king of Man at a time when Brittonic-speaking elites held power on the island. His own pedigree is short, comprising only four generations from himself to his great-grandson Idwal. The latter's sister was the aforementioned Celeinion, great-grandmother of Merfyn Frych. A plausible interpretation of the Welsh genealogical data is that Merfyn Mawr's royal dynasty on Man ended with Idwal whose authority then passed to his nephew Elidir, son of his sister Celeinion.[17] From Elidir the Manx kingship then passed to his son Gwriad who likewise bequeathed it to Merfyn Frych. All of these men can probably be identified as kings of Man. They ruled either the whole island or some part of it, perhaps as vassals of Gwynedd. It is tempting to see Gwriad ab Elidir as the individual commemorated on Guriat's Cross. Indeed, many historians accept the identification. A date in the early 800s has been assigned to the cross and would fit with Gwriad ab Elidir's chronological context according to the pedigree. Other candidates for the Guriat of the inscription should also be acknowledged. One, a Gwriad who died in 878, perished alongside Rhodri Mawr in a battle against the Mercians. He is usually identified as Rhodri's brother and would thus belong to a later generation than his namesake on the Manx cross-slab. Another possibility is that Guriat's Cross did not commemorate a secular figure but rather a high-ranking cleric who lived and died in the monastery at Maughold. Nevertheless, the coincidence of names and chronological context tips the balance of probability in favour of Gwriad ab Elidir, the father of Merfyn Frych.[18]

A further link between the Merfynion dynasty and the Isle of Man appears in a poem written in the margin of the *Annals of Ulster*. The poem appears alongside the year entry for 878, in which the deaths of Rhodri Mawr and three other men are noted.[19] Aside from Rhodri, the others are an Irish king, an Irishman who was either a king or a prince, and a Pictish king. Linguistic features in the poem suggest that its composition may be contemporary with the events it describes. The preceding annal describes Rhodri as *rex Brittonum*, 'king of the Britons', while the poem calls him Ruaidri Manann, 'Rhodri of Manau', usually interpreted as 'Rhodri from the Isle of Man'. At his death, Rhodri was king of Gwynedd, so the Manx connection requires some explaining. The simplest explanation is that his contemporaries in Ireland believed him to be a Manxman. In Wales in the following century the author of the *Cyfoesi* believed that Rhodri's father Merfyn Frych came from Man. Both men were kings of Gwynedd and, presumably, both were also kings of Man.[20] Drawing all the information together, we seem to be seeing a prominent family of Manx Britons holding kingship on Man before obtaining the throne of Gwynedd in the early ninth century. Moreover, if Gwriad ab Elidir is the individual commemorated on Guriat's Cross, his family's main centre of power may have lain in the very district where the monument was found, near Kirk Maughold in the northern part of Man.

Assigning a Manx origin to the Merfynion kings of Gwynedd goes some way to explaining the lack of evidence for Gaelic-speaking rulers on Man in the seventh, eighth and ninth centuries. There is nothing in the sources to suggest anything other than British rule on the island in this period. The fifth and sixth centuries seem rather to mark the high point of Irish intervention, with ambitious kings like Báetán mac Cairill targeting Man in the late 500s. From the late 600s to the late 800s, the few Manx-related events in the sources refer to people with Brittonic names. This obviously changes quite dramatically in the Viking Age, when people with Norse names took control of the island. Nevertheless, some modern commentators see Man as predominantly Gaelic in culture and language on the eve of the Norse takeover, with a Gaelic-speaking elite holding power. As we have seen in this chapter, the information in the Welsh and Irish texts – fragmentary though it is – weighs against such a view.[21] With the true picture arguably more nuanced than the sources suggest, we should probably envisage Man entering the 800s with a bicultural population comprising Brittonic-speaking and Gaelic-speaking communities. The two groups appear to have co-existed amicably, their dealings no doubt including some intermarriage and bilingualism. Overall control nevertheless seems to have resided in British hands from c.600 to the coming of the Norse in the late ninth century. It is likely that the chief kindred on Man throughout this period was the one to which Merfyn Frych belonged and that it had held power since at least the time of Merfyn (*Muirmin*) Mawr in the late seventh century. Alternative contexts for Merfyn Frych require special pleading, such as the idea that his father Gwriad ab Elidir was a dispossessed Venedotian prince who, while living in temporary exile on Man, raised there a son who would eventually seize the kingship of Gwynedd.[22] While such a scenario can be accommodated by the information in the Welsh pedigrees, it adds complexity to what is otherwise a straightforward picture of dynastic change in Gwynedd in 825. We should therefore retain the identification of Gwriad ab Elidir, Merfyn Frych and Rhodri Mawr as Manx Britons, members of a family that had amassed sufficient military forces and sea power at home to mount a strong challenge for the throne of Gwynedd. What motivated them to take such a step, and the means by which it was achieved, are questions to which we shall now turn.

I have argued that Merfyn Frych was most likely a king of Man when he became king of Gwynedd in 825. Later Welsh pedigrees show him as the son or husband of Esyllt, daughter of the Venedotian king Cynan ap Rhodri who died in 816. It seems likely that Cynan had been a client or ally of his powerful English neighbour King Cenwulf of Mercia whose lands adjoined Gwynedd's eastern border.[23] After Cynan's death, his rival Hywel ap Caradog ruled Gwynedd for the next nine years until his own passing paved the way for Merfyn Frych to take the throne. Hywel had contested Cynan's claim on the kingship of Gwynedd in the years 813 to 816 and this had led to a war fought partly on Anglesey. As Cynan's grandson or son-in-law, Merfyn Frych no doubt aligned himself with Cynan's faction and may have refused to recognise Hywel when the latter became king of Gwynedd in 816. Unlike Cynan, Hywel had a turbulent relationship with the Mercians who, in 822, invaded Gwynedd and destroyed the ancient fortress of Degannwy. In 825, however, the Mercians were decisively defeated by their fellow English rivals the West Saxons. This effectively ended Mercia's status as a major power. Rulers in other lands who had been clients of Mercian kings were obliged to look elsewhere for protection and support. Some turned to the West Saxons, the new overlords of southern Britain, whose military capabilities would soon be tested against the Vikings. Mercia's defeat came in the same year as the death of Hywel who seemingly left no designated heir to succeed him as king of Gwynedd. Instead, the throne was seized by Merfyn Frych, a kinsman of Hywel's former rival Cynan. Whether Merfyn became Gwynedd's new king by consent or coercion is unknown. It is certainly possible that Cynan's erstwhile supporters among the Gwynedd aristocracy invited Merfyn to take the throne and that Hywel's faction grudgingly accepted him. There might have been no other suitable candidates, or perhaps none to match Merfyn's political ambition and military resources. As a prominent figure on the Isle of Man, where he probably ruled as a king, Merfyn offered the prospect of protection and stability in a time of upheaval. Alternatively, he may have simply taken the kingship of Gwynedd through force of arms, arriving at the head of a Manx war fleet. Force might indeed have been his only option. Despite his kinship with King Cynan, Merfyn was not a legitimate claimant to the Venedotian throne under Welsh laws of succession.[24] A plausible reconstruction of events begins to emerge, in which Merfyn brought a Manx fleet and army to Anglesey, taking control of the island before crossing the Menai Strait to vanquish rival claimants. There is little doubt that Anglesey would be the obvious springboard for such a campaign, not only because of its proximity to Man but also because anyone who controlled Anglesey could dominate the rest of Gwynedd.

We should note that this reconstruction is not the only one that has been proposed. While many historians see Merfyn as a Manxman, others take a different view.[25] One theory locates his origins in the Welsh kingdom of Powys, while another sees his family as a displaced royal kindred from Gwynedd, one that merely used Man as a temporary base from which to compete for the Venedotian throne. Both alternatives bend and stretch the otherwise simple descriptions of Merfyn and his son Rhodri being 'of the land of Man' and 'of Man' respectively. Doubts have also been raised about the notion that Brittonic was the language of the Manx ruling elite when the first Viking settlers arrived at the end of the ninth century. A key argument for the doubters is the absence of Brittonic elements in the island's modern place-names, in contrast to many examples of Gaelic elements. The argument hinges on a philological theory that sees enough early (pre-Norse) Gaelic place-names to make a case for Gaelic being the main language spoken on Man from c.600 to c.900.[26] Against this we can point to a counterargument that few, if any, of the Gaelic names can be confidently assigned to the pre-Viking period. Many, if not all, might be no older than the twelfth or thirteenth centuries.[27] Some Gaelic elements that have been put forward as early, such as *sliabh* ('hill'), could have come to Man *after* the Viking Age, as was apparently the case in Galloway. That there were communities of Gaelic speakers on Man in pre-Norse times seems undeniable, but they might not have been numerous enough, or of sufficiently high status, to leave a heavy footprint on the island's placenames. Nor is there any need to imagine these folk rejecting or resenting the authority of Brittonic-speaking rulers.[28] Having said all this, we cannot ignore the absolute dearth of Brittonic place-names in today's Manx landscape. While many of the island's Gaelic names are of uncertain date, the Brittonic names that must have been present in pre-Norse times do not exist today. Non-survival of these names is highly significant, especially in light of what the Welsh and Irish sources seem to be saying about the contemporary political situation. As we shall see in the next chapter, there may be a good reason for this.

Man, Anglesey and the Vikings

The Viking Age began in the late eighth century when seaborne raids by pagan Scandinavian warriors came to the notice of contemporary chroniclers. The first recorded attacks on Britain and Ireland occurred in the 790s when major monasteries such as Lindisfarne in Northumbria and Iona in the Hebrides were targeted. The first known raid in the Irish Sea region was an attack on the island of *Rechru* – either Rathlin off the Antrim coast or Lambay near Dublin – in 795.[29] These and other early raids were carried out by Vikings of Norse (most likely Norwegian) origin whose main objective was plunder in the form of high-value items. Gold, silver and gemstones were obviously much sought after as precious and portable commodities. So, too, were human captives who could be traded as slaves. As the eighth century passed into the ninth, Viking raids became more frequent and more wide-ranging.[30] The seaways around Britain and Ireland, from the northern isles of Orkney and Shetland to the English Channel, became thoroughfares for fleets of Norse longships. Although the raiders did not make permanent settlements at this time – generally preferring to sail home across the North Sea with their loot – some of them established temporary bases from where they could launch hit-and-run raids. Given the Isle of Man's location we might expect that it, too, was attacked during this early raiding phase, but the sources are silent on the matter. An entry in the *Annals of Ulster* for the year 798 reported a raid on *Inis Phatraic*, 'Patrick's Island', in which a monastery containing the shrine of the seventh-century saint Mochonna was ransacked. It was once thought that this referred to St Patrick's Isle at Peel, but most historians now think Holmpatrick near Dublin is a more likely location. Holmpatrick's name, derived from Old Norse, means 'Patrick's island' and its monastery is said to have been founded by St Mochonna.[31]

By the second quarter of the ninth century, the Norse raids on Ireland were increasing in severity. This was partly due to a change in the pattern of relationships between the Irish kingdoms, resulting in a shift in the balance of power from north to south. A key moment came in 819 with the death of Áed Oirdnide, a powerful king of the northern Cenél nEógain kindred.[32] Áed was the high king of Ireland, the nominal overlord of all other kings. He had successfully retained this paramount status for more than twenty years and had a formidable military reputation. In the north his authority extended to the coasts of Ulster, which looked out towards the isles of the Hebrides where Norse raiding fleets prowled. The Norse may have been deterred from attacking Ulster's shorelands because of Áed's ability to launch counter-raids with his own forces. His death removed this threat of effective retribution. So, too, did the subsequent failure of his kinsmen to retain the high kingship of Ireland, which passed instead to a rival dynasty further south.[33] The transfer of power left the north weaker, presenting an opportunity for Norse Vikings to plunder the coasts of Ulster. As time went by, these assaults became more frequent, more severe and more ambitious. Emboldened by easy pickings, the Vikings extended their range southward to target the kingdoms of Brega and Leinster, both of which were attacked in 827. The onslaught on these lands continued throughout the 830s and, in 841, the Norse seized Dublin, a place that was to become their principal stronghold in the Irish Sea region.

There can be no doubt that the upsurge in raiding activity in the 820s had major implications for the Isle of Man. Lying so close to Ulster, it probably endured more attacks than ever before. If the Manx ruler at this time was Merfyn Frych, the increasing intensity of Viking raids on Ireland provides an additional motive for his taking power in Gwynedd: he may have hoped to strengthen his position in the Irish Sea by gaining control of Anglesey, an offshore province of the Venedotian kingdom.[34] Control of both Anglesey and Man, and of the waters in between, would have put Merfyn in a much stronger position than if he held Man alone. Man, as we have already surmised, must have had a considerable number of ships that could be deployed by the island's rulers as a war fleet, crewed by native Manxmen. This was certainly the case in the twelfth century and was no doubt true in the ninth as well.[35] Such a naval asset, operating in tandem with the fleet of Gwynedd, may have kept predatory Vikings at bay for many years. It is interesting to note that there is no evidence for a Viking conquest of Man during the period 825 to 844 when Merfyn held the kingship of Gwynedd, nor in the reign of his son Rhodri Mawr who held the same authority from 844 to 878. In fact, archaeological data tells us that there was no significant phase of Norse settlement on Man before the late ninth century. Was the colonisation of such a strategic island delayed because the Vikings were unable to inflict a decisive defeat on Merfyn and Rhodri before the 870s, on land or sea, on Man or in Gwynedd? In 856, Irish chroniclers noted a battle between Rhodri and a Viking warlord called Orm whose base probably lay in Ireland. The location is unknown, but Orm may have been the leader of a Viking force that is said to have raided Anglesey around this time. The battle brought death to Orm and victory to Rhodri.[36] Given that Rhodri, like his father, arguably ruled Man and Gwynedd together, his defeat of Orm may have helped to alleviate Viking pressure on both territories. His victory reminds us that Viking armies, notwithstanding the ferocious image they often present to modern eyes, were by no means invincible. Indeed, they sustained many setbacks during their period of activity in Britain and Ireland. Yet we should also consider the possibility that Merfyn and Rhodri negotiated with some Viking forces instead of fighting them, to avoid bloodshed and to secure mutual agreements benefiting both sides. The use of Manx harbours might even have been offered to one or more Norse fleets in exchange for promises of non-aggression. Another possibility is that Merfyn and his son became allies or vassals of powerful Norse warlords, perhaps those based at Dublin, in return for protection from other Vikings. In this scenario, tribute payments from Gwynedd and Man would have been handed over, accompanied by oaths of friendship or allegiance. The Norse leader Orm whom Rhodri defeated in 856 might even have been the rival of another Viking warlord whose protection Rhodri had accepted.[37]

The foregoing discussion proposes that Vikings were deterred from conquering and colonising Man for much of the ninth century. It envisages the island as the domain of a royal dynasty of Britons who, from 825 onwards, ruled simultaneously in Gwynedd. This was a time when Vikings were making substantial gains in the Irish Sea region, a time when Norse raiding fleets were plundering freely from bases in the Hebrides. On the Irish mainland, one group of Norsemen established a permanent settlement at Dublin. Yet, in the midst of all this aggressive activity, the Isle of Man seems to have remained in the hands of its own rulers. As we shall see in the next chapter, the key data is archaeological rather than textual, for no contemporary source tells us what happened. What the archaeology will show us is that the physical evidence for Norse settlement on Man does not pre-date the final quarter of the ninth century. That the Vikings did not conquer the island sooner is one of the most remarkable aspects of Manx history.

Vikings in the Irish Sea, c.790 to c.950

6

THE EARLY VIKING PERIOD

The dynasty of Ivar

By the middle of the ninth century, Viking activity in Britain and Ireland was switching from hit-and-run attacks to military campaigns on a much larger scale. In 851, a force known to Irish chroniclers as *Dubgaill* ('Dark Foreigners') seized control of the Norse stronghold at Dublin. To the Irish, all Vikings were *gall* ('foreigners') but a distinction was now being drawn between 'Dark' and 'Fair'. The precise meaning of these terms is unclear. Although the 'Fair Foreigners' were often assumed to be the Norse and the 'Dark Foreigners' the Danes, the former might simply be the initial wave of Vikings and the latter a subsequent wave.[1]

In 853, a Norse warlord called Olaf set himself up as king of Dublin and as overlord of all the Scandinavian settlers in Ireland. Olaf then used Dublin as a base for launching raids on Ireland and Britain. Two of his kinsmen came to join him: Audgisl and Ivar who were probably his brothers. All three seem to have been associated with a Viking host known as the 'Great Army' which first appears in the historical record in the 860s. Contemporary English chroniclers described this force as Danish, but its composition was undoubtedly more varied.[2] While a majority of its warriors might indeed have been Danes, there were also many Norwegians and probably a few contingents from other lands.

In 865, the main strength of the Great Army invaded England via the North Sea, landing in the kingdom of East Anglia. There it remained for a time before moving against Northumbria and Mercia. The Northumbrian royal centre at York was captured in 866 and a new 'Anglo-Danish' kingdom was established there. At York the Great Army initially acted as a power broker before eventually installing its own leaders in the kingship. By 874, large swathes of English territory lay firmly in Viking hands, including eastern Mercia, most of Northumbria and all of East Anglia. English rule was restricted to lands in the west and south, but these were under constant threat of raids from what later historians called the 'Danelaw'. An English fightback was spearheaded by the kings of Wessex, most famously by Alfred the Great in the final quarter of the ninth century. Alfred achieved some notable victories, but the new century began with much of the Scandinavian gains still intact.

The current view among historians is that Olaf, Audgisl and Ivar were Norsemen who led sections of the Great Army in England but who also pursued their own ventures in the Irish Sea. Little is known of their origins, but Ivar might be Ivar the Boneless, one of many sons of a famous, semi-legendary Viking called Ragnar Lothbrok ('Hairy-Breeches'). Alternatively, Ivar may have been a prince from one of the royal families of Norway.[3] Whatever their origins and kinship with one another, and whatever their relationship with the Great Army, we can be certain that Olaf, Audgisl and Ivar had become leading figures among the Dublin Norse by 870. Ivar is the most significant of the three, being remembered long after his death as the progenitor of the 'Hiberno-Norse' dynasty of Dublin, an extended family known to Irish chroniclers as the Uí Ímair, 'descendants (or grandsons) of Ivar'.[4]

In 870, a huge fleet of 200 ships sailed into the Firth of Clyde, carrying a Viking army from Dublin. It was led by Olaf and Ivar. Their primary target was Alt Clut, the mighty fortress of the Clyde Britons on Dumbarton Rock, which they surrounded and besieged. Remarkably, the defenders held out for several months, yielding only when their water supply failed. The Vikings then thoroughly ransacked the fortress.[5] So devastating was the siege and its aftermath that the ancient kingdom ruled from Alt Clut for the previous 400 years collapsed in disarray. Large numbers of Britons were taken captive before being shipped over to Dublin to be traded as slaves. Yet their royal dynasty survived – or was permitted by the Vikings to continue – at an alternative centre of power higher up the Clyde. Ten miles upstream from Dumbarton, a successor kingdom arose phoenix-like in the *strath* or river valley around Govan and Partick. As we shall see, this new political entity – known as Strat Clut, 'Strathclyde' – was to become a significant power in the tenth century.[6] It retained the Brittonic language but assimilated aspects of Scandinavian culture and undoubtedly accommodated Norse settlers. It is likely that Strathclyde's rulers reached some kind of accord with their Dublin counterparts, eventually putting aside old enmities to forge a more nuanced relationship. Their erstwhile royal citadel on Dumbarton Rock seems to have become a Norse stronghold after the siege of 870, at least for a while. Its strategic location at the head of the Firth of Clyde would certainly have made it an attractive proposition for future development as a major ship haven like Dublin. For some reason, however, this seems not to have happened and Dumbarton was evidently back in British hands by the mid-tenth century: the site has yielded sculptured stones carved in the 'Govan School' style associated with the kingdom of Strathclyde.

Vikings on Man

As noted at the end of Chapter 5, the first Viking settlements on the Isle of Man appear to have been established towards the end of the ninth century.[7] This is not so much a firm date as a 'best guess' made in the absence of a contemporary historical narrative, such as a set of Manx annals, that might otherwise have provided an account of Norse colonisation. Lacking a textual source, we must look to other types of evidence. Archaeology provides one important avenue, yielding artefacts that can, in some cases, be dated fairly precisely. Place-names, too, can indicate locations where speakers of the Norse language made their homes. Even the written record is not a total blank if we broaden our scope to consider texts from beyond the Irish Sea region, some of which might offer useful analogies for what was happening on Man.

One event that has sometimes been seen in a Manx context is the death of Tomrar, a Norse *jarl* ('earl') who was slain at 'Port Manann' in 866. His demise was noted in the *Fragmentary Annals of Ireland*, a chronicle in which individual year entries were embellished with detailed narratives drawn from storytelling and legends.[8] As with the raid on *Inis Phatraic* in 798, the geographical context could be Ireland rather than Man, for *Manann* occurs in a number of Irish place-names. Since other information on Tomrar shows him raiding Irish territory, his death at Port Manann should probably be assigned to an Irish rather than to a Manx context.[9] As far as can be judged, the Irish chronicles make no mention of Viking activity in Man during the ninth century. Nor, indeed, does any other written source from Ireland or Britain. The only certain allusions come from the Icelandic sagas. In these late and controversial works we encounter the Viking warlord Ketil Bjornsson, nicknamed 'Flatnose', depicted as ruling a large maritime domain comprising the Hebrides and Man. If such a polity ever existed, it would rightly attract our interest as a potential forerunner of the famed Kingdom of the Isles of later times. From the Viking Age onwards, contemporary references to 'The Isles' refer specifically to the Hebrides and Man, drawing a clear distinction between these 'southern' islands and the Northern Isles of Orkney and Shetland. The saga accounts of Ketil's career differ slightly, but the basic storyline is the same: during the reign of Harald Fairhair, king of Norway, Ketil is said to have conquered Man and the Hebrides on behalf of the king but decided to set himself up as a ruler in his own right. Some historians, accepting this story as true, see Ketil as an early 'king of the Isles', pre-dating the oldest known bearer of the title by a hundred years.[10] Yet it is more likely that the story is a fictionalised version of ninth-century events and that it reflects a much later perspective. The sagas in question are compositions of the twelfth and thirteenth centuries, created in an era when kings of Norway were seeking to reaffirm what they saw as their rightful authority over the Norse colonies in Britain and Ireland.[11] By depicting Ketil as conqueror of Man and the Hebrides on behalf of the ninth-century King Harald Fairhair, the saga writers were strengthening later claims of Norwegian royal overlordship by projecting them 300 years backwards, thus giving them greater antiquity. While we might suppose that Ketil really existed and that he may have raided parts of the Irish Sea region, we should probably treat his alleged rule over Man and the Hebrides with scepticism.

The earliest certain reference to Viking activity in a Manx context relates to a sea battle fought in 914. This is discussed in more detail below, but its date should make us wonder why Man seems to have been avoided by Norse settlers during the greater part of the 800s. In the previous chapter, we considered the possibility that the British (Brittonic-speaking) rulers of Man may have deterred Viking settlement by force of arms or via negotiated agreements. We identified two of these rulers as Merfyn Frych and his son Rhodri Mawr, each of whom probably ruled Man and Gwynedd simultaneously between the 820s and the 870s. In this chapter we will consider what change in circumstances at the end of the ninth century may have encouraged or enabled the first Norse colonists to arrive on Man.

What presumably changed was the relationship between Man's rulers and their Norse counterparts in Ireland. Dealings may have become openly hostile from c.870 after previously being amicable. The date is an informed guess, based on the actions of Rhodri Mawr after a battle on Anglesey where, in 877, he suffered a defeat at Viking hands.[12] The victors were 'Dark Foreigners', perhaps the same group whose leader Orm had been slain by Rhodri twenty-one years earlier. This time Rhodri was on the losing side, his defeat being so severe that he fled Gwynedd to seek refuge in Ireland. We might have expected him to flee to Man, especially if it was his family's ancestral home. The fact that he went elsewhere suggests that Man had already fallen under Viking control and was no longer under Rhodri's authority. Seven years earlier, a Norse fleet from Dublin had captured the royal stronghold of the Clyde Britons at Dumbarton, toppling their king and enslaving large numbers of his people. Did another force of Dubliners – or perhaps the same one – seize Man in similarly violent fashion and at roughly the same time?[13] It is even possible that Ivar and his kinsmen had resolved to subdue not one but two power bases of the Britons, both of which had strategic value in a maritime context: Dumbarton on the Firth of Clyde and the sea-girt Isle of Man. Bereft of its great fortress, the royal dynasty of Alt Clut withdrew to an inland site and would henceforth be restricted in terms of naval warfare. Likewise, without access to Manx ships and harbours, the Merfynion dynasty of Gwynedd would have been less able to challenge Uí Ímair domination of the seaways. It is therefore possible that Rhodri's flight into exile in 877 took him to Ireland because Man had already been seized by the Dublin Norse. Whatever the true sequence of events, the eventual outcome seems clear: British rule on Man gave way to Norse rule sometime in the late ninth century.

The Viking colonisation of Man: archaeological evidence

Conventional wisdom once assumed that the first Scandinavian settlements on Man were established in the early tenth century. More recently, this date has been pushed back into the final decades of the ninth. A phase of colonisation at some point during the 800s would indeed be unsurprising, given that this was when Norse settlements were being established in Ireland. On Man, the pertinent archaeological evidence comes from a number of graves containing artefacts, such as personal jewellery, that can be dated to the period 850–900.[14] Burial with grave goods, a practice usually shunned by Christians, indicates that the first Norse colonists on Man were pagans. They do not appear to have come directly from the ancestral homelands across the North Sea. Indeed, none of their graves on Man contains objects that can be securely identified as having been made in Scandinavia. What these graves do contain are things that originated in areas already colonised by the Norse, such as Ireland and the Hebrides. In all likelihood, then, the first Norse settlements on Man were founded by migrants from these areas.[15] Where the sex of an individual buried in a grave can be determined, the associated objects ('grave goods') imply traditional gender roles. Martial equipment such as swords, spears and shields have been found in male burials, indicating the presence of high-status warriors – a military aristocracy – among the Norse colonists. Of the small number of female burials, one contained what appears to be a pestle and mortar that may have been used for mixing cosmetics or medicines. This grave was found on St Patrick's Isle at Peel and seems, from the richness of the objects interred, to be the grave of a woman of high status. An iron rod buried at her side, traditionally interpreted as a spit for roasting meat, might be connected with sacred rituals or spell casting. The woman is now often described as the 'Pagan Lady' of Peel. Analysis of her skeleton has shown that she was not a native of Man but came to the island from elsewhere, perhaps from one of the Norse colonies around the Irish Sea.[16]

Some of the early Norse graves on Man have been found inside mounds, a type of burial seen in other parts of the Viking world. The individuals buried in these mounds were warriors, interred with weapons rather than with farming tools.[17] In the Irish Sea region, mound graves are known from Cumbria, Lancashire, the Hebrides, Ireland and Man. Burial in a mound indicates that the deceased held pagan beliefs and was a person of high status. Being a prominent feature in the landscape, a burial mound could be used as a territorial marker as well as a memorial. It is possible that one or more Manx Viking-Age mounds served this dual purpose, marking a place of burial while visibly reinforcing a claim to land ownership by the family of the deceased. One such mound was erected on the site of a Christian cemetery at Balladoole in the south of the island. It contained a ship burial that obliterated or damaged the graves of local Christians.[18] A Viking interred in such a tomb was someone of very high status indeed, a warlord of renown, perhaps even a king.

The burial evidence from Man implies that the initial phase of Norse settlement did not involve large numbers of people, with one estimate proposing a figure of 400.[19] On a small island, such a group could have a massive impact, especially if it included a significant percentage of armed men. What the warrior-graves may be telling us is that the Norse colonisation of Man began with a violent takeover. The alternative is some kind of negotiated agreement between the native rulers and the incoming Norse, with the latter being allowed to settle on the island in exchange for serving the former as mercenaries. Yet such an accord can hardly have endured for more than a generation or two for, as we shall see in the next chapter, Man was completely under Norse control by the middle of the tenth century. By then, the Brittonic-speaking elite that had formerly ruled the island was gone. We can thus imagine a rapid conquest in which this elite – essentially the pre-Norse rulers of Man and their landed aristocracy – were ejected or destroyed. Some Brittonic-speaking islanders of lesser status – tenant farmers who worked the land, herders in the uplands

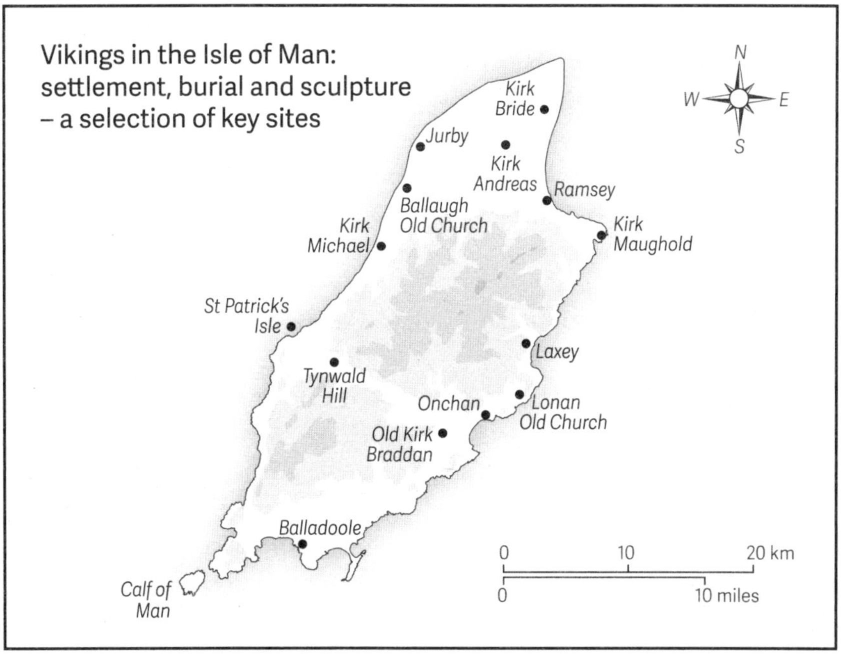

and fisherfolk plying the inshore waters – may have been permitted to remain *in situ* as subjects of the incoming Norse. The fate of their Gaelic-speaking neighbours may have been broadly similar.

Despite their paganism, the first Viking colonists on Man had a preference for burying their dead in locations previously used by native Christian communities. The use of stone cists in some burials containing pagan objects suggests that the settlers engaged local people as grave diggers. At Maughold, the principal Christian site on Man, pagan Norse settlers made use of the monastic cemetery for their own burial rites. At least two Viking swords have been discovered there. At Jurby, an unexcavated mound in the churchyard most likely contains a Viking burial.[20] What we appear to be seeing at a number of Christian sites on the island is continuity of cemetery use during the early Norse period, possibly after a brief hiatus in the aftermath of a violent conquest. Continuity does not necessarily mean that peaceful relations between settlers and natives became the norm, in the Maughold area or elsewhere. It merely suggests that not all interactions between the two groups were hostile. As discussed below, Christian sculpture was being produced at Maughold in the tenth century, indicating that the monastic community and its stone-carving workshops survived – or were revived – after Man fell under Norse rule.

While the monastery may have endured looting and damage by Viking raiders throughout the 800s, the sculptural evidence shows that it had recovered by c.950. Other places on Man, both religious and secular, might have witnessed less continuity than Kirk Maughold, or none at all. A varied pattern of conquest and colonisation, with violence and destruction across some parts of the island, but negotiation and co-existence in others, can probably be envisaged.

Viking settlement on Man: language and place-names

The Vikings who raided the Irish Sea region in the late eighth and early ninth centuries spoke the Old Norse language. Those who subsequently settled in Ireland and the Hebrides were exposed to the Gaelic speech of the native populations. Some settlers would have learned how to speak Gaelic themselves. Furthermore, there would have been numerous instances of Viking men marrying Gaelic-speaking Irishwomen or Isleswomen and raising families with them. In many cases, the offspring of these unions would have been bilingual in Gaelic and Norse.[21] By the late 800s, when the first Norse settlers arrived on Man, it is likely that there were already many people of mixed Norse-Gaelic parentage living around the shores of the Irish Sea and in the Hebridean isles. Nevertheless, on Man a large number of Scandinavian place-names suggests that Norse was the main language of the first Viking colonists and that it remained dominant on the island for a considerable time, probably to the end of the Norse era in the thirteenth century.[22] Names such as Jurby (*djúra-by*, 'deer settlement), Laxey (*laks-á*, 'salmon river') and Ramsey (*hrams-á*, 'wild garlic river') all indicate the presence of Norse speakers. What happened to the pre-Norse languages of Man? In the case of Brittonic there is every indication that it completely disappeared from the island, this being the most straightforward explanation for the dearth of Brittonic elements in today's place-names. In the case of the Gaelic place-names of present-day Man, we come to an intriguing question: can any be shown beyond doubt to pre-date the Norse colonisation? Linked to this question is another: did the Gaelic speech of pre-Norse times survive the Viking colonisation? These questions need to be asked, not least because the very substantial number of Norse place-names on Man implies not only a political takeover by a Norse-speaking elite, but also colonisation on a large scale, across the whole island and at every level of society, by people whose main language was Norse rather than Gaelic.[23] Both questions have, unsurprisingly, been debated by specialist scholars for a long time. On one side of the debate is the argument that the Gaelic names in today's Manx landscape should not be seen as survivals from pre-Norse times but as names created *after* Norse rule ended in the thirteenth century. This scenario sees pre-Norse Gaelic, like Brittonic, being obliterated by the Viking takeover. It then sees a much later revival of Gaelic in the post-Norse period (after 1266) when Man became part of the kingdom of Scotland and when settlers of Scottish origin may have devised new names in Scottish Gaelic for places that had previously had Norse names.[24] On the other side of the debate stands an argument for widespread survival of pre-Norse Gaelic names. This envisages Norse colonists arriving on Man in the ninth and tenth centuries but co-existing alongside the island's Gaelic-speaking communities, who thus continued to use their own names for places.[25]

Both arguments have been eloquently presented by their respective supporters and it is difficult for the non-specialist to choose one over the other. Yet, amid the uncertainty, there is one point on which both sides agree: only three places on Man have names for which a pre-Norse origin seems certain. These are Douglas, Rushen and the island's own name.[26] It is worth pointing out that none of these three can be shown to derive from Gaelic rather than from Brittonic. Viewed in isolation, such a tiny percentage of confirmed pre-Norse names lends weight to the idea that the Viking takeover of Man destroyed the older linguistic landscape, pushing Gaelic speech as well as Brittonic speech into oblivion. Some historians think that this is what happened in Orkney and Shetland where Pictish, the Celtic language of pre-Norse times, has left hardly any trace in a modern landscape dominated by Norse names. There has been much debate over what this says about the fate of local Picts. A grim scenario of violent conquest followed by deliberate slaughter of Pictish men and enslavement of Pictish women is one possibility. Mass evacuation by Pictish families to avoid these fates is another, while peaceful, albeit unequal, co-existence with Norse settlers has also been proposed.[27]

Place-name data from other Scottish islands has prompted a similar range of interpretations. On the Hebridean isles of Lewis and Skye, for example, we find Gaelic names attached to landscape features such as hills and bogs rather than to settlements. This suggests that indigenous Gaelic-speakers survived but as a subjugated, low-status group serving Norse colonists as shepherds and peat cutters.[28] By the same token, on those Hebridean isles where the percentage of Gaelic place-names is much greater, are we seeing substantial survival of native populations throughout the Viking period or a later resurgence of Gaelic speech? If minimal survival of pre-Norse names could be proved on any one island, it might mean that Norse-speaking colonists expelled or killed the

Gaelic-speaking inhabitants before devising new names in their own language for settlements and landscape features alike. Is this what happened on Man: an almost total wipeout of pre-Norse place-names, not only those of Brittonic origin but the Gaelic ones too? A compromise in the debate between survival and non-survival of pre-Norse Gaelic speech on Man sees a nuanced picture, one that accepts *some* Gaelic names as genuine relics from pre-Norse times rather than seeing all of them as creations of a later age. In this scenario, some of the pre-Norse communities of Manx Gaels survived into the Viking Age, living alongside Norse colonists in a bilingual society that nevertheless gave precedence to the Norse language. I envisage this situation continuing until the late 1200s, when the Norse-speaking Crovan dynasty came to an end. We may note that Gaelic speech, unlike Brittonic, is likely to have been used by some of the early Norse-speaking settlers who came to Man, especially those who had been born to Irish mothers in Dublin or elsewhere. Perhaps this type of linguistic affinity eased the initial contact and subsequent relations between Norse settlers and Manx Gaels, in some parts of the island at least? In other parts, merely speaking the language of Ireland might not have been enough to save indigenous Gaelic-speaking families from being slain or enslaved.

Norse or post-Norse?

Assigning dates to place-names is notoriously difficult, hence the long-running debate about the Gaelic names of the Isle of Man. The island's Norse names, too, have come under similar scrutiny. It was once suggested that some of these might have been created not in the Viking Age but considerably later, by people from north-west England who arrived on Man *after* the end of Norse rule in the thirteenth century.[29] The historical backdrop lies in the 1400s when the Stanleys, a family of wealthy English landowners, became the rulers of Man. It is known that a number of tenant farmers from the Stanley estates in Lancashire came to live on the island. Although these people were English speakers, their home county has many place-names of Scandinavian origin. Hence a theory arose that some Stanley tenants may have transferred familiar Norse-sounding names from Lancashire to their new settlements on Man. However, it has since been largely withdrawn, leaving a broad consensus among philologists and historians that the Norse place-names on Man do indeed belong to the Viking Age.[30]

'Hiberno-Norse'

The Vikings who settled in Ireland in the ninth century are sometimes referred to as 'Hiberno-Norse'. This is a term of modern origin incorporating *Hibernia*, a Roman name for Ireland, and 'Norse', a word unattested before the late sixteenth century.[31] 'Norse' was coined in English from an old Dutch word *noordsch* and originally meant 'Nordic' in the sense of a group of Northern European languages. There is a possibility that the similar-sounding Scandinavian word *Norsk* ('Norwegian') might explain why 'Norse' eventually became a specific label for Norwegian Vikings. Throughout this book I have tended to follow this narrow usage, while at the same time keeping in mind that not all 'Norsemen' or 'Norsewomen' necessarily had ancestral roots in Norway. Some may have been of Danish or even Swedish heritage. In the case of the term 'Hiberno-Norse' we can, I believe, apply a precise geographical meaning. It is a useful label for people of Scandinavian heritage who lived in Ireland during the Viking Age, as well as for those among them who later migrated from Ireland to establish new colonies elsewhere.[32] We should note that 'Hiberno-Norse' is not applicable to Scandinavian settlers in other Gaelic-speaking areas, such as the Hebrides, unless they originated among the colonies in Ireland.

The Norwegian connotation of 'Hiberno-Norse' has meant that it often appears in modern historical studies as a counterpart to 'Anglo-Danish', the latter being a label commonly applied to those Viking warriors and their descendants who colonised the eastern parts of England. There is always a risk that such labelling promotes a false perception that Scandinavian raiders and settlers in Britain and Ireland comprised two homogenous groups separated along ethnic lines, the one having Norwegian ancestry and the other Danish. As stated above, such a distinction is unlikely to reflect the reality of the situation, which undoubtedly presented a more complex picture of ethnic and cultural identities. English chroniclers in the ninth and tenth centuries were using broad brushstrokes when they routinely described their country's Scandinavian invaders as 'Danes'. Even if a majority of Scandinavians in the so-called Danelaw did indeed have Danish ancestry, it is hard to believe that all of them did, still less that their English contemporaries knew this to be the case or even gave the matter much thought. Modern distinctions between Danish and Norwegian Vikings have sometimes gone as far as imagining the latter as wilder and more barbarous than the former. Needless to say, such notions are wide of the mark. We only need to look at connections and similarities between the 'Norse' Uí Ímair dynasty of Dublin and the 'Danish' Great Army in England, to see that all Vikings were essentially cut from the same cloth.[33] These folk mingled and co-operated regardless of which part of the Scandinavian homelands their ancestors had called home. The lines between their various groupings were undoubtedly less clear-cut than some of our modern labelling fancifully suggests.

Lochlann and Laithlind

One of the more puzzling terms associated with the Uí Ímair dynasty is a place called *Lochlann*, sometimes written as *Laithlind*. Olaf, brother of the dynasty's eponymous founder Ivar, is described in the *Annals of Ulster* as 'son of the king of Laithlind'.[34] The location of this place is not indicated in *AU*, nor in any other medieval source. One theory is that it is a contemporary Irish name for Norway. In the eleventh century this was indeed the case, but it might not have been so in the ninth. Another theory sees Lochlann or Laithlind as an umbrella term encompassing all Norse colonies in the Isles (Man and the Hebrides), the Northern Isles (Shetland and Orkney) and on the west coast of Scotland.[35] A further suggestion is that Laithlind may be a compound name comprising the old Gaelic words for 'mud' (*lath/loth*) and 'pool' (*lind*), hence 'The Muddy Pool', a possible alternative name for Dublin (Gaelic *dubh+lind*, 'dark pool'). Finally, we may note that the synonymity of Lochlann and Laithlind is based on a modern assumption and that the two names may have referred to separate locations in the Viking Age.[36]

Conversion and assimilation

At some point in the first half of the tenth century, the Norse colonists on Man adopted Christianity. We know this because the pagan practice of mound burial ceased, as did the placing of grave goods. The process of conversion appears to have been gradual rather than rapid, with reverence for the gods of Scandinavian paganism being slow to fade.[37] Nowhere is the pagan-to-Christian transition more visible than in the sculptured stones that the colonists erected in memory of their deceased. For them, this was a new custom: pagan Scandinavia had no home-grown tradition of monumental stone carving. Commemorative stones bearing names were not present in the funerary rituals of pre-Christian Norway and Denmark. Although some graves in these lands appear to have been marked with wooden posts, it is not possible to ascertain whether or not they were carved with runes identifying the deceased.[38] Sculptured gravestones in Christian cemeteries around the coasts of Britain and Ireland were probably the first such monuments encountered by the Vikings when they began raiding these areas in the late 700s. Descendants of these same plunderers became the colonists of the Irish Sea region in the ninth century whose own descendants began to adopt Christianity in the tenth.

Alongside a new set of religious beliefs, the Norse Christian converts engaged with local traditions relating to sculptured stone memorials. On the Isle of Man there are approximately 100 such monuments, carved during the period of Viking rule yet bearing Christian motifs. Expert study of their style of decoration has assigned the majority to the tenth century. The date is significant: it suggests that there was a substantial break in Manx stone carving in the ninth century, between the last pre-Norse monuments (such as Guriat's Cross) and those of the Norse settlement.[39] Most of the surviving examples are fragments of various sizes and shapes rather than complete monuments. The original monument in nearly every case was a slab carved with a cross on one or both sides. Crosses were often decorated with, or surrounded by, intricate patterns of interlace. What these stones show quite clearly is that the Norse converts did not abandon the traditions and beliefs of their forebears. The carvings often combine Christian imagery with Scandinavian artistic styles or with motifs from Scandinavian mythology. Four distinct styles of Scandinavian artwork – Borre, Jellinge, Mammen and Ringerike – are identifiable on Manx stones. These are named from places in Scandinavia where they appear on objects of Viking-Age provenance. Each style is recognisable by its variations, such as in the way patterns and animals are carved. Many of the stones from Man include inscriptions in the Norse runic alphabet, identifying the deceased by name. One famous inscription, from Kirk Michael, commemorates Maelbrigde (a Gaelic name) and his father Athakan the smith. It adds that the stone was carved by a man called Gaut who 'made this and all in Man'. The stone has an interlace pattern in the Borre style. Other Manx stones, with Borre patterns carved in a recognisably similar fashion, are likewise considered to be Gaut's work. He is thought to have been active during the middle third of the tenth century.[40]

Even where no distinctly Scandinavian designs are evident, the deceased may have been a Christianised Norse settler rather than a Manx native. One example is an ornately carved cross-slab from Onchan near Douglas, carved with a large, ringed cross-head above a tapered shaft adorned with interlace. Each corner of the cross-head and its centre contain a raised circular boss. A date in the late ninth or early tenth century has been proposed for this monument, placing it within the initial phase of Norse colonisation.[41] Of similar date, although with less ornamentation, is a slab from Maughold depicting a tapered, ring-headed cross with a single boss in the centre. Neither of these two stones displays overtly Scandinavian influence but, on chronological grounds, both may commemorate Christian Norse colonists. A third slab, from Lonan Old Church, is roughly contemporary but has a different sculptural style. Its ringed cross-head is huge in comparison with the shaft, which is narrow and straight. There are no bosses and no interlace, but the shaft contains a mysterious carved object at the top and two spirals at the base. The upper carving is reminiscent of a common Pictish symbol identified as a 'mirror' and might have been inspired by it. The spirals look like those adorning other Manx stones from the Viking Age.[42] Paired spirals are also seen in pre-Christian Celtic art, but in this context can probably be interpreted as the roots of a living tree, the 'tree of life', here presenting an alternative image of the cross of Christ. Elsewhere on Man, multiple spiral ornamentation occurs on a cross-slab from Onchan and on two from Kirk Michael, all three monuments dating to the early tenth century. Interlace patterns on Manx sculpture of this period range from the simple to the intricate. At Lonan, a stone carved in the shape of a large ringed cross-head above a short, undersized shaft is almost completely covered with interlace. The only unadorned parts of the cross are four circular armpits, left bare by the stone carver, their lack of decoration making them stand out all the more.[43]

The artisans who carved the Manx stones of the late ninth to tenth centuries did not operate in isolation from those in other lands. They were open to ideas and techniques, especially from places that were not very far away. Particular influences upon their work have been identified, with varying degrees of confidence, by noting certain similarities. One place that seems to have influenced the Manx carvers was Whithorn in Galloway, where a distinctive style or 'school' of ornamentation developed in the tenth century. Another was the north-west coast of Northumbria in what would later become the county of Cumberland (now part of Cumbria), an area that shared Galloway's close proximity to Man.[44]

A new development in Manx sculpture of the tenth century was the practice of carving both sides of a slab and, in many cases, the edges as well. This innovation, not previously seen on the island, is characteristic of monuments that have been identified as contemporary with the first phase of Norse settlement.[45] Another new feature from around the same time is imagery associated with hunting. Carvings of human figures riding horses, often accompanied by dogs, are seen on Pictish sculpture of the eighth century but appear considerably later in Man. Hunting with hounds was a distinctly aristocratic activity in early medieval society and allowed young noblemen to hone their skills for war. When reproduced in sculpture, a hunting scene made a clear statement about the wealth and status of the people it depicted. Similarities between hunting scenes on Pictish sculpture of the eighth century and on Manx sculpture of the tenth suggest that the former provided inspiration for the latter, despite the 200-year gap between them.

Man and Dublin in the tenth century

Rhodri Mawr, king of Gwynedd, died in 878 during a battle against English forces from Mercia.[46] His sons divided the kingdom between them, with Anarawd the eldest succeeding to the kingship. Anarawd forged an alliance with the Vikings of Northumbria whose leaders were now firmly established at York. In 881, he avenged his father by thwarting a Mercian invasion at a battle on the River Conwy. However, by the early 890s he had shifted towards the English, eventually aligning with King Alfred of Wessex. Several raids on Gwynedd were launched from the Danelaw around this time and probably indicate Viking displeasure at Anarawd's changing loyalties.[47]

Moving forward to the start of the tenth century, we come to an event of enormous significance for the Irish Sea region. In 902, an alliance of Irish kings captured Dublin and ejected the Uí Ímair.[48] Members of the dynasty, together with large numbers of people from Dublin and other Norse settlements in Ireland, fled into exile. Most of the refugees sailed to Britain, constituting a substantial diaspora that led to new colonies being established on the western coast of Northumbria, from the Solway Firth down to the Ribble and Mersey estuaries. Others landed in Wales while some sailed much further north to make new homes in the Hebridean isles.[49] Having had dealings with the Irish for many years, it is likely that many Hiberno-Norse migrants had a basic understanding of Gaelic speech. Some may even have used it in their everyday discourse. Nevertheless, the place-names that they gave to their new settlements were usually coined in the Old Norse language.

Among the Hiberno-Norse arrivals in Wales was one group, led by a certain Ingimund, who landed on Anglesey. Confronted there by the king of Gwynedd, a grandson of Rhodri Mawr, they were forced to return to their ships. They eventually settled near Chester, most likely on the Wirral peninsula, on English land granted by the rulers of Mercia. Archaeological evidence from Anglesey shows that Ingimund's people were not the only Hiberno-Norse migrants seeking refuge on the island. Another group succeeded in making its home there in the early tenth century, taking over a native settlement and producing craft objects.[50] Not far away, a Viking burial with grave goods has also been discovered.

Although no equivalent data exists for Man, we need not doubt that it, too, was a destination for Norse groups fleeing Ireland after the fall of Dublin in 902.[51] The new arrivals would have added to an existing Norse population established a generation earlier. In the following decade, Man reappears in the historical record. An entry in the *Annals of Ulster* under the year 914 reports a sea battle in Manx waters between Rognvald, a grandson of Ivar, and Bardr, son of Ottar. Rognvald was victorious and Bardr was slain. This encounter between two Viking warlords may have been a contest for control of Man.[52] Rognvald was at that time emerging as a dominant figure in the Irish Sea region and Man's strategic advantages are likely to have featured in his ambitions. After his victory, Manx harbours may have been obliged or compelled to welcome his ships. Indeed, his raiding fleet, or Bardr's, was most likely already using one or more of these havens before the battle.[53] Rognvald was a prince of the Uí Ímair dynasty that had been exiled from Dublin twelve years earlier, his grandfather being its eponymous founder Ivar. Another of Ivar's grandsons was Sihtric, probably a cousin to Rognvald. He, too, was carving a formidable military reputation in the second decade of the tenth century. In 917, both Sihtric and Rognvald appeared off the west coast of Ireland, leading separate fleets. Rognvald seized Waterford, a haven that another Viking force – possibly led by his adversary Bardr – had taken from the Irish three years earlier. Meanwhile, Sihtric landed further north and met the men of Leinster in battle. After defeating them he marched on Dublin, wresting the city out of Irish hands before setting himself up as its new king. This violent restoration of Norse power in Ireland signalled that the fifteen-year exile of the Uí Ímair was over.[54] Rulers elsewhere watched the unfolding situation closely, not least the English king Edward the Elder and his sister Lady Æthelflæd. These siblings, respectively the rulers of Wessex and Mercia, were cast in the tough mould of their late father Alfred the Great. Like him, they were determined to curtail the Viking predilection for raiding and land-taking. In Mercia, they were steadily restoring to English control a broad swathe of territory long held by sections of the Great Army. As well as fighting on this eastern front, Æthelflæd strengthened the defences of north-west Mercia to guard against raids from Viking York (*Jorvik*). The events of 917 meant that she also had to contend with the additional menace of a resurgent Uí Ímair dynasty in the Irish Sea. According to the *Fragmentary Annals of Ireland*, she formed an alliance with the Scots and Strathclyde Britons against an unnamed Norse king. The latter was almost certainly Rognvald. Although the source is a late and controversial chronicle, it may here be reporting authentic history. It goes on to describe a Norse raid on Strathclyde that the Britons withstood and repulsed.[55] Rognvald was arguably the culprit, leading or sending his fleet to the Firth of Clyde to punish Æthelflæd's northern allies for aligning with her against him. In 918, the year of Æthelflæd's death, Rognvald sailed to Northumbria and seized the kingship of York. The city's Anglo-Danish elite – a group of English secular and ecclesiastical leaders together with senior figures from the Great Army – offered him their allegiance. The third decade of the tenth century thus began with two of Ivar's grandsons holding power on both sides of the Irish Sea. We can be fairly certain that the Isle of Man, lying on an axis between Dublin and York and already a Norse colony, became increasingly useful to the Uí Ímair. It would have been a convenient stepping stone on the route between the two Viking cities, as well as serving as a base for seaborne raiding expeditions. It undoubtedly had plenty of ships that could be mustered as a war fleet in support of Dublin's interests.

In 920, two years after Æthelflæd's death, Rognvald attended a meeting at Bakewell in northern Mercia. Other attendees included the kings of Alba and Strathclyde. The gathering was summoned by King Edward of Wessex in the hope of establishing peace between the various parties. Contemporary English chroniclers depicted it as a ceremony of submission to Edward's overlordship, but this is probably tenth-century 'spin'.[56] Rognvald was no doubt seen by his fellow attendees as the bogeyman, but whatever agreement was reached is unlikely to have been tested. He died in the following year. His successor as king of York was Sihtric whose former kingship at Dublin now went to Guthfrith, another of Ivar's grandsons. The ensuing years saw a bitter rivalry between the Norse in Ireland as those of Dublin and Waterford fought against those of Limerick on the Atlantic coast. Limerick had its own royal dynasty, either a branch of the Uí Ímair or a separate kindred to which Bardr Ottarsson had belonged.[57] Wars between these three Norse colonies and their Irish neighbours meanwhile continued, with mixed results and a varied pattern of alliances. Guthfrith left Dublin in 927, travelling to York where he succeeded Sihtric who had died. The vacant Dublin kingship was then contested between Guthfrith's and Sihtric's sons until Guthfrith himself returned to take charge of the city. In the late 920s and early 930s Guthfrith led Dublin and Waterford in the continuing strife with Limerick, a war that seems to have embroiled many Irish kingdoms too. Hostilities did not end with Guthfrith's death in 934 but raged for a further three years until his son Olaf decisively defeated the Limerick Norse in a battle on the River Shannon.[58] Across the sea in Northumbria, the kingship of York had lain vacant since the departure of Guthfrith in 927. Power there had been seized by the English king Athelstan, a son of Edward the Elder. In 937, shortly after vanquishing his Limerick foes, Olaf Guthfrithsson sailed over to Britain with a mighty army. Forming an alliance with the Scots and Strathclyde Britons, he came against Athelstan at the famous Battle of Brunanburh, no doubt expecting that a big victory would win the prize of York for himself. Instead, the victor was Athelstan who forced Olaf to sail back to Dublin with heavy losses. The English chronicler John of Worcester, writing some 200 years later, called Olaf 'king of the Isles', a plausible addition to the career of such a renowned Viking warlord.[59] The title implies the existence of a tenth-century kingdom comprising the Hebrides and Man. To what extent this can be seen as an embryonic version of the great 'Kingdom of the Isles' that flourished in the twelfth and thirteenth centuries is uncertain, but we can probably envisage the two as broadly coterminous. In other words, the later kingdom should, to some extent, be seen as the successor of the earlier.[60] Although Olaf Guthfrithsson's main residence no doubt lay at Dublin, his chief centre of power in the Isles was probably Man.

Athelstan's death in 939 presented a new opportunity for Olaf who duly arrived in York to claim the kingship that his father had held briefly twelve years earlier. At Dublin a cousin and namesake, Olaf Sihtricsson, became the new king. This man bore the curious nickname *Cuarán* (Gaelic: 'Sandal') which is commonly used to distinguish him from other Olafs.[61] The death of Olaf Guthfrithsson in 941 led to another round of crown swapping among the Uí Ímair, with Olaf Cuarán moving across to York and Blacaire Guthfrithsson replacing him at Dublin. The Uí Ímair had also taken power in Limerick by this date, for Olaf Cuarán's brother Harald Sihtricsson was now ruling there. In 944, the combined armies of two allied Irish kings ransacked Dublin. In the same year, Olaf Cuarán was expelled from York by King Edmund of Wessex, half-brother of Athelstan. Cuarán returned to Dublin in the following year,

Chapel Hill, Balladoole: a small chapel or 'keeill', one of several archaeological features indicating religious activity on the hill from the Bronze Age to the Viking Age [© Barbara Keeling]

Jurby Church: stained-glass window showing St Maughold's conversion by St Patrick [© Barbara Keeling]

Lonan Old Church (St Adamnan's). Dedicated to Adomnán, abbot of Iona (679–704), this part-renovated medieval church stands on what may have been a much older Christian site [© Barbara Keeling]

St Patrick's Isle: the curtain wall of Peel Castle and the Round Tower [© Barbara Keeling]

Left. Kirk Maughold: Crux Guriat, 'Guriat's Cross' (early ninth century)
[© Barbara Keeling]

Below. The Crux Guriat inscription, with a sketch by P.M.C. Kermode
[photo © Barbara Keeling]

Right. Balladoole: the Viking ship-burial on Chapel Hill [© Barbara Keeling]

Below. Kirk Andreas: detail of a rider on the tenth-century Sandulf's Cross [© Barbara Keeling]

Kirk Andreas: Scandinavian runic inscription (not yet deciphered) alongside a cross-shaft [© Barbara Keeling]

Kirk Michael: one edge of this cross-slab has the runic inscription 'Gaut carved this and all in Man'. Gaut (Gautr) was active c.900 [© Barbara Keeling]

Kirk Bride: the tenth-century Thor's Cross with its carved figures, including one supposedly representing the Scandinavian god Thor [© Barbara Keeling]

Kirk Maughold: the surviving portion of this Viking-Age monument has a hunting scene carved below the cross [© Barbara Keeling

Right. Lonan Old Church: wheel-headed cross in the churchyard, probably carved in the tenth century
[© Barbara Keeling]

Below. Lonan Old Church: detail from a late nineteenth-century window in the north wall, commemorating the kings of Man and the Isles
[© Barbara Keeling]

Castletown: the fourteenth-century south tower of Castle Rushen. A seat of royal power in the time of the Crovan dynasty, the castle may have succeeded an older fortification built in the 900s [© Barbara Keeling]

Durham Cathedral: the tomb of Bishop Antony Bek (died 1311). Bek was 'Lord of the land of Man' during the reigns of the English kings Edward I and Edward II [© Barbara Keeling. Reproduced by kind permission of the Chapter of Durham Cathedral.]

Tynwald Hill: the traditional site of Manx law-making and justice, taking its name from Norse *þingvollr*, 'field of the assembly' [© Barbara Keeling]

Kirk Maughold: the cross house [© Barbara Keeling]

ousting Blacaire and retaking the kingship of the city. Blacaire made a brief comeback but eventually fell in battle against Irish foes. Cuarán then departed for Northumbria to make a final bid for power at York, but its future was now English and its days of giving allegiance to Scandinavian kings were coming to an end. In 951, Cuarán returned to Dublin. There he continued to rule as king until his retirement to the monastery of Iona in 980.

Tynwald

The present-day government of the Isle of Man is based in Douglas. It comprises three elements: a body of twenty-four elected representatives called the House of Keys; an eleven-member Legislative Council, responsible for reviewing laws proposed by the House of Keys; and the Lord of Man – the monarch of the United Kingdom – usually represented by a Lieutenant Governor. Together, the House of Keys and the Legislative Council constitute the Tynwald Court. Each year, on or around 5 July, the Court assembles at Tynwald Hill for a ceremony presided over by the Lieutenant Governor or by a member of the UK royal family. The hill, an artificial feature with a distinctive stepped profile, stands in the village of St John's. It forms part of a 'ritual landscape' that includes a Bronze Age mound burial and St John's Chapel – a church connected to the hill by a processional path. Manx tradition claims that the ceremony at Tynwald Hill originated in mass gatherings of the island's population in the Viking Age or earlier. This is supported by the name of the hill which derives from *þingvollr* (Old Norse: 'assembly field' – the first syllable is pronounced as *thing*). Unfortunately, the documented history of the site cannot be traced back earlier than 1228 when it is mentioned in the Manx Chronicle. References to assemblies and ceremonies taking place there commence in 1417. Many historians nevertheless take the view that Tynwald Hill was probably used by early Norse settlers as a venue for large public assemblies where laws were promulgated and justice was dispensed. Furthermore, Tynwald is clearly analogous with other sites in the Viking world where the former presence of a *þing* is acknowledged in a much later place-name. Among these other sites are Dingwall in Easter Ross (Scotland), Tingwall in Shetland and Thingmote in Dublin. The hill at Dublin, although no trace of it survives, is believed to have been a stepped mound like its Manx counterpart. Some, perhaps many, of the Viking-Age *þing* sites may have functioned as ritual venues as far back as prehistoric times.[62]

A Viking-Age carving of the Crucifixion

In the eighteenth century, part of a finely sculptured slab was unearthed by workmen on the Calf of Man, a small island lying off the south-western extremity of the Manx coast. Local tradition associates the place of discovery with a keeill, but no trace of such a structure has been found to date. The stone is now held in the Manx Museum at Douglas. Its carving is unique on Man, depicting the Crucifixion in a style reminiscent of Irish or Byzantine representations. The bearded figure of Christ is shown wearing a robe and a round breastplate, the latter adorned with a circle of double-strand interlace. At one side of the cross stands Longinus, the Roman soldier who supposedly pierced Christ's body with a spear. The other side would have depicted Stephaton, the soldier who offered Christ a vinegar-soaked sponge, but this part of the slab has not been found. The complete slab is thought to have originally served as the front panel of an altar or as one of the side panels of a tomb. It was formerly dated to c.800 because of its similarity with Crucifixion imagery from around this time, but is now seen as having more in common with images from the late 900s.[63]

7

RÍ INNSE GALL

The sons of Harald

Near the end of the previous chapter, we encountered the Viking warlord Olaf Guthfrithsson, a famous member of the Uí Ímair dynasty. His death in 941 removed one of the key political players from the Irish Sea region, but his energy and ambition lived on through his sons. By the 960s these men, the Olafssons, were launching raids on Ireland from a power base located most probably on Man or in the Hebrides.[1] Their presumed connection with these areas is implied by the presence in their army of certain *lagmainn* (Gaelic: 'lawmen', in the sense of 'law speakers'). References to *lagmainn* in Irish chronicles are usually associated with Norse forces from the Isles, hence these 'lawmen' are presumed to have Manx or Hebridean origins.

Following in their father's footsteps, the Olafssons wielded considerable influence for a decade or more. After their disappearance from the historical record c.970, a new power arose in the shape of the Haraldssons. These two brothers, named as Maccus and Godred in contemporary texts, similarly originated among the Hiberno-Norse in Ireland. Their father can be identified as Harald Sihtricsson, another scion of the Uí Ímair and a great-grandson of the dynastic forefather Ivar. Harald, who may have been a brother of the renowned Olaf Cuarán, was king of the Norse stronghold at Limerick until his death in 940. His sons Maccus and Godred came to the notice of contemporary chroniclers some thirty years later, when they raided Anglesey in 971 and 972. In one twelfth-century English chronicle, Maccus is described as *archipirata*, 'chief of pirates', a label that seems to place him above other sea-going raiders in a position of superiority – or notoriety.[2] He and his brother may indeed have viewed themselves as paramount figures among the various Norse warlords prowling the waters between Britain and Ireland. They certainly aspired to royal status and might even have issued their own coinage – an activity usually associated with powerful overkings. Coins made in imitation of contemporary English

The Irish Sea region, c.950 to c.1060
N
W
E
S
Shetland
Orkney
ALBA
Iona
Argyll
'The Isles'
Fife
North Sea
Govan
STRATHCLYDE
Arran
Galloway
Carlisle
Solway Firth
NORTHUMBRIA
Ulster
Man
York
Irish Sea
Connacht
Dublin
BREGA
Anglesey
Gwynedd
Chester
Limerick
Leinster
Powys
EAST ANGLIA
Waterford
MERCIA
Munster
Wales
Dyfed
Gwent
WESSEX
KENT
SUSSEX
English Channel
0 50 100 km
0 50 miles

types were produced in the Irish Sea region in the late tenth century and may have been minted on behalf of the Haraldssons, perhaps on the Isle of Man.[3]

The predatory activities of the Haraldssons were serious enough to be viewed as a threat by the English king Edgar, grandson of Athelstan and great-great-grandson of Alfred the Great.[4] In 973, Edgar convened a meeting of rulers at Chester, the former Roman fortress city near the mouth of the River Dee. Although a forlorn, derelict place at the dawn of the tenth century, Chester had been restored by Lady Æthelflæd in 907 as a Mercian fortress and trading centre. It was connected to the maritime economy of the Irish Sea region and, by the late 900s, its streets were home to a cosmopolitan populace that included people of Scandinavian heritage. The high-level meeting in 973 was attended by the two most important kings in northern Britain at the time: Cináed of Alba and Máel Coluim of Strathclyde. Also present were a couple of Welsh kings – Hywel and Iago – together with a man called Dyfnwal who was most likely Máel Coluim's father. King Edgar, in whose territory Chester lay, took the role of host. The final three attendees were two men with Scandinavian names – Siferth (Sigfrith) and Ulkil – alongside Maccus who is here described as 'king of many islands'.[5] Nothing is known of Sigfrith and Ulkil, but they may have been prominent Vikings whose activities were impacting on Edgar's political and economic interests. Maccus was undoubtedly the son of Harald and brother of Godred. The 'many islands' over which he ruled were almost certainly Man and the Hebrides, with the former a likely location for his main headquarters.[6]

During the meeting the attendees boarded a small boat in which Edgar, as host, acted as steersman while the others each took an oar. This international crew of high-ranking individuals made a short voyage along the Dee from Edgar's royal residence to St John's Church. There they paused to pray before making the return journey. English chroniclers claimed that the event saw Edgar receive oaths of allegiance from the others, his steering of the boat supposedly confirming his superiority. This is almost certainly an embellishment of the true facts. The meeting was more probably a conference of ambitious, powerful rulers who regarded one another as equals.[7] The outcome sought by Edgar was no doubt a peaceful resolution of differences to offset the ever-present danger of conflict. If so, the event may have been a success, at least from an English viewpoint. No conflicts involving Edgar's forces are recorded for the remaining two years of his reign. Nevertheless, news from beyond his borders suggests that he was right to be concerned about Maccus Haraldsson who, with his brother Godred, went on to pursue aggressive policies for the next ten years. In 980, Haraldsson forces from Man and the

The name 'Maccus'

Some historians suggest that Maccus Haraldsson's forename derives from the Norse name *Magnus*. They point to an entry in the *Annals of the Four Masters*, an Irish chronicle compiled in the seventeenth century from various medieval texts, in which Maccus is referred to as *Maghnus*. However, this form of his name appears in a nineteenth-century edition of *AFM* and not in the earliest manuscript. Most historians therefore see *Maccus* as a name of Gaelic origin, deriving from *macc*, 'son'. More particularly, occurrences of the name seem to be associated with places where Gaelic-speakers and Scandinavian colonists lived side by side.[9]

Hebrides were probably the 'Islesmen' who fell in defeat as allies of the Dublin Norse in a battle against the powerful Irish king Máel Sechnaill. Two years later, Godred Haraldsson raided the Welsh kingdom of Dyfed, plundering the great monastery of St Davids. In 984, both he and Maccus were in action again, this time at the Viking fortress of Waterford where they fought in alliance with Brian Bóruma, king of Munster.[8]

After the battle of Waterford, we hear no more of Maccus. It is possible that he perished there. His brother Godred survived to keep the family ambitions alive and was soon launching a new wave of attacks on Wales. In 987, Godred defeated the Welsh on Anglesey, taking 2,000 prisoners. He is probably the unnamed 'son of Harald' who won a battle on Man against unidentified foes in the same year.[10] If, as seems likely, Man was the main Haraldsson base, Godred was here fighting a defensive action. His victory may have thwarted a takeover of the island by a rival Norse group, either from within Man itself or from further afield. Godred won with the assistance of Danes, a people who were relative newcomers in the volatile politics of the Irish Sea region. What circumstances lay behind their alliance with Godred is unknown, but it occurred at a time when large raiding fleets from Denmark were roaming the seaways around Britain.[11] Although the name of Godred's Danish ally is not recorded, we might wonder if it was Sweyn Forkbeard, the newly anointed king of Denmark. As we shall see, Sweyn was soon to become a significant presence in the affairs of Britain and Ireland. It may be that his growing power was noticed at an early stage by Godred, who made good use of it by forming an alliance. At some point, according to *Njáls saga*, Godred fought against Sigurd the Stout, the Norse earl of Orkney. What caused these two mighty warlords to clash is unknown, if indeed their conflict ever happened outside the imagination of the saga-makers. *Njáls saga* was written in the 1200s and, like other works in its genre, cannot be considered a completely reliable witness to tenth-century events. Its mention of warfare between Godred and Earl Sigurd is nevertheless consistent with what other sagas say about Sigurd's activities. In *Orkneyinga saga* we hear of him raiding in the Hebrides and taking tribute. *Eyrbyggja saga* depicts him raiding Man in 989 and imposing a tax on the islanders.[12] If these episodes are based on real events and are more than mere storytelling, they firmly connect Sigurd to the history of Man and the Hebrides. His taking of tax and tribute implies that some among the Norse elite in these territories submitted to his overlordship. A possible example is Earl Gilli who lived on either Coll or Colonsay and who became Sigurd's henchman in subsequent campaigns.[13] Turning back to Godred Haraldsson, we find that his last appearance in the sources is in an entry in the *Annals of Ulster* noting his death in 989. There he is described as *rí Innse Gall*, 'king of the Isles of the Foreigners', a title that reinforces the idea that he and his brother had ruled a kingdom comprising Man and the Hebrides.[14] Godred died in battle in Dál Riata, the ancient maritime realm spanning the islands and coastlands between Argyll and Antrim. The precise location of his demise is unknown, as is the identity of his foes.

Royal raiders

In 995, according to the Welsh chronicles *Brut y Tywysogyon* and *Brenhinedd y Saesson*, the Isle of Man was raided by King Sweyn Forkbeard of Denmark.[15] Sweyn was not the only royal warlord from the Viking homelands to arrive in Manx waters. His contemporary Olaf Tryggvason, a prince of Norway, is said to have fought at least one battle on Man while raiding Scotland and the Hebrides. Our source for this information is *Óláfs saga Tryggvasonar*, part of a collection of sagas compiled by the thirteenth-century Icelandic historian Snorri Sturluson.[16] Despite being a blend of fictional stories and historical facts, the saga's reference to Olaf Tryggvason's Manx venture can cautiously be accepted as authentic.

Another powerful royal figure attacked Man in the first year of the new millennium. This time, the raider was no Viking, but an English king. His name was Æthelred and he was a son of the aforementioned Edgar. Twelfth-century

English chroniclers gave Æthelred the epithet *Unræd*, meaning 'poorly advised'. This was later misinterpreted as 'Unready', a more damning term that implies weakness or ill-preparedness in the face of aggression. Æthelred did indeed come under intense pressure from Vikings, but he emerges from the sources not as a weak king but as one who tried to use diplomacy as well as warfare in his dealings with external foes. In the year 1000, he launched a seaborne expedition against the Cumbrians, the Britons of Strathclyde. Our source is the *Anglo-Saxon Chronicle*:

> In this year the king went into *Cumberlande* and ravaged nearly all of it. His fleet went out around Chester and should have come to meet him, but could not, so it plundered the Isle of Man.[17]

In Æthelred's time the name *Cumberlande* did not refer to a county in north-west England but simply meant 'land of the Cumbrians'. The latter were the Brittonic-speaking inhabitants of Cumbria, a large territory that extended from Loch Lomond to the River Eamont south of Carlisle.[18] Cumbria was the expanded realm of the kings of Strathclyde, several of whom had played important roles in the turbulent international politics of the tenth century. Why Æthelred chose to attack their land is unknown. Perhaps the current Cumbrian monarch had given allegiance or support to England's Viking foes? This is what one twelfth-century chronicler gave as a motive for the attack, implying that Cumbrian territory was being used as a base by Danish warbands.[19] A large part of the Cumbrian kingdom was duly ravaged by Æthelred and his soldiers. His fleet, however, failed to rendezvous with his land forces and instead went on a diversion to Man, where it took plunder. We might wonder who held authority on Man at that time. The most plausible candidate is Rognvald, described in Irish chronicles as 'king of the Isles', whose reign spanned the years 989 to 1005. Rognvald's father was a man called Godred whom we can identify as Godred Haraldsson, 'king of the Isles of the Foreigners'.[20] It was Godred's brother Maccus who had attended the meeting at Chester convened by Æthelred's father Edgar in 973. There might even be a connection between Edgar's meeting and his son's attack on Man twenty-seven years later, in which case the attack may have been more than an afterthought prompted by an unscheduled diversion. Were the oaths of peace sworn by Maccus Haraldsson and Edgar in 973 cast aside by their respective heirs as the new millennium dawned? Clearly, whoever ruled Man at the time of the English assault in 1000 was not on friendly terms with Æthelred. Like the kings of Strathclyde/Cumbria, the Norse rulers of Man were uneasy neighbours for their English counterparts.[21] Man was essentially a Viking pirate base posing a constant threat to English interests in the Irish Sea. We may note here that Anglesey, not Man, has also been suggested as the place attacked by Æthelred's fleet. Although the form of name used in the *ASC* entry (*Monige*) might feasibly apply to either island, the fact that the English fleet was heading north from Chester towards *Cumberlande* makes Man the more likely of the two.

Echmarcach

Rognvald Godredsson, king of the Isles, died in the kingdom of Munster in south-west Ireland in 1005. The Irish chronicler who noted his death gave no more information, so we are left to guess the circumstances.[22] Munster was ruled at that time by Brian Bóruma ('Brian Boru'), one of the most famous figures in Irish history. Brian was king of the Dál gCais, a people of Munster whose heartlands lay in what are now the counties of Limerick and Clare. He is best known for winning a great victory over a coalition of Irish and Scandinavian forces at Clontarf near Dublin in 1014, a battle that he himself did not survive. The background to this momentous clash lay in a long-running contest for the high kingship of Ireland, a position of overlordship held by Brian from c.1002 but frequently challenged by other kings. Among the latter was Máel Mórda, the king of Leinster, whose nephew and ally was Sihtric Silkbeard, king of the Dublin Norse, a son of Olaf Cuarán. By 1013, a showdown between Máel Mórda and Brian had become inevitable. To counter the threat from Brian's impressive coalition of allies and vassals, Máel Mórda sent Sihtric to gather additional forces among various Viking groups outside Ireland. Sihtric returned in 1014, having persuaded Earl Sigurd of Orkney and a Danish warlord called Brodir to bring their respective fleets to Dublin. According to *Njáls saga*, the warlord Brodir is said to have come from the Isle of Man where he and his brother Ospak had a pirate lair on the west coast.[23] The brothers' origins are far from certain. One Irish source associates Brodir with York, a connection that would be consistent with his alleged Danish ancestry, so perhaps he went from there to Man.[24] In the *Annals of Ulster*, Brodir's half-brother Conmael is identified as an Islesman and, significantly, had a Gaelic name. This fraternal connection might have played a part in bringing Brodir to the Irish Sea region and to Man. With no source hinting that Brodir or Ospak held royal status on Man, we should probably see them as adventurers who used the island as a base for their fleet rather than ruling it as kings. *Njáls saga* goes on to say that Sihtric Silkbeard secretly promised the high kingship of Ireland to both Brodir and Earl Sigurd in exchange for military assistance in the coming war. A special bonus, thrown in as an extra incentive, was a promise of marriage to Sihtric's mother, Gormflaith, a woman who at that time was the embittered ex-wife of Brian Bóruma. The great battle of Clontarf eventually took place, claiming many lives including Brian's and Brodir's.[25] In *Njáls saga*, Brodir personally slew Brian before being cut down by Brian's followers. Meanwhile, Brodir's brother Ospak is said to have fought on Brian's side, losing two of his own sons in the carnage. How much of the saga's account of Brodir and Ospak is genuine history rather than later storytelling is a matter of debate. Brodir's existence and his Manx connection do seem to be accepted as authentic by modern scholars, notwithstanding the possibility that his name might not be Norse but Gaelic. Ospak, on the other hand, may be nothing more than a 'ghost', a figure created for the saga.[26]

Looking back to the death of Rognvald Godredsson in 1005, the Munster location suggests that he was connected with Brian Bóruma, but whether as ally or enemy is uncertain. It is also possible that Rognvald had been ousted from the kingship of the Isles and was living in exile at Brian's court.[27] Whatever the circumstances behind his presence in Ireland, Rognvald was survived by a brother whose name was Lagman ('Lawman'). It is not at all clear that Lagman became the next king of the Isles. He nevertheless emerges as an important figure in a sequence of events that begins with the passing of Sweyn Forkbeard, king of Denmark, in 1014. At the end of the previous year, Sweyn had forced Æthelred the Unready into exile in Normandy. Sweyn had then seized the English throne for himself, but his death after only five weeks paved the way for Æthelred's return. Any stability that followed was short lived, for Sweyn's half-Polish son Cnut appeared on the scene. Cnut was eager to consolidate his position as heir to the Danish throne and had an eye on England too. He also began to take an interest in the Irish Sea where Brian Bóruma's death at Clontarf had altered the regional patterns of power.[28] Cnut saw an opportunity and set about forging alliances with Viking warlords. One of these was the aforementioned Lagman Godredsson, who clearly had military forces at his disposal or he would have been of little use to Cnut. The unanswerable question here is whether Lagman was a king in his own right, ruling the Isles like his brother had done, or simply a Viking adventurer leading a band of warriors. The second of these possibilities is implied by a contemporary source in which Lagman appears as a mercenary in the service of a duke of Normandy.

However, another text – written by a Norman – describes Lagman as a king, calling him 'king of the Swedes' (Latin: *rex Suerorum*). At first glance, this seems a rather strange title for a man whose ancestry lay in the Irish Sea region. If it has any historical basis, it might be an error for 'king of the *Sudreyjar*', the latter being a Norse term for the 'Southern Isles' (otherwise known as 'The Isles'), meaning Man and the Hebrides.[29] Perhaps Lagman pursued a mercenary career in Normandy and elsewhere before attaining the kingship of the Isles? What eventually became of him we do not know. He had a son, Olaf, who fell at Clontarf among the forces defeated by Brian Bóruma. Had Olaf survived, he might have succeeded his father in the kingship. It is possible, of course, that the Haraldsson dynasty's fortunes waned during or after Lagman's lifetime. If this was the case, they seem to have been revived again by a man called Echmarcach.

We first hear of Echmarcach in 1031 when he was one of three kings invited to a meeting with Cnut, an event reported in the *Anglo-Saxon Chronicle*. Cnut was at that time ruling the three kingdoms of England, Denmark and Norway as an empire spanning the North Sea. England, however, was his main country of residence. He had seized the English throne in 1016 after waging war against Æthelred the Unready and Æthelred's son Edmund Ironside. Cnut's reasons for convening the meeting in 1031 are not explained, but the broad context can be inferred from the geographical associations of the other attendees: Maelcolm, Maelbaethe and Iehmarc.[30] This trio can be identified as Máel Coluim, king of Alba, Mac Bethad (Shakespeare's 'Macbeth'), the king or *mormaer* ('great steward' or 'sea steward') of Moray, and lastly Echmarcach, a man whom Irish chroniclers described as king of Dublin and the Isles. Echmarcach's name is of Gaelic origin, but we know from Irish sources that his patronym was mac Ragnaill, 'son of Ragnall (Rognvald)', which implies Scandinavian ancestry. Echmarcach's maritime kingdom stretched from Dublin to the Hebrides and thus included Man. Indeed, he is no doubt the unnamed 'son of Ragnall' whom Irish chroniclers identified as ruling Man in 1061.[31] The close connection between Dublin and Man in Echmarcach's time is shown by coins minted on Man in the early to mid-eleventh century. These were similar to coins minted in Dublin and may have been produced on Man when Echmarcach was at the height of his power.[32] From Irish sources we learn that he held the kingship of Dublin twice, from 1036 to 1038 and again from 1046 to 1052. He was not ruling the city when he attended the meeting with Cnut in 1031, but presumably still held Man and the Hebrides at that time.[33]

Which Ragnall?

The identity of Echmarcach's father 'Ragnall' is a matter of debate. Some historians think he was a certain Rognvald, king of Waterford, who died in 1018, or perhaps this Rognvald's son and namesake whose death is recorded seventeen years later. Yet it seems more probable that he was Rognvald Godredsson, son of Godred Haraldsson and nephew of Maccus, who died in Munster in 1005.[34]

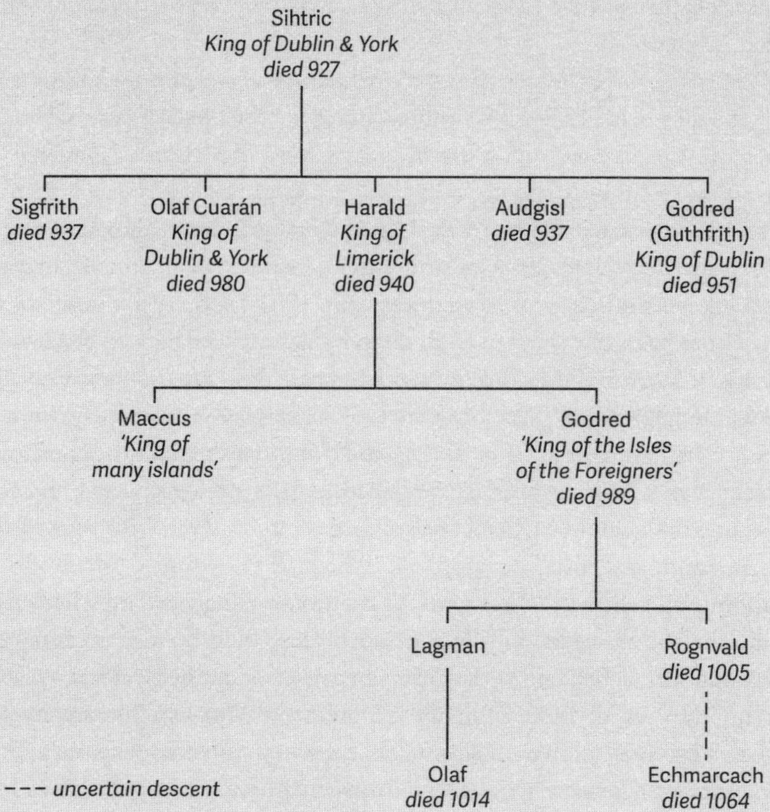

The year entry reporting the royal meeting in 1031 exists in several versions of *ASC*, two of which say that it took place in Scotland. This would put the location in Máel Coluim's kingdom. In a work called *Knútsdrápa*, composed by a contemporary Icelandic *skald* (poet), the setting is identified more specifically as Fife. The purpose of the meeting is not explained in any surviving source, leaving us to make informed guesses based on what we know of the prevailing political circumstances. Cnut, as the most powerful of the four attendees, surely convened the meeting, but what did he hope to gain from it? One possibility is that he was seeking a four-way alliance to thwart the ambitions of Earl Thorfinn of Orkney, a man who – like Cnut himself – sprang from a family of Viking warlords.[35] Several Icelandic sagas and skaldic verses depict Thorfinn, a son of Early Sigurd the Stout, as a prolific raider in Hebridean waters and in the Irish Sea as far south as Dublin. If the depiction is accurate, Thorfinn was raiding Echmarcach's territory and disrupting the balance of power in the seaways. Other saga material refers to Thorfinn clashing with Mac Bethad's father and with Mac Bethad himself on the frontier of Moray. At the meeting in 1031, Cnut may have hoped to secure from Mac Bethad and Echmarcach their sworn oaths to stand firm against Thorfinn and to refrain from making any deals with him. Moreover, Echmarcach's power and influence in the Irish Sea meant that he, too, posed a potential threat to Cnut's ambitions. This may have been keenly felt in the coastlands of Northumbria on the western edge of Cnut's kingdom, areas vulnerable to predatory fleets from the Isle of Man. In the case of Máel Coluim, Cnut no doubt wished to forge a lasting peace with a powerful neighbour with whom he had recently been at war.[36]. It is also possible that Mac Bethad and Echmarcach attended the meeting as vassals of Máel Coluim and that this pattern of relationships was itself a bone of contention for Cnut. Whatever points were discussed at the meeting, and whatever agreements or promises were made there, the outcome for Echmarcach seems to have been positive: there is no record of hostilities between him and Cnut in the ensuing years. Nor did Echmarcach make any attempt to install himself on the throne of Dublin while Cnut remained alive. Since 989, Cnut's ally Sihtric Silkbeard had ruled the city. Echmarcach nevertheless moved to strengthen his own position, securing a useful alliance with the family of Brian Bóruma when his sister Cacht married Brian's son Donnchad.[37] Moreover, as soon as Cnut died in 1035, it may have been support from Brian's heirs that enabled Echmarcach to launch a new bid for the Dublin kingship. Assuming that he still held Man, he may have used the island as a springboard for his assault on Dublin in 1036. The attempt was successful and Sihtric was forced to abdicate, dying in exile six years later. As things turned out, Echmarcach held Dublin for only two years before being ousted again, this time by a certain Ivar, a fellow scion of the Uí Ímair dynasty. Ivar became the new king of Dublin and was ruling there when Earl Thorfinn of Orkney, accompanied by his nephew Rognvald Brusason, launched a series of raids in the Irish Sea. *Orkneyinga saga* depicts Thorfinn as overlord of the Hebrides in the 1030s, adding that his army included Hebridean Vikings as well as others from Ireland and Scotland. If Thorfinn's overlordship really was so extensive – and we cannot completely trust the saga on this point – it may have encompassed Man.[38] In such circumstances Echmarcach, presumably still ruling Man and some at least of the Hebridean islands, may have been forced into a tributary relationship with Thorfinn. Alternatively, the saga might simply be exaggerating Thorfinn's power. For instance, its assertion that he controlled a number of Scottish earldoms is a very bold claim and should arouse our scepticism. His alleged authority in lands around the Irish Sea might likewise be open to doubt. In reality, he may have raided in Ireland, Man and the Hebrides with considerable success but without imposing overlordship on fellow Vikings in these lands.[39]

At Dublin, Ivar seems to have reigned until 1046 when Echmarcach made another successful comeback by again seizing the kingship. Six years later, in 1052, Echmarcach was forced from the city by Diarmait mac Máel na mBó, king of Leinster, whose raid escalated into a full-scale battle.[40] Echmarcach survived the loss of Dublin but was forced to leave Ireland. He is said to have fled across the sea and there is good reason to believe that his destination was Man.[41] He was, as already noted, probably ruling the island in 1061. In that year, an invasion of Man by Diarmait's son, Murchad – whom his father had installed as king of Dublin – forced an unnamed 'son of Ragnall' to offer a tribute payment.[42] If Ragnall's son was Echmarcach, as is likely, then this submission to Irish enemies was the last known episode in a long and eventful career. Three years later, we encounter Echmarcach a long way from his domains, travelling to Rome as a religious pilgrim. His companion on this journey was his brother-in-law Donnchad, king of Munster. The two men seem to have voluntarily abdicated their thrones to go on pilgrimage together. They reached the Eternal City, but their sojourn turned out to be brief, both of them dying in the following year.[43] The Irish annalists who noted Echmarcach's pilgrimage and death called him 'king of the Foreigners' (Gaelic: *rí gall*), one of their standard labels for a ruler of Norse ancestry. More surprising is the title given by the eleventh-century chronicler Marianus Scotus, an Irishman living in Germany, who called Echmarcach *rex innarenn*. This is usually translated as 'king of the Rhins' and is seen as evidence that Echmarcach's kingdom included the Rhins of Galloway, the hammerhead peninsula jutting out into the North Channel. Although we would not be surprised to learn that this area was indeed under his authority, it is possible that *rex innarenn* is a scribal error for *rex insularum* and that the true meaning here is 'king of the Isles'.[44]

The Kingdom of the Isles

The maritime realm associated with the Haraldsson brothers and their successors Rognvald and Echmarcach is described in the sources as the 'Isles of the Foreigners' or as simply 'The Isles'. Defining what this name actually meant in the context of tenth- and eleventh-century political geography will be a useful exercise at this point. It is also a necessary one, enabling us to better understand the subsequent history of the Irish Sea region in general and of Man in particular. By the twelfth century, as we shall see in the following chapters, a formal political entity known as the 'Kingdom of the Isles' had come into being. What, then, was the connection between this later realm and the one we have been discussing in the present chapter?

Modern historians seem to be in agreement that an identifiable Kingdom of the Isles began to take shape around the mid-tenth century.[45] It comprised various islands off the coast of north-west Britain that had been colonised by Norse Vikings during the 800s and early 900s. Each colony or group of colonies was, we can assume, initially ruled by the chieftain who founded it, before falling under the control of a more powerful ruler whose authority covered a much larger area. What appears to have happened over time is a process of amalgamation in which these larger lordships fell under the sway of ambitious individuals like Maccus Haraldsson who ruled very extensive territories. To what extent Maccus or any subsequent 'king of the Isles' was able to exercise real political control over what was essentially an assemblage of dispersed territories is hard to estimate. In practice, local chieftains on the more remote islands are likely to have maintained enough independence to ensure that the king's authority operated there in name only.[46]

It is clear that contemporary observers outside the early or 'proto' Kingdom of the Isles in the tenth and early eleventh centuries regarded it as culturally and politically Scandinavian rather than Gaelic. To Irish chroniclers it was sufficiently Norse for its ruler to be described as *rí Innse Gall*, 'king of the Isles of the Foreigners'.[47] The geographical limits of the kingdom seem to have been fairly fluid, with different islands included within its bounds at different times, but it essentially encompassed Man and the Hebrides. As we have already seen, Man and the Hebrides together were known to the Vikings as *Sudreyjar*, the 'Southern Isles', to distinguish them from the *Nordreyjar* of Orkney and Shetland. Man, although separated from the Hebridean archipelago by many miles of seawater, was regarded by Vikings not only as one of the *Sudreyjar* but as the most valuable, not least because of its fertile soils. The historian Clare Downham has aptly described Man as the 'jewel in the crown' of the renowned Kingdom of the Isles that had emerged by c.1100.[48] Man was certainly the principal seat of this later kingdom and had arguably served the same purpose in the 'proto-realm' that preceded it, as far back as the days of Olaf Guthfrithsson in the mid-tenth century. Indeed, it may be no coincidence that the first mention of *Innse Gall* in Irish sources refers to the 940s, only a couple of generations after Man fell under Norse control. The conquest and colonisation of Man might thus have been a major catalyst in creating a large maritime kingdom, stretching northwards into the Hebridean seaways, during the tenth century.[49] Man can plausibly be seen as the original core of this entity, as the principal domain from which other islands in the *Sudreyjar* were subsequently brought under control. Man's position has always made it a good choice as a hub of maritime power. Moreover, as a stepping stone between Ireland and Britain it is ideally suited to play a key role in the affairs of the two larger land masses. This role undoubtedly came to the fore when the great Viking strongholds of Dublin and York began to forge links with one another from the late ninth century onwards.[50]

The earliest individual whom we can identify as ruling the Isles of the Foreigners as a single entity is, of course, Olaf Guthfrithsson. A leading member of the Uí Ímair dynasty, at the time of his death in 941 Olaf held the kingships of both Dublin and York. According to the twelfth-century English chronicler John of Worcester, he was also 'king of the Isles'. Whether Olaf himself ever used such a title is doubtful, for John was neither a contemporary witness nor a stranger to literary embellishment. Likewise, although Olaf's sons may have used Man and the Hebrides as pirate bases, there is no record of their using royal titles in relation to their authority in these places. Hence we have no idea whether they regarded themselves as kings of a specific political entity that was already known as 'The Isles' in their lifetimes. Not long afterwards, Maccus Haraldsson was described as *rí Innse Gall* by Irish chroniclers and 'king of many islands' by their English counterparts. The same can be said of his brother Godred, nephew Rognvald and great-nephew Echmarcach. The kingdom ruled by these men was more scattered than other Viking polities in the seas around northern Britain. It was much less compact than the Earldom of Orkney, which had emerged as a recognisable entity in the late ninth century. A dispersed realm stretching across the Hebrides was inevitably more difficult to control then the fairly compact Orcadian archipelago, especially by kings whose chief centre of power lay on Man at the southern extremity.[51] Yet it was Man rather than a Hebridean territory such as Skye or Islay that would be chosen as the seat of royal authority in the Kingdom of the Isles. This is why present-day historians refer to rulers of this later realm as 'kings of Man' or as 'Manx kings'. Both labels are accurate, being borrowed from contemporary sources in which the first mention of a Norse 'king of Man' (*rex Manniae*) refers to the 1070s.[52] Man is likely to have had the same status as a 'royal capital' in the proto-realm of the tenth and early eleventh centuries that we have discussed in this chapter. It would therefore not be anachronistic to describe Maccus Haraldsson, 'king of many islands', and his brother Godred, 'king of the Isles of the Foreigners', as kings of Man, given that the island probably served as their headquarters.[53] On the other hand, it would not be strictly accurate to speak of a 'Kingdom of Man' in their time. This is a term that becomes meaningful only after the mid-1100s when, as we shall see, the Kingdom of the Isles was partitioned between Manx-based and Hebridean-based dynasties.

Sudreyjar

The Norse term *Sudreyjar* appears in the Icelandic sagas where it distinguishes a group of 'southern' isles from the *Nordreyjar* (Shetland and Orkney). The southern group comprises the Hebrides and Man together with other islands such as Arran and Bute in the Firth of Clyde.[54] A common Anglicised form of *Sudreyjar* is Sudreys, often preceded by the definite article as '*the* Sudreys'. Another variant of *Sudreyjar* is Sodor, usually in the context of an ecclesiastical diocese founded in the twelfth century and known since the 1500s as 'Sodor' or 'Sodor and Man'. The formal Latin name for the diocese is *Ecclesia Sodorensis* (literally 'Church of the Sudreys') for which Sodor is an abbreviated form. The extra words 'and Man' are superfluous, having been added c.1600 at a time when Man and the Sudreys were assumed to be separate. St German's Cathedral on St Patrick's Isle at Peel, founded c.1230, remains the seat of the bishops of Sodor and Man to this day.

Gall-Gaedhil

The middle of the eleventh century saw the appearance of a new power in the Irish Sea: the Gall-Gaedhil or 'Foreigner Gaels'. Irish chroniclers had used this name two centuries earlier to describe one or more bands of warriors who were active in Ireland. Its precise meaning is debatable, but in the ninth century it probably referred to Gaelic-speaking people who behaved like Vikings. Whether these folk were of Norse or native parentage (or some mixture of the two) is hard to say.[55] We hear of Gall-Gaedhil again in the tenth century, as military forces, and in the early eleventh when the death of one of their kings, Suibhne mac Cináeda, was noted by the chroniclers. In Suibhne's time the Gall-Gaedhil seem to be settled in Galloway as well as further north in the Ayrshire coastlands.[56] The fact that Galloway takes its name from Gall-Gaedhil tells us that its population was regarded as having a hybrid Norse-Gaelic identity in the period when the name was bestowed. Who originally devised the term, and when they devised it, remain unanswered questions. It must have been in existence in the ninth century, when Irish tradition knew of it. One suggestion is that it first appeared in the kingdom of Strathclyde in the speech of local Britons and was similar to *Gallwyddel*, the Welsh name for Galloway. The Gaelic equivalent *Gall-Gaedhil* would then be derived from the original Brittonic name. Whatever its true origin, *Gall-Gaedhil* is considerably older than the territorial name *Galloway*. When we encounter the Galwegians – the people of Galloway – in the next chapter, their leaders have already become significant players in the turbulent politics of Britain and Ireland.

Manx sculpture in the eleventh century

The new millennium heralded the demise of the ornately carved cross and the upright cross-slab on the Isle of Man. Elsewhere, too, this type of sculptural activity entered its twilight phase. In the former 'Danelaw' areas of eastern and northern England, the free-standing cross that had been such a striking feature of stone carving in the 900s ceased to be produced before c.1050. In Scotland and Ireland we see a similar picture. The change was most likely driven by a Europe-wide reform of ecclesiastical responsibilities that included, among other things, giving the clergy tighter control of burial customs. This meant that the setting up of memorials was effectively taken out of the hands of individual families and regulated by the Church. On Man, the last gasp of the ancient sculptural tradition may be represented by a cross-slab from Maughold. Most likely erected in the early eleventh century, it has a carved cross on both sides and a runic inscription. Each cross contains a roughly incised pattern of geometric shapes, but the overall impression is of a debased artistic style having little in common with the finely worked decoration of earlier monuments.[57]

8

THE FOUNDING OF THE CROVAN DYNASTY

The year 1066 was a momentous one in the history of Britain. It marked both the beginning of the Norman era and the twilight of the early medieval period. It bore witness to a number of events that would permanently change the patterns of political power on both sides of the Irish Sea. The first of these occurred in the first week of January when Edward, king of England, died at the end of a twenty-four-year reign. Known to posterity as 'the Confessor', Edward was a son of Æthelred the Unready but left no son of his own to succeed him. His death sparked a crisis in which the vacant throne was claimed by several competing rivals. One of these, the English nobleman Harold Godwinsson, was proclaimed king by a council of senior courtiers the day after Edward's passing. His right to rule was challenged by Harald Hardrada, the formidable king of Norway, who claimed the English throne for himself. Another claimant was William, duke of Normandy, who declared that *he* was Edward's designated heir and that Harold Godwinsson had previously promised to accept this. In September, Hardrada launched an invasion of England, landing in Northumbria at the mouth of the River Tyne. His campaign began with a battle at Fulford near York where he defeated an English force led by the earls of Northumbria and Mercia. A more decisive clash took place five miles east of York at Stamford Bridge after Harold Godwinsson marched north with his army. There the Norwegians were utterly vanquished, suffering a huge number of casualties including their king. Harold Godwinsson then began the southward trek back to London, even as Duke William landed on the south coast of England with a Norman army. Near Hastings in present-day East Sussex, the two sides fought a battle in which William emerged victorious. Harold was slain, his death enabling William to become England's first Norman monarch.[1]

The Isle of Man was not directly affected by these conflicts. They did, however, influence its subsequent history by paving the way for ambitious Norman lords to become involved in the Irish Sea region. Moreover, the Norwegian defeat at Stamford Bridge brought Godred Crovan, one of the most famous figures in Manx history, into the spotlight. We first hear of Godred in the Manx Chronicle, which states that he escaped from the battle having fought on the Norwegian side. He may have managed to reach one of the two dozen ships that sailed to Orkney with the battered remnants of Hardrada's army.[2] Godred eventually found refuge with his namesake Godred Sihtricsson, described in the Manx Chronicle as *rex Manniae*, 'king of Man'. The choice of destination was not random, for Crovan had spent at least part of his childhood on the island. After staying for a time, he left, perhaps after Sihtricsson's death in 1070. The king's son Fingal succeeded to the throne, but of him we know nothing outside the Chronicle, where he is mentioned only once. We cannot even be sure that he existed but, if he did, his reign may have witnessed an assault on Man reported in the *Annals of Ulster* under the year 1073.[3] The attacking force came from Ireland where the dominant power was still the royal dynasty of Munster, the descendants of Brian Bóruma. Leading the attack was a man called Sihtric Olafsson, together with two unnamed grandsons of Brian: all three were slain. Why they targeted Man is uncertain, but they presumably hoped to impose Munster overlordship and install Sihtric Olafsson as king of the island.[4]

Six years later, Godred Crovan reappeared in Manx waters, this time at the head of a large fleet from the Hebrides. He launched an invasion but was defeated in battle by Manx forces, perhaps those of King Fingal. Sometime afterwards, Godred mounted a second invasion which was likewise thrown back into the sea. Victory finally came during a third attack, largely through the use of a cunning tactic. Godred's fleet sailed into the haven of Ramsey under cover of darkness, bringing an army of Hebrideans. A detachment of 300 warriors disembarked to hide in a wood on nearby Sky Hill. At dawn the next day, the main invasion force engaged the Manx in battle. At the height of the fighting, Godred unleashed his concealed warriors against the Manx rear to gain a great victory. Yet he refrained from slaughtering his beaten foes, instead showing them clemency when they surrendered. To his own army he offered a choice between settling on Man as a new elite or looting the island and going home. The Hebrideans chose the second option and an orgy of pillaging ensued. Afterwards, the greater part of Godred's army sailed back home with its plunder. The rest remained with Godred, who went on to establish himself as the new king of Man. He partitioned the island in two, allocating the southern half to his Hebridean followers and the northern half to the Manx.[5] Thus began the Kingdom of the Isles, the realm of the Crovan dynasty, with Man as its primary centre of power.

Who was Godred Crovan?

The Manx Chronicle tells us that Godred was the son of Harald the Black of Ysland. The identity of this Harald is uncertain. So, too, is the location of Ysland, which has been variously interpreted as Iceland, Islay or Ireland. Of the three, Ireland is generally more favoured by present-day historians, chiefly because of an Irish chronicle entry in which Godred Crovan is called 'son of the son of Harald'. This is seen as a more correct description of Godred's parentage than the one given by the Manx Chronicle. His father, an unnamed 'son of Harald', can then be cautiously identified as Ivar Haraldsson, a king of Norse Dublin who died in 1054.[6] This is the same Ivar who had competed with Echmarcach in a struggle for the Dublin throne. He was a grandson of the renowned Olaf Cuarán and, if he was indeed Godred Crovan's father, the latter would be yet another scion of the Uí Ímair dynasty. Such a genealogical connection would be consistent with Godred's own tenure of the kingship of Dublin, a part of his career discussed below.

Godred's kingdom is generally assumed to have encompassed parts of the Hebrides, from where he had raised ships and soldiers for the invasion of Man. It is thus appropriate to describe him as 'king of the Isles', not merely as king of Man.[7] He had an affinity with the inhabitants of both Man and the Hebrides, sharing with them a cultural heritage rooted in the Norse colonies around the Irish Sea. He was essentially a Viking warlord ruling a dispersed maritime realm inhabited by descendants of Vikings. From a Manx perspective he was the latest in a series of rulers who arrived on the island fitting this description. Like his predecessors, he looked towards Dublin with an eye on the kingship there. At the same time, he needed to be alert to potential challengers for the Manx throne. In 1087, he had to defend Man against an attack by an Ulster prince who had teamed up with 'the grandsons of Rognvald'. The latter can be identified as the same Rognvald whose son Echmarcach had ruled Dublin and the Isles earlier in the century.[8] Godred's forces repulsed the attack and slew its leaders. Four years later, Godred seized the kingship of Dublin for himself, thereby becoming the most powerful figure in the seaways between Ireland and Britain. It is no surprise that other men of ambition sought to align themselves with him, whether as allies or vassals. One was Gruffudd ap Cynan, a prince of Gwynedd, who needed a fleet for a campaign against Norman encroachment on his lands. The twelfth-century Welsh text *Historia Gruffud vab Kenan* says that the ships required by Gruffudd were provided by his ally 'King Gothrei' whose realm lay among 'the isles of Denmark'. There can be little doubt that Gothrei is Godred Crovan. The isles of 'Denmark' are more correctly the *Sudreyjar* of Man and the Hebrides where a Scandinavian elite – mainly of Norse rather than of Danish ancestry – continued to hold power. Sixty vessels, crewed by Godred's Manx and Hebridean sailors, were loaned to Gruffudd, who was thus able to launch a seaborne attack against his Norman foes on Anglesey.[9] We may note that Gruffudd's approach to a Norse ruler like Godred is unsurprising, given his own parentage: his mother Ragnhild was a princess of the Uí Ímair dynasty.

After taking the kingship of Dublin, Godred is likely to have made the city his main place of residence. His reign there lasted only a few years. In 1094, the Munster king Muirchertach Ua Briain arrived with a large army, seeking to oust Godred. The latter withstood the assault with the help of northern Irish allies but, after these departed, Muirchertach attacked again and with greater success.[10] Godred was forced to leave Dublin but did not return to Man, presumably because it was not safe for him to do so. Instead, he sailed north to the Hebridean part of his kingdom, perhaps to the large island of Islay where, in the next year, he died of plague. Local tradition on Islay points to a prehistoric monolith, the Carragh Bhan, as a monument erected in his memory.[11].

Crovan

Godred's epithet appears only in the Manx Chronicle. Its meaning is obscure, with a number of possible explanations. One suggestion is that *Crovan* derives from *kruppin*, an Old Norse word meaning 'cripple'. Other theories see an Irish Gaelic derivation from *crúbach*, 'claw' or *crobh-bhán*, 'white hand'. In some Irish chronicles Godred appears with a different epithet *meránach* which can mean 'mad' or 'furious' as well as being related to the word *mear*, 'finger'. Taking all the various interpretations into consideration, we might wonder if there was something about Godred's hands that prompted contemporaries to turn it into a nickname.[12]

Bishop Roolwer

Appended to the Manx Chronicle is a list of 'bishops of Man and the Isles', from the eleventh century to the fourteenth. The list begins with Roolwer, described as 'the first bishop before the reign of Godred Crovan'. Whether this means that Roolwer was bishop when Godred took the kingship is hard to say. It could equally mean that Godred became king *after* Roolwer's epsicopate.[13] Roolwer's name is usually interpreted as a form of the Old Norse name *Hrolfr*, from which the names Rolf and Rollo are derived. Although there is no mention of him outside the Manx Chronicle, it has been suggested that his name could be based on a shortened form of *Thorolf* and that he may be the same man as Bishop Thorolf of Orkney.[14] Thorolf held the Orcadian see in the time of Earl Thorfinn the Mighty and his identification as Roolwer would fit chronologically with Thorfinn's supposed overlordship of the Hebrides and Man. However, as we saw in the previous chapter, the true extent of Thorfinn's power in the Irish Sea is uncertain and may have been inflated by the saga writers. An alternative suggestion is that Roolwer and Thorolf were close contemporaries but separate individuals, the former being bishop of Man while the latter held the bishopric of Orkney. Both may have claimed or exercised ecclesiastical authority over parts of the Hebrides, reflecting the ever-changing patterns of secular overlordship.

The Manx Chronicle asserts that Roolwer's grave lies at Kirk Maughold and that his immediate successor was Bishop William, a man whose name suggests Norman ancestry.[15] Such a name suggests an ecclesiastical link between the rulers of Man and the new Norman elite of England.[16] William was in turn succeeded by Hamond, said in the Chronicle to have been 'a Manxman by birth'. Hamond is the first bishop of Man and the Isles to whom we can assign a specific chronological context, for the Chronicle adds that he 'ruled the bishopric in the days of Godred Crovan'. It is possible that the sequence of bishops from Roolwer to William to Hamond represents the infancy of a newly created diocese of 'Man and the Isles', founded in the second half of the eleventh century. In this scenario, the diocese emerges after a period in which Manx Christians had no bishop, a hiatus spanning the years between the last pre-Viking bishop – presumably in the late ninth century – and Roolwer in the eleventh. If there was indeed such a gap it was most likely caused by the activities of pagan Vikings. Of the pre-Viking bishops we glean nothing from any source. The Manx Chronicle states that Roolwer was the 'first' bishop because he is the earliest for whom the chronicler had reliable information.

Although the chronicler was aware that there had been 'many bishops in Man' since St Patrick's supposed mission in the fifth century, he adds that 'we are very much ignorant of who the bishops were before Roolwer or of what sort they happened to be, as we have no record of them, nor can we learn for sure from what our elders tell us'.[17] The chronicler claimed that Roolwer's grave lay at Kirk Maughold. He might have been aware that a sculptured stone at the same place commemorated a much earlier bishop, an individual whose name we now interpret as Irneit and whose memorial stone we discussed in Chapter 5. On the question of 'what sort' of people the Manx chronicler's 'many bishops' were, we can assume that some were Britons, holding office in the period when Brittonic-speaking kings ruled Man. Others may have been Scots, Irishmen, Englishmen or Picts. The chronicler's belief that nothing is known about any of these men is somewhat chilling. It implies that not only were the written accounts of their episcopal careers totally destroyed, but also any folk memory of their names. That they had existed was plainly not in doubt, but information about them had utterly disappeared. Whatever had once been known was most likely swept away during the Norse takeover of Man in the late 800s and early 900s.

Bishop Roolwer may have been associated with a certain Dunan, described in the *Annals of Ulster* as *ardescop Gall*, 'high bishop of the Foreigners' at his death in 1074. The description locates the Christian communities over whom Dunan presided in the Norse colonies. His successor Gilla Patraic was 'bishop of Dublin', a title that may reflect a reorganisation of Dunan's 'high bishopric'. Such reorganising may have become necessary in the wake of an event that occurred two years before Dunan's passing: the conquest of Dublin by the Munster king Toirrdelbach Ua Briain. Toirrdelbach, who dominated Ireland at that time, perhaps sought to weaken Dublin's links with Man and the Hebrides. If so, he may have used the occasion of Dunan's death to give the city a bishop of its own. Dunan, then, can be tentatively identified as the last bishop of a diocese comprising a broad swathe of Norse colonies. His authority may have encompassed Dublin, Man, the Hebrides and other places. If his death facilitated the separation of Dublin from the rest, then his successor Gilla Patraic can be regarded as the city's first bishop. Roolwer might then be identified as the first bishop of whatever remained of the diocese of the 'Isles of the Foreigners'.[18]

After Godred Crovan

The Manx Chronicle tells us that Godred was succeeded as king by his eldest son Lagman, whose name in Old Norse means 'lawman' (or 'law speaker'). Lagman's authority was disputed by his younger brother Harald who soon mounted a rebellion. This was snuffed out and Harald was taken captive. In an act of gruesome vengeance, he was blinded and castrated, a deed that later filled Lagman with remorse. The Chronicle assigns to Lagman a seven-year reign and says that he gave up his crown to go on a religious pilgrimage to Jerusalem but died along the way. Seven years from his father's passing in 1095 should mean that Lagman's reign ended c.1102, but this puts the Manx Chronicle at odds with other texts and even with its own chronology. For instance, it later gives a detailed account of a military expedition to Orkney, the Hebrides and Man by King Magnus 'Barelegs' of Norway, apparently placing this after Lagman's death but in the year 1098. Magnus ruled Norway from 1093 to 1103. His first campaign in the west, intended to subjugate the Norse colonies to his overlordship, was reported in the Icelandic sagas as well as in the Manx Chronicle and the date 1098 can be accepted as correct.[19]

Reconciling the Norwegian expedition with what the Chronicle says about Lagman's reign is no easy task, but a number of possible scenarios can be proposed. The one I currently favour sees Lagman succeeding to his father's kingdom in 1095 but, from the outset, being opposed by factions who supported his younger brothers Harald and Olaf. Harald he successfully eliminated but Olaf, the youngest and still a child, became the main focus of opposition. I envisage Lagman being toppled from the throne after reigning only a few months and withdrawing to the northern part of the kingdom, probably to Skye and the Western Isles. The Manx Chronicle says that the chieftains of the Isles sent envoys to Ireland to ask King Muirchertach of Munster for a regent who would rule until Lagman's youngest brother Olaf came of age. The chronicler places this request *after* Lagman's death but is here surely in error. The correct date may be 1095. Muirchertach responded by sending his nephew Domnall mac Taidc as a caretaker ruler. Domnall actually had a reasonable claim on the kingship of the Isles, being a grandson of the earlier king Echmarcach. However, he abused his power and ruled as a brutal tyrant. After three years, the chieftains of the Isles ejected him, forcing him to return to Ireland. This would have happened in 1098, the year when Magnus Barelegs launched his first expedition to the Isles.[20] Before the Norwegian king came to Man, rival factions from the northern and southern sides of the island fought a battle at Santwat, an unlocated site probably in the vicinity of Peel. The event is reported in the Manx Chronicle but without any context. The northerners won but the respective commanders – MacMaras and Earl Ottar – were slain. These men are otherwise unknown.[21]

Later in the same year, Magnus Barelegs brought a Norwegian fleet of 160 ships into the west. Drawing together various pieces of information provided by the Manx Chronicle and the Icelandic sagas, we can trace the expedition's progress fairly closely. The Norwegian king began by subjugating Orkney. According to *Orkneyinga saga*, he captured the Orcadian earls Paul and Erlend, sons of Thorfinn the Mighty, before sending them to Norway and taking Erlend's sons as hostages. He then made his own son Sigurd, a child of eight, the new ruler of Orkney before resuming his journey. After sailing around the northernmost tip of Britain, the Norwegian fleet turned south towards the Hebrides. On Skye they found Lagman, son of Godred Crovan, and took him prisoner. One thirteenth-century Icelandic text, a chronicle known as *Morkinskinna* ('rotten parchment'), describes Lagman as ruling the 'northern islands' and as the lord of North Uist, the island immediately south of Lewis and Harris in the Outer Hebrides or Western Isles. This information from *Morkinskinna* is found in verses allegedly composed by the skaldic poet Gisl Illugason. Gisl's words carry considerable weight: he was a member of the Norwegian expeditionary force and thus a contemporary witness.[22] Gisl adds that King Magnus treated Lagman Godredsson with considerable leniency, keeping him as a member of his own entourage. The likely political context here is that Lagman, having probably been barred from Man since his father's death, was a man of thwarted ambitions whose hopes of glory now lay in tatters. On the other hand, living as a landless vassal among the Norwegian king's courtiers was doubtless preferable to the cruel punishment he had inflicted upon his brother.

The Manx Chronicle relates that Magnus Barelegs eventually came to Man. Soon after his arrival at St Patrick's Isle he visited the battlefield of Santwat, still littered with corpses. In spite of this grim sight, he became so enamoured of Man that he decided to make it his permanent home. He also built fortresses on the island that were named after him. The Manx Chronicle adds that he went on to subdue Galloway, an area already colonised by the Norse. Sailing afterwards to Anglesey, he defeated a force of Normans who had invaded Gwynedd and slew one of their leaders, a significant event mentioned in several sources. He then sailed back to Man, from where the Icelandic sagas show him returning home to Norway. A statement in the Manx Chronicle that he remained permanently on Man is erroneous. He left the island, and we have no idea who ruled there after his departure. The Manx Chronicle refers to a man called Ingimund whom Magnus appointed as king of the Isles.[23] This appears in the Chronicle *before* the 1098 expedition, but perhaps we should move it to the period *after* Magnus returned home. Ingimund was essentially a sub-king tasked with governing the Isles under his patron's overlordship. However, he seems not to have exerted control in Man, instead establishing his seat of power on Lewis. He and his companions are said to have violated women of all ages, thereby incurring the wrath of the chieftains of the Isles who responded by setting fire to his house and killing everyone inside.

Turning to the fortresses on Man that were supposedly named after Magnus Barelegs, we may note that these are absent from the Icelandic sagas but seem to be mentioned in the thirteenth-century Welsh chronicle *Brut y Tywysogyon* (hereafter *ByT*). According to *ByT*, Magnus erected and garrisoned three castles on Man.[24] The context here is not the expedition of 1098 but a later one launched in 1102. What brought Magnus back to the Irish Sea was his political relationship with King Muirchertach, still the dominant figure in Ireland at the dawn of the twelfth century. On the second expedition Magnus sailed from Norway to Man where he again established his headquarters. He then engaged in diplomacy with Muirchertach, forging an alliance that was sealed by betrothing his now-twelve-year-old son Sigurd to the Irish king's five-year-old daughter.[25] However, whatever stratagems the fathers of the young couple intended to pursue were soon extinguished, for Magnus was slain in the summer of 1103 in a battle against the Ulaid. At his death, he was described by an Irish chronicler as 'king of Norway and the Isles'. He had successfully reinforced the notion that the Norwegian crown wielded sovereignty over the people of the Isles, these being the inhabitants of Man and the Hebrides. Like him, the Islesfolk were descended from Norse Vikings. Notwithstanding the miles of sea that separated them from the homeland of their ancestors, Magnus regarded them as his subjects. To him, they were still Norwegian.

Lagman Godredsson: crusader or pilgrim?

In 1095, Pope Urban II urged Western Christendom to raise an army for the task of wresting the sacred sites of the Holy Land out of Muslim hands. His plea was answered with great enthusiasm in many countries and by people of every social class, both rich and poor. Thus began the Crusades, the first of which set out from European shores in 1096. Some historians think that Lagman, Godred Crovan's eldest son, could have been one of many highborn crusaders.[26] The Manx Chronicle states that he travelled to the Holy Land on pilgrimage, 'marked with the sign of the Lord's Cross'. This has been interpreted as a reference to the traditional image of the crusader knight wearing a cross-embroidered surcoat. We know from other sources that the crusades attracted soldiers of Scottish, Irish, English and Scandinavian origin, so it is not difficult to imagine the son of a Manx king among them. Indeed, for all we know there may have been a substantial crusading contingent from the Isles, including from Man. If Lagman did become a crusader, a likely venture for him to have joined is the Norwegian crusade of 1107–11. This was led by Sigurd, son of Magnus Barelegs. According to *Morkinskinna*, Sigurd withdrew from a royal triumvirate in which he and his two brothers had shared power in Norway after their father's death. Leading a fleet of 60 ships, Sigurd set out in 1107 to fight in the Holy Land. He sailed first to England where he spent the winter as a guest of the Norman king Henry I, resuming his journey in the following spring. Passing south into the Mediterranean he eventually reached the port of Acre in present-day Israel in 1110. He then visited Jerusalem, which at that time lay under crusader rule. Over the next couple of years, Sigurd and his Norwegian warriors fought alongside other crusaders. The Manx Chronicle says that Lagman Godredsson died while on 'pilgrimage' to Jerusalem. In reality he may have gone there as a soldier in Sigurd's army.[27]

We can see that the political situation on Man around the beginning of the twelfth century is hazy. Any attempt at reconstructing a coherent picture is hindered by the confused chronology of the Manx Chronicle, which is unclear as to who held authority in Man and the Hebrides after the death of Magnus Barelegs in 1103. Norwegian overlordship may have continued in some form, although it is hard to envisage such a distant sovereignty being enforced unless the sons of Magnus appointed someone to rule on their behalf. Not until the second decade of the century does the picture become somewhat clearer. In 1111, according to the *Annals of Inisfallen*, the Irish prince Domnall mac Taidc subjugated the Isles. There he set himself up as king, presumably ruling from Man. If we accept the testimony of the Manx Chronicle, this was his second stint in the role. In 1114 he was back in Ireland, his uncle Muirchertach having been ousted from the throne of Munster. Domnall then became embroiled in a dynastic conflict and was slain while making his own bid for the Munster kingship.[28]

Olaf Godredsson

In about 1113, the senior nobles ('chieftains') in the Kingdom of the Isles chose Olaf, the youngest of Godred Crovan's three sons, to be their king. Olaf ruled for forty years, an impressively long reign in an era when kings could expect to fall in their prime to enemy swords or to an assassin's knife. Norse tradition, preserved in the Icelandic sagas, remembered Olaf as *Kliningr* ('the Dwarf') or *Bitlingr* ('Little Bit'), perhaps denoting small stature or – by way of jest – extremely large stature. In a seventeenth-century history of Clan Donald (the MacDonald clan) he was 'Olaf the Red', no doubt an allusion to red hair or a ruddy complexion. When we first encounter him in the Manx Chronicle, he was living in England at the court of King Henry I. Henry was a son of William the Conqueror, the duke of Normandy who had destroyed his English rival Harold Godwinsson at Hastings in 1066. Why Olaf was in Henry's entourage is nowhere explained. Either his father or one of his older brothers may have sent him to England as a child. No doubt the Anglo-Norman court soon began to seem to Olaf a safer place than anywhere back home in the Isles. As a high-status guest of King Henry, and as a royal prince, he would have mingled with people of similar rank. His contacts would have included not only highborn folk of English and Norman stock but those who, like him, had come from other lands. He would almost certainly have been acquainted with the young Scottish princes Alexander and David, both of whom dwelt at Henry's court, and also with their sister Matilda whom Henry had married. Both Alexander and David were destined to become kings, the former being succeeded by the latter on the Scottish throne.

Olaf was probably in his twenties when he became king of the Isles. He married Affrica, daughter of Fergus, the lord of Galloway.[29] The couple may have met at the English court, for Affrica's father was King Henry's son-in-law. Their marriage was undoubtedly a political union, sealing a treaty or alliance between their respective families. Twelfth-century Galloway, like Man and the Hebrides, was part of the Hiberno-Norse maritime world. It was an autonomous entity whose rulers had not yet become fully subordinated to the Scottish crown. Affrica bore Olaf a son called Godred. Three more sons were born to the king's concubines, of whom the Manx Chronicle says that there were many. Concubinage was a common practice among powerful men in medieval times, but was regarded by their Christian clergy as a vice.[30] It is little surprise that the monastic scribes who wrote the Manx Chronicle withheld the names of Olaf's concubines. Elsewhere we seem to find the name of one of them: Ingibjorg, daughter of Earl Hakon of Orkney. This lady, although described in one Norwegian text as Olaf's wife, was doubtless his concubine, albeit one of high noble birth.[31]

No wars involving the people of the Isles are recorded during Olaf's reign. The Manx Chronicle says that he was 'a peace-loving man who entered into such a close confederacy with the kings of Ireland and Scotland that no man dared disturb the peace in the Kingdom of the Isles in his lifetime'.[32] From this we might infer that his time at the Anglo-Norman court had been well spent in nurturing friendships with those who would eventually become powerful fellow rulers and neighbours. Amicable relations with the Scottish kings Alexander (reigned 1107–24) and David (1124–53) would have been especially useful, given their interests in the western coastlands of their realm. The lack of warfare that characterised Olaf's reign probably owed more to shrewd dealings with Scottish and Irish kings than to his supposedly peace-loving character.

The fall of Strathclyde

Alexander I became king of Scotland in 1107. He appointed his brother David as *princeps Cumbrenses* ('Prince of the Cumbrians'), a new role created to fill a void left by the Scottish conquest of Strathclyde in the previous century. Strathclyde had also been known as *Cumbria*, a Latin name meaning 'land of the *Cumbri*', the latter being synonymous with 'Northern Britons' and usually anglicised as 'Cumbrians'. Sometime between 1050 and 1070, Strathclyde/Cumbria had been conquered by Malcolm Canmore, the father of Alexander and David.[33] Its kings had long benefitted from contact with the Irish Sea region via the Firth of Clyde, a great artery that connected them with Man and the Hebrides as well as with Dublin and other parts of Ireland. Prince David, the new ruler of what had been the last kingdom of the *Cumbri*, inherited this same network of maritime links.

In 1152, Olaf's son Godred sailed across the North Sea to pay homage to the Norwegian king Inge Haraldsson. The visit shows that Norwegian overlordship was still acknowledged by the ruling dynasty of the Isles. Godred may have been sent by his father to discuss high-level ecclesiastical matters, not least the recent designation of the Trondheim diocese as the first Norwegian archbishopric. As we shall see, Olaf had created a new episcopal headquarters in his own kingdom and its bishops were nominally subject to those of Trondheim, just as he himself was nominally a vassal of King Inge.[34] Godred had not yet returned from Norway when his father was brutally murdered. King Olaf's death, according to the Manx Chronicle, occurred on 29 June 1153. It came after he agreed to a meeting with three of his nephews who had turned up on Man demanding a half share of his kingdom. This trio were the sons of Olaf's middle brother Harald and had lived in Dublin for many years. Olaf met them at Ramsey to discuss their demands, but they had already decided to kill him. During the meeting, one of them produced an axe and decapitated the king. The trio then divided Man among themselves before launching an invasion of Galloway. This was fiercely repulsed and the sons of Harald fled back to Man. There, however, they ruthlessly persecuted any Galwegians who dwelt on Man, slaying some and forcing the rest to depart. For several months the three siblings held the reins of power, stirring much resentment among the chieftains of the Kingdom of the Isles. In the autumn, their cousin Godred left Norway and sailed for home. After a brief stop on Orkney, he came to Man where the people proclaimed him as their new king. His murderous cousins were captured and punished, two having their eyes torn out while the third was executed.[35] So began the reign of Godred Olafsson, of which more will be told in the next chapter.

Rushen Abbey

Godred Crovan's youngest son Olaf had spent his formative years at the royal court of King Henry I of England. It was around this time – the early 1100s – that the churches of Western Christendom underwent a major reform. The impetus for change was driven by new religious orders that were emerging in France: the Cistercians, the Augustinians, the Savignacs and others. From France the reformist movement spread to England where the young Olaf Godredsson no doubt became aware of it. As King Henry's fosterling he would have witnessed the close relationship between royal and ecclesiastical authority in ceremonies taking place at the great Benedictine abbey of Westminster, by then a centre of religious power as well as a mausoleum of mighty kings.[36] Olaf knew there was nothing like it back home. After succeeding to the throne of the Isles, he was keen to establish something similar in the heart of his own kingdom.

In 1134, Olaf invited the Cistercian abbey of Rievaulx in Yorkshire to establish a daughter-house on Man. He had set aside a portion of land at Rushen for this purpose. However, the invitation was turned down. Why, we do not know, yet the fact that Rievaulx was itself newly built may have influenced the decision. Although founded a few years earlier, in 1131, the work of construction at Rievaulx did not commence until 1132. Undeterred, King Olaf sent out a second invitation, this time to Furness Abbey on the coast of what is now Cumbria. Founded in 1123, Furness Abbey originally housed a community of Savignac monks, members of a religious order that lived by a more relaxed set of rules than the strict, ascetic Cistercians.[37] Olaf's invitation was accepted by Abbot Ivo who sent a group of Furness monks to Rushen to begin the work of founding a daughter-house.

At around the same time, Olaf sent a letter to the archbishop of York, informing him that the bishop of Man and the Isles would henceforth be a 'chief bishop' (Latin: *pontifex*) and that all future appointees to the role would be chosen by the monks of Furness.[38] The likely context here is that Olaf was seeking to align the ecclesiastical affairs of his kingdom more closely with his dynasty. Similar reorganisation was happening in other lands, not least in England and Scotland. Kings were increasingly recognising that 'church and state' (to use a modern term) worked best when they worked closely together. In another document, Olaf bemoaned the fact that 'strangers' and 'mercenaries' had been allowed to oversee the religious needs of his people. What he probably meant was that episcopal responsibilities in Man and the Hebrides had sometimes been assigned to bishops whose seats lay outside the Kingdom of the Isles.[39] Under the new system initiated by Olaf, a bishop of 'Sodor and Man' (Sodor = *Sudreyjar*, 'Southern Isles') was duly elected by the monks of Furness. The latter chose one of their own brethren who had been part of the original group sent to Rushen. This individual also happened to be the preferred candidate of the people of Man, his presence among them having enabled them to witness his talents.[40] Confirmation of his appointment was duly given by King Olaf and the new bishop took up his duties. His name was Wimund, and he turned out to be one of the most enigmatic figures in the entire history of the diocese. At first, he seems to have had a fairly conventional episcopal career. We hear nothing unusual about him for fifteen years until, in 1147 or thereabouts, he announced that he was the son of a senior Scottish nobleman – the Earl of Moray. Mustering a band of warriors, Bishop Wimund then launched an attack on Scottish territory. His objectives are not clear, but they presumably included a desire for lordship over lands that he regarded as his rightful inheritance.[41] He also attacked the lands of an unnamed fellow bishop, possibly the incumbent of Whithorn in Galloway. Wimund's rapid career switch from cleric to marauder came to the notice of the Scottish king David, who had succeeded his brother Alexander in 1124. David tried to calm the situation by granting Wimund substantial estates in the vicinity of Furness Abbey, perhaps those that constituted the Norman barony of Copeland.[42] Wimund accepted the gift and proceeded to roam around his new domain with his warriors. These men eventually turned against him. After holding him captive, they delivered him to King David who had him blinded and castrated. Wimund survived to spend his last years as a monk at Byland Abbey in Yorkshire, living there in obscurity. One final piece of information about him comes from the fifteenth-century Scottish historian Walter Bower who implies that Wimund's challenge to David's authority, albeit a minor one posing little real threat, was instigated by King Olaf Godredsson of the Isles.[43]

9

'FEALTY AND OATH'

After disposing of his three cousins and avenging the brutal assassination of his father, Godred Olafsson began his reign. It was actually a reign of two parts with a break in between. The first part commenced with his accession to the throne in 1153 and lasted until 1158. During this brief span of four or five years he is said to have engaged in a war in Ireland. Our only source for the war is the Manx Chronicle, for no Irish text mentions it. According to the Chronicle, hostilities broke out in the third year of Godred's reign, the catalyst being his acceptance of an invitation from the citizens of Dublin to be their new king.[1] Soon afterwards he sailed over to Ireland, accompanied by a large fleet and army. The presence of these forces implies that he was expecting trouble, which duly arrived in the shape of Muirchertach mac Lochlainn.

Muirchertach was the king of Tír Eoghain (Tyrone) in the north and also held the high kingship of Ireland. Marching south to confront Godred, he sent 3,000 cavalrymen towards Dublin but these were cut down by a deadly torrent of spears. Muirchertach then withdrew, returning to his northern domain. A few days later, Godred returned to Man and disbanded his own army. So ends the Manx Chronicle's account of how Godred Olafsson became king of Dublin in 1156, an otherwise undocumented episode in the city's history. In the absence of corroboration from the Irish annals, the whole thing looks suspiciously like an invention by the Manx chronicler. On the other hand, we should perhaps not dismiss it too swiftly. At the very least, Godred's alleged kingship of Dublin would be consistent with the Crovan dynasty's previous involvement in the city's affairs. One possibility is that the Manx Chronicle is here reporting real events but dating them six years too early, for Irish sources do indeed describe an attack on Dublin by Muirchertach mac Lochlainn, assigning it to 1162. However, they do not mention Godred Olafsson. He seems to have been in Norway at that time. Whatever the truth behind the story of his battle against Muirchertach, Godred eventually forged a less hostile relationship with the Tír Eoghain dynasty when he married Muirchertach's

Man and the Isles in the era of the Crovan dynasty
N
W
E
S
Shetland
Orkney
Caithness
Lewis
Western Isles
Harris
Uist
Skye
Ross
Moray
Atholl
Scotland
Mull
Iona
Argyll
'The Isles'
Fife
North Sea
Islay
Glasgow
Kintyre
Arran
Galloway
Tír Eoghain
Whithorn
Ulster
Strangford Lough
Dundrum
Carlingford
Man
Furness Abbey
Stamford Bridge 1066
York
Irish Sea
Connacht
Dublin
Anglesey
Gwynedd
Leinster
Powys
England
Waterford
Wexford
Munster
Wales
Dyfed
Gwent
London
English Channel
0 50 100 km
0 50 miles

granddaughter Fionnula in 1176. This was undoubtedly a political marriage, forged against a backdrop of inter-dynastic rivalries in the Irish Sea region.[2]

Somerled

In 1158, Godred Olafsson received a challenge from his brother-in-law Somerled, an ambitious lord who had established himself as a major force in the Hebrides. Somerled is one of the most famous figures in Scottish history. Indeed, his fame is so great that he has become an almost legendary character. He is sometimes seen as a hero of Celtic Scotland who fought against Viking invaders, but in reality he sprang from the same Norse-Gaelic milieu as the Crovan kings of the Isles. Like many significant players of the era, he comes to us with a story containing many gaps and questions. The oldest record of him is an entry for the year 1153 in the *Chronicle of Holyrood*, a Scottish text compiled in the late twelfth to early thirteenth centuries. This says that he rebelled against King Máel Coluim IV of Scotland in November of that year.[3] Máel Coluim, at the tender age of 12, had succeeded his grandfather David six months earlier. The same eventful year had also witnessed the assassination of Olaf Godredsson, king of the Isles, a killing that was soon to have implications for Somerled's own situation. In the meantime, the young Scottish monarch Máel Coluim IV found himself having to deal with Somerled's rebellion. This depiction of Somerled as a rebel rather than as an external foe suggests that he had previously accepted Scottish overlordship. He was nevertheless a powerful ruler in his own right, holding sway over a number of Hebridean islands as well as a swathe of mainland territory in Argyll (*Airer Goidel*, 'the coastland of the Gaels').[4] King David had expanded his own authority into Argyll and had probably compelled Somerled to recognise him as overlord. Warriors from Argyll and the Hebrides fought in David's army during his invasion of England in 1138 and some of these men may have been sent by Somerled. The *Chronicle of Holyrood* adds that Somerled's revolt against David's grandson Máel Coluim IV in 1153 was made in alliance with the sons of yet another Máel Coluim. There is some uncertainty over the identity of these unnamed sons, but it is likely that their father was one of David's nephews and that they had a valid claim on the Scottish throne.[5] In the end, their rebellion fizzled out, freeing their ally Somerled to pursue policies that furthered his own territorial interests.

Somerled's origins lay among the mixed Norse-Gaelic population of the Hebrides. While his father Gille Bride had a Gaelic name, Somerled's own name derives from Old Norse *Sumarlidi* ('summer traveller'). He was related by marriage to the Crovan dynasty, his wife being an illegitimate daughter of Olaf Godredsson, son of Godred Crovan. This lady's name, according to *Orkneyinga saga*, was Ragnhild. The Manx Chronicle, while not naming her, says that her marriage to Somerled caused 'the ruin of the entire Kingdom of the Isles'.[6] Meanwhile, her brother King Godred Olafsson was making himself unpopular with his chieftains, depriving some of their status and others of their estates. One of the most powerful among them, Thorfinn Ottarsson, asked Somerled to intervene. Thorfinn proposed that Godred should be ejected from the Manx throne and that Somerled's son Dougal should replace him. The ambitious Somerled was happy to give his full support. Thorfinn duly escorted Dougal around the Isles, presenting him as a king in waiting. However, not everyone was favourable to the plan. One dissenter, a chieftain called Paul, travelled in secret to Man to inform King Godred of the conspiracy stirring against him. Godred immediately mustered a war fleet, intending to strike first. Somerled responded by assembling his own fleet of eighty ships. The two sides clashed in a sea battle on 6 January 1156, both sustaining heavy casualties. With no clear result in sight, Godred and Somerled agreed a peace treaty that partitioned the Kingdom of the Isles between them. Although the precise division of territory is unknown, Somerled seems to have received a central bloc comprising Mull and Islay together with a number of smaller islands while Godred retained Man as well as the northern part of the Hebrides including Skye and Lewis.[7]

Both Godred and Somerled were now kings of the Isles, each ruling a separate division of the original realm. We can call these divisions 'Kingdom of Man and the Isles' and 'Kingdom of Argyll and the Isles', the former preserving Man's continuing role as the headquarters of the Crovan dynasty, the latter acknowledging Somerled's territories in mainland Argyll as well as those in the Hebrides. Yet the negotiated peace did not long endure. In 1158, Somerled again sailed south with his fleet, this time directly to Man where he defeated Godred in battle. So ended Godred's first period of kingship. Somerled followed up his victory by plundering the whole of Man. He then departed, sailing back to his Hebridean domains. He spent the remaining six years of his life reigning over both parts of the Kingdom of the Isles. Meanwhile, his beaten adversary Godred fled to Norway, a land where he had been welcomed before, hoping there to obtain support for a new war. Godred also visited England and Scotland for the same purpose. In the end, he had no need to renew hostilities, for Somerled died in 1164 while fighting the Scots on their own territory, in a battle at Renfrew on the Firth of Clyde.[8] Somerled's demise was regarded as a significant event, being mentioned by contemporary writers on both sides of the Irish Sea. The Manx Chronicle asserted that he had invaded Scotland because he wanted to conquer it for himself, a notion that seems rather far-fetched. It is more likely that he had a specific grievance with the Scottish king Máel Coluim IV, perhaps stemming from a recent Scottish campaign in Galloway which had forced Somerled's kinsman Fergus from power.[9] One of the contemporary texts is a Latin poem, *Carmen de Morte Sumerledi* ('Song of the Death of Somerled') in which the last phase of the battle of Renfrew is vividly described. It tells of the mighty Hebridean warlord being slain by sword and spear, adding that one of his sons – whose name, Gillebrigte, we learn from other sources – was wounded in the fray and drowned while trying to flee to the ships. Somerled's corpse was decapitated, the severed head being presented to the bishop of Glasgow. Yet body and head were subsequently reunited for a dignified burial on Iona, a monastery in which Somerled had taken a close interest in life.[10]

Somerled and Maughold

The Manx Chronicle has few positive things to say about Somerled. This is not surprising, given his ravaging of Man after his victory over Godred Olafsson in 1158. To the chronicler, Somerled and his henchmen were enemies of the Crovan dynasty and hence deserved to be cast in a bad light. The Chronicle contains a story that serves this purpose. It concerns a holy miracle that supposedly occurred when Somerled and his army were camped on Man, near Ramsey. One of Somerled's senior chieftains, a man called Gilcolm, suggested looting the religious site at Kirk Maughold. Somerled, although initially opposed to the idea, eventually gave his assent. Gilcolm decided to launch a dawn assault but, in the meantime, went to his tent to sleep. During the night, an apparition of Saint Maughold chastised him for planning the attack. It then pierced his heart with a staff, inflicting a mortal wound. His followers, attempting to save him, were prevented from doing so by a huge swarm of flies. News of his death reached Somerled and the rest of the army, filling them with such terror that they sailed away from Man as fast as the tides would allow.[11]

After Somerled

Somerled's demise on the battlefield of Renfrew in 1164 paved the way for Godred Olafsson's homecoming. Godred left Norway and returned to Man, resuming the kingship from which he had been deposed six years earlier. With the Kingdom of the Isles still divided in two, he now ruled a somewhat smaller realm than before. The other portion had been ruled by Somerled and was now controlled by his sons, of whom there were at least five. How these siblings distributed power among themselves is unclear, for little is said on the matter in any contemporary source. One of them, Dougal, had been put forward for the kingship of the Isles before the treaty of partition and may therefore have been the eldest. His chief claim to fame is as the eponymous ancestor of Clan MacDougall, a notable Scottish family in later times. Another of Somerled's sons was Ranald who sired the progenitors of the MacDonald and MacRuairi clans. Ranald fought against Angus, one of his own brothers, in a battle reported by the Manx Chronicle under the year 1192. The circumstances behind this fraternal strife are obscure. Amid the uncertainty, however, there is no doubt that the second half of the twelfth century witnessed the emergence of a new maritime power in the Hebridean region: the sons and descendants of Somerled, known in Gaelic as *Clann Somhairle*.[12] An alternative name – the one I tend to use throughout this book – is MacSorleys, an Anglicised form of *Meic Somairle* ('the sons of Somerled').

Turning back to Godred Olafsson, the second phase of his reign after his return from Norwegian exile coincided with an event of great significance for the Irish Sea region: the arrival in Ireland of a band of Anglo-Norman mercenaries. This marked the beginning of more than 700 years of English domination in Ireland. A key moment in the chain of events leading to the Anglo-Norman invasion came in 1166 with the death of Muirchertach mac Lochlainn, king of Tír Eoghain, one of the mightiest kings in Ireland, whose power was waning. Muirchertach's death had serious repercussions for his remaining allies, one of whom was Diarmait Mac Murchada ('Dermot MacMurrough'), the king of Leinster. With Muirchertach gone, Diarmait's situation became more vulnerable. He soon found himself facing a coalition of Irish kings who were determined to oust him. The coalition's forces invaded Leinster and Diarmait was pushed into exile. Fleeing to England, he came to the royal court of King Henry II. There he sought assistance in raising an army so that he could recover his throne. Henry allowed him to seek recruits among the Norman knights of England, one of whom was Richard de Clare, known as 'Strongbow'. Diarmait pledged his daughter in marriage to Strongbow and made him heir to the Leinster throne. Other Norman lords also offered their services to Diarmait, bringing their own military retinues comprising soldiers from various parts of England and Wales. Having acquired these formidable allies, Diarmait sailed back to Ireland to await their arrival. In May 1169 the first Anglo-Norman contingents sailed over to join him, adding their muscle to a military campaign that soon brought Leinster under his sway.[13]

In the following year, 1170, Strongbow himself landed in Ireland. He and his lieutenant – a cousin of the Welsh historian Gerald of Wales – linked up to besiege the former Viking fortress of Waterford. It soon fell into their hands, becoming an Anglo-Norman stronghold, and later serving as the venue for Strongbow's wedding to Diarmait's daughter. It also became the springboard for an assault on Dublin. Diarmait initially engaged in peace talks with Ascall, Dublin's Hiberno-Norse king, but while these were in progress the Anglo-Normans broke into the city and captured it. Ascall fled by ship to what Gerald of Wales described as 'the northern isles', a term that in modern parlance denotes Orkney and Shetland. Gerald, however, is most likely referring to Man and the Hebrides, which from a Welsh perspective would indeed lie northward.[14] Soon after Diarmait's death in May 1171, Ascall returned to Dublin with a fleet of more than sixty ships and a large army. Among his troops were warriors from the Isles who, according to one Irish text, were sent by Godred Olafsson. An assault on the city's new Anglo-Norman garrison followed but, despite a hard-fought battle, Ascall's forces were defeated and he himself was taken captive. He was executed in public, his death marking the end of Hiberno-Norse rule in Ireland.[15]

A grand alliance of Irish kings then attempted to take Dublin. Their armies encircled the city, while its harbour was blockaded by 30 ships from the Isles sent by Godred Olafsson. After a siege lasting two months, Strongbow and his henchmen sought a negotiated peace. The ensuing discussions allowed the Anglo-Normans to retain control of Dublin, Waterford and another former Viking stronghold at Wexford. The Irish armies then withdrew and Godred's ships ended their blockade. Godred's participation in the siege is explained by Gerald of Wales as 'fear of the threat of English domination'.[16] Such fear was justified, especially given the speed of the Anglo-Norman gains in Ireland. Godred knew that the Isle of Man, his principal seat of power, lay in a vulnerable position if the Anglo-Normans acquired a strong presence on both sides of the Irish Sea. Looking further north, we may note that Gerald's account makes no mention of the rival Hebridean kingdom ruled by Somerled's sons, the MacSorleys. They presumably refused to help Ascall of Dublin, or perhaps they were not approached by him, unless some of the Islesmen in his army were from the MacSorley realm as well as from Godred's.

The capture of three major havens in Ireland was a major success for the Anglo-Normans. It was not so much a triumph for King Henry II as a series of land grabs by opportunistic individuals from his entourage. It was only when Henry himself landed at Waterford in October 1171 that a more systematic takeover began. Henry claimed that Pope Adrian, the only Englishman ever to hold papal office, had issued a document in 1155 granting Henry the sovereignty of Ireland. Whether such a document ever existed is hard to say, but the claim was seemingly accepted by many Irish kings, who offered Henry their allegiance. This was, however, only one of the motives behind Henry's invasion of Ireland. Another was a desire to bring Strongbow and his fellow-adventurers back into the orbit of the English crown before their Irish gains made them too powerful.[17]

With the Viking Age in Ireland now effectively over, and with Dublin and other key places firmly in Anglo-Norman hands, the remaining Norse-Gaelic elites in the Irish Sea region reassessed their alliances and allegiances. Godred Olafsson, king of Man and the Isles, decided to align himself with the new power. In 1180 or thereabouts, he forged a bond of kinship with John de Courcy, one of the most powerful Anglo-Norman lords in Ireland, via a marriage alliance. Gerald of Wales reported the event with these words: 'John took as his lawful wife the daughter of Godred, king of Man'.[18] More information is provided by the Manx Chronicle, which gives the bride's name as Affrica. The marriage marked an important moment in the history of the Crovan dynasty, a clear acknowledgment by Godred and his family that a new political era had begun.

In any case, John de Courcy was not a figure who could be easily ignored. In 1177, he had established himself as ruler of Ulster after invading with a small army and ousting the native king. This gave him control of the strategic coastlands of what are now the counties of Down and Antrim, making him an important player in the Irish Sea region. His marriage to Affrica of Man was mutually beneficial to both him and his father-in-law. It gave de Courcy a key ally among the older maritime powers while, for King Godred, it turned a potentially dangerous Anglo-Norman warlord into a kinsman. In addition, Godred may have been glad to see the demise of the native Ulster kings, given their past hostility to the Isle of Man.[19]

Myroscough Abbey

The priest who solemnised King Godred Olafsson's wedding to Fionnula of Tír Eoghain in 1176 was Silvanus, abbot of the great Cistercian house at Rievaulx in Yorkshire. The king showed his gratitude by giving the abbot a piece of land in the northern part of Man. The location was Myroscough in what is now the parish of Lezayre. Our sole source of information is the Manx Chronicle in its notice of the royal wedding:

'The same day King Godred gave, as an offering to the venerable abbot Silvanus, a portion of land at Myroscough, on which he presently built a monastery. But in the course of time the whole estate, monks and all, was ceded to St Mary's Abbey, Rushen.'[20]

The date of Rushen Abbey's acquisition of the Myroscough ecclesiastical estate is unknown. By c.1280, when a list of Rushen's landholdings was drawn up (and appended to the Manx Chronicle), Myroscough was among them. It is not known if an abbey was ever actually built at Myroscough, for no trace of it has yet been discovered.[21] Construction may have commenced before being halted abruptly when the estate was transferred to Rushen Abbey. Thereafter, the land may have been used by the Rushen monks as a distant farm or 'grange'. Such use is implied by the name of Grange Farm, a site within the bounds of the Myroscough monastic estate. The estate itself was known locally as 'abbeyland' as late as the nineteenth century.

Rognvald Godredsson

In November 1187, at St Patrick's Isle on Man, King Godred Olafsson died. He was buried on the sacred island of Iona, where his old foe Somerled already lay in perpetual repose. Iona had once been part of the Crovan dynasty's Hebridean territories. Like Mull, its larger neighbour, it had been granted to Somerled by the partition of 1158 and was now under the authority of his sons. Nevertheless, despite mutual antipathy between the two kingdoms of the Isles, the MacSorleys allowed Iona's hallowed ground to accept the Manx king's remains.

Before he died, Godred nominated his younger son Olaf to succeed him. He had an older son, Rognvald, who appears to have been illegitimate. According to the Manx Chronicle, Olaf was the product of a lawful marriage and was his father's designated heir. Godred's only legitimate wife, in the eyes of the Church, was the Irish princess Fionnula. She can therefore be identified as the mother of Olaf but not of Rognvald. The latter is likely to have been born to one of Godred's concubines. However, Rognvald was not destined to be sidelined from the kingship for long. When their father died, Olaf was only ten years old, an age deemed in some quarters as too young for kingship. At that time, Rognvald was not residing on Man but somewhere in the Hebrides, at a location not specified in the Manx Chronicle. A deputation from Man visited him with an invitation to replace the boy-king Olaf on the throne. Rognvald, described in the Chronicle as a sturdy man of mature years, was happy to accept. He duly arrived on Man to begin a reign that would prove to be long and eventful. He wasted no time in showing the warlike spirit that would prompt *Orkneyinga saga* to describe him as 'the greatest warrior in all the western lands'.[22] Like his Viking ancestors he was an accomplished pirate, leading a fleet of longships on raiding expeditions around the shores of Ireland. Among his targets were Dublin and the Boyne Valley as well as the more distant Aran Islands off the west coast. This, at least, is what a contemporary Gaelic bard tells us in a praise poem.[23] The bard, an Irishman, extolled the Manx king's martial reputation through the medium of heroic verse. Although Rognvald's own main language was Norse, this poem is a clear indicator that he understood Gaelic speech. No doubt he was much pleased when the bard described him as 'a bright, slim, blue-eyed, noble war-god'. His raids on Ireland were celebrated in the poem, yet they receive no mention in the Irish chronicles. This need not make us sceptical of the poem's testimony, for there is nothing implausible in the idea of a Manx king leading his fleet on plundering expeditions against Irish targets. The MacSorleys were doing the same, raiding Ireland from their Hebridean realm, the only difference being that their raids were reported by Irish chroniclers.[24]

If raiding Irish territory was one of Rognvald's martial pursuits, another was his involvement in the military ventures of others. Quite early in his reign, in 1193, he helped Prince Rhodri of Gwynedd to victory over dynastic rivals in a battle on Anglesey. This comes from a Welsh source – a chronicle written in the 1200s – which identifies Rhodri's ally as 'Godred, king of Man', but Godred had died six years earlier and his son Rognvald is surely the king intended here. The identification is strengthened by other links between Rognvald and Rhodri, namely the latter's betrothal to Rognvald's daughter. Here our source of information is a papal document from 1199 which adds that, after Rhodri died in 1195, before the marriage took place, a new prospective husband was found for Rognvald's daughter in the shape of Rhodri's nephew Llewelyn. As things turned out, this wedding also did not happen, and Llewelyn went on to marry an English princess.[25]

Around the year 1200, Rognvald gave assistance to the Scottish king William the Lion in a conflict with Harald Maddadsson, the earl of Orkney. The cause of this war was the mainland territory of Caithness which Earl Harald claimed as one of his own domains. The thirteenth-century English chronicler Roger of Howden mentions the involvement of Rognvald 'son of the king of Man', although a subsequent emendation of Roger's original text curiously changed the patronymic to 'son of Somerled, king of Man'. Somerled did indeed have a son of this name, namely 'Ranald' whom we encountered above, but we should not confuse him with William's Manx ally Rognvald Godredsson.[26] Contemporary with Roger's chronicle is *Orkneyinga saga* which, as well as describing Rognvald as 'the greatest warrior in all the western lands', added the interesting note that 'for three whole years he had lived aboard longships'. From the same saga we learn that Rognvald led a force of warriors from the Isles, Kintyre and Ireland in support of William the Lion. Kintyre is usually associated with the MacSorleys but, in this instance, it was being used as a recruiting ground for a king of the Crovan dynasty. MacSorley sympathies in the Caithness war may have lain not with William but with Harald Maddadsson, whose war fleet was reinforced by ships from some part of the Isles. *Orkneyinga saga* goes on to say that Rognvald subjugated Caithness on behalf of William before leaving it in the care of three stewards. Earl Harald killed one of these but eventually submitted to William.

Relations between Rognvald and William remained amicable through the final years of the Scottish king's long reign. Around the year 1207, Rognvald's younger brother Olaf was imprisoned by William at Rognvald's request. The cause of this serious breakdown in the siblings' relationship was Olaf's discontentment with his share of their father's realm. Having been denied the throne in 1187 because of his tender age, he had received instead the Hebridean island of Lewis as his own domain. Despite its large size, Lewis was too poor to support Olaf's household and warband. He complained to his brother, King Rognvald, who responded by placing him under arrest. Chained as a prisoner, Olaf was sent to Scotland to be locked up in one of King William's dungeons. There he languished for nearly seven years.[27]

If Rognvald's dealings with William the Lion were cordial and stable, those with the king of England were rather more volatile, shifting to and fro between friendship and hostility. England's monarch at this time was John, a son of Henry II. Rognvald came into contact with John at a time when the career of the latter's namesake, John de Courcy, was on a downward spiral. At the start of the thirteenth century, de Courcy still held power in Ulster but did so without seeking King John's formal consent. He was also embroiled in a feud with the de Lacys, one of the most powerful Anglo-Norman families in Ireland. The feud turned into a war and the de Lacys, with King John's encouragement, invaded Ulster. They eventually captured de Courcy and seized his lands. King John then appointed Hugh de Lacy as the new lord of Ulster, conferring upon him the rank of earl. At some point, de Courcy was released from captivity and set free. He made his way to the Isle of Man, seeking refuge at the court of his brother-in-law King Rognvald. In the following year, de Courcy and Rognvald sailed to Ulster with a fleet of 100 ships. They besieged a fortress near Strangford Lough, probably the castle of Dundrum, but the arrival of a large army led by Walter de Lacy, brother of Earl Hugh, brought a swift end to the campaign. There were to be no more comebacks for de Courcy, who thereafter fades into the background.[28] His downfall did not, however, prove detrimental to those of his Manx ally and kinsman. In February 1205, Rognvald Godredsson came under the formal protection of King John, in exchange for an oath of allegiance. The English king's confirmation of this new relationship appears in a document issued by his court: 'Know that we have taken our beloved Rognvald, king of Man, under our keeping, protection and defence, and all his lands and people. And we forbid any person to inflict injury or annoyance upon him or his, wherefore if any offence be committed against him, we will reckon the same done to ourself.'[29] In April of the following year, Rognvald was invited to England to spend Easter with his new patron. Over the next few years, he received gifts of cash and land. For John, the arrangement turned a dangerous sea kingdom on his western flank into a useful ally.

By 1210, however, the relationship between the English and Manx crowns had soured. In June, King John invaded Ireland to reimpose his authority on the Anglo-Norman elite, including the de Lacys. The latter were sheltering one of John's former favourites, William de Braose, who had fallen out of favour at court. Accompanying de Braose in exile were his wife Matilda and their two adult sons. Their daughter Margaret was already in Ireland, having married Walter de Lacy ten years earlier. News of King John's invasion prompted de Braose to send his wife and sons on another journey, this time back across the Irish Sea to Galloway. The fugitives did not sail straight to Galloway but went first to the Isle of Man, spending four days there.[30] That their brief visit had the blessing of King Rognvald is strongly implied by King John's subsequent action, which looks like a punishment meted out to his Manx vassal. After subduing Ireland, John sent part of his army to Man under the command of his lieutenant Fawkes de Bréauté. John was doubtless aware that Rognvald and his chieftains were not there at that time. Over the ensuing couple of weeks, Fawkes and his men comprehensively ransacked the island. After seizing some Manx people as hostages, they then sailed home to England. If this was John's retribution for the hospitality shown by Rognvald to the fugitive family of William de Braose, it may not have seemed disproportionate to contemporary observers. For the fugitives themselves, a grim fate lay in store. Matilda de Braose and her sons arrived safely in Galloway but were captured by a Scottish lord who sent them to King John. Matilda and one son, named William like his father, were imprisoned on John's orders and died of starvation.

Rognvald's involvement in the de Braose affair provides a likely reason for the ravaging of Man by English forces. Another factor is a recent change in Rognvald's relationship with Norway, whose kings were once again gazing westward. Throughout the twelfth century, Norwegian eyes had tended to look inward rather than outward. A series of civil wars, fuelled by inter-dynastic rivalry, had occupied the thoughts and energies of the royal house. By the early 1200s, a brief lull in these internal troubles offered an opportunity to reimpose Norwegian overlordship in the Norse-Gaelic lands of the west. In 1210, during the reign of King Inge Bardsson, a Norwegian fleet entered Hebridean waters and plundered the monastery on Iona. Earl Harald Maddadsson of Orkney was compelled to travel to King Inge's court where he and his sons offered allegiance and a tribute payment. Anxious that he would be next on the Norwegian list of targets, King Rognvald of Man did the same, sailing to Norway with his son Godred to pay homage to their overlord.[31] Our source here is the thirteenth-century Norwegian or Icelandic text *Boglunga sogur*, or rather a later version of it, in which Rognvald is styled 'king of Man in the Hebrides' (Norse: *konge aff Möen i Syderö*) while his son is confusingly described as 'king of Man' (*konge paa Manö*).[32] This was a somewhat awkward period for Rognvald. Having previously accepted the patronage and protection of King John of England, he now found himself forging the same kind of bond with a different sovereign. To John this may have seemed like a betrayal, one that required a suitably strong response. It could also be an additional or alternative reason behind his decision to send Fawkes de Bréauté to ravage Man in Rognvald's absence.[33] Indeed, Rognvald and his son might even have been paying homage in Norway when Fawkes attacked.

Within a couple of years, John's displeasure had receded enough for him to again draw Rognvald under his wing. In 1212, on the sixteenth day of May, John and his entourage of courtiers and vassals assembled at Lambeth in London. Also present was Rognvald, whose public renewal of loyalty was recorded in a charter:

> Know that I have become liegeman of our lord John, king of England, against all men, as long as I shall live, and that I have performed fealty and oath to him.[34]

Several documents associated with this charter have survived and in these we find John's reciprocal pledges to Rognvald. In one, John issued an instruction to his subordinates in Ireland, telling them that 'if any *Wikini* (Vikings) or others should offend in the territory of Rognvald, king of Man, you shall assist him in the destruction of his and our enemies, since he is bound to us by fealty and oath, to perform the same for us against those who offend in our territory'. The *Wikini* in this context were undoubtedly the Norwegian royal raiding fleets whose vessels had reappeared in the Isles two years earlier. While John was wise to feel anxious about the threat from Norway, the irony of engaging a pirate king of Man – a descendant of Viking warlords – to protect England's coasts from Norwegian pirates whose own forebears were Vikings too has not been lost on modern historians.[35] In another document, John gave Rognvald the former de Lacy domain of Carlingford in Ulster, a valuable gift that included a strong castle as well as a harbour giving access to the Irish Sea. A third document issued by John ordered the release of certain subjects of Rognvald who were being held captive in England. Who these people were is not explained, but it is tempting to identify them as the hostages taken from Man by Fawkes de Bréauté in 1210.[36]

The documents associated with the May 1212 ceremony at Lambeth suggest that mutual concerns over the growing menace of Norway helped to heal the rifts between John and Rognvald. Other factors in their rapprochement probably include a desire by John to place a loyal vassal on the eastern shore of Ulster after the de Lacys' fall from grace. Additionally, we can look beyond the English texts to take notice of the wider political context. Thus, while Norwegian Vikings were once again posing a threat to stability in the Irish Sea, other powers closer to home could similarly not be ignored. For example, both Rognvald and John were mindful of what the king of Scotland might be up to. Likewise, the Norse-Gaelic lords of Galloway had ambitions of their own and operated more-or-less independently of the Scottish crown. Also in the mix were Somerled's descendants, the MacSorleys, still ruling their own portion of the former Kingdom of the Isles, and further north the earls of Orkney whose natural allegiance lay with Norwegian kings.

King John and his Scottish counterpart William the Lion forged a treaty in February 1212. This gave stability to Anglo-Scottish relations at a time when both kings had concerns over the situation in Ireland and the ambitions of Norway. The treaty enabled John to give land in Ulster to Alan, the lord of Galloway, who was nominally William's vassal. This donation was probably made around the time when Rognvald Godredsson received the nearby lands of Carlingford.[37] Alan received a huge tract of territory comprising most of the northern part of what is now County Antrim. He and his kinsmen then attacked other lands to the west, their army being joined by Islesmen led by the grandsons of Somerled. Whether Rognvald's forces also took part, venturing from his recently acquired stronghold at Carlingford, is an open question. Besides, he soon had his own troubles to deal with. In 1214, William the Lion died. The Scottish king's passing spelled the end of seven years of captivity for Olaf Godredsson, Rognvald's younger brother, whom William had kept as a prisoner at Rognvald's request. Olaf's newfound freedom was soon to bring Rognvald's reign – and his life – to a violent end.

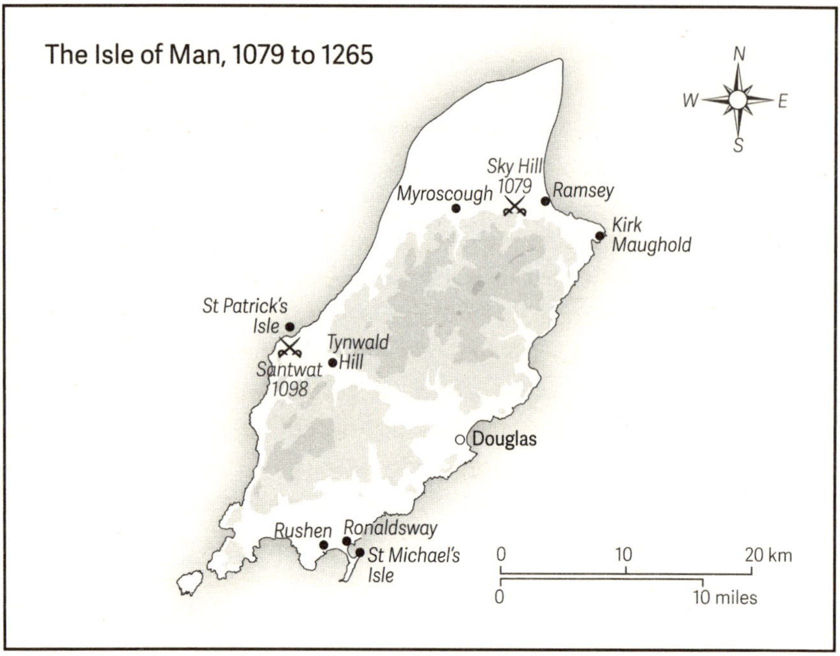
The Isle of Man, 1079 to 1265
N
W
E
S
Sky Hill
1079
Myroscough
Ramsey
Kirk
Maughold
St Patrick's
Isle
Tynwald
Hill
Santwat
1098
Douglas
Rushen
Ronaldsway
St Michael's
Isle
0
10
20 km
0
10 miles

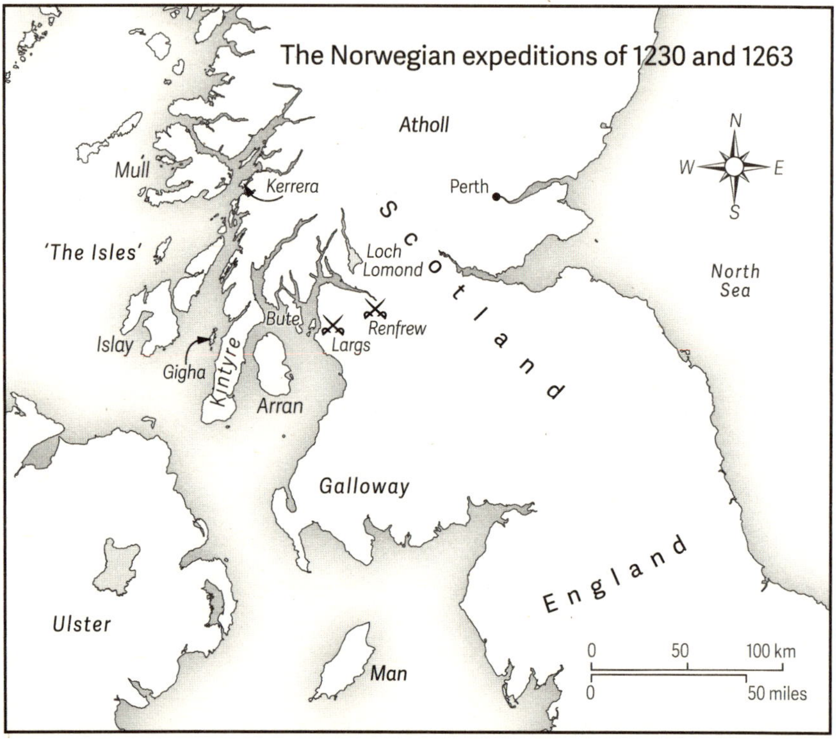
The Norwegian expeditions of 1230 and 1263
Atholl
N
W
E
S
Mull
Kerrera
Perth
'The Isles'
Loch
Lomond
Scotland
North
Sea
Bute
Renfrew
Largs
Islay
Gigha
Kintyre
Arran
Galloway
England
Ulster
Man
0
50
100 km
0
50 miles

10

'WEST ACROSS THE SEA'

Olaf the Black

William the Lion, king of Scots, died in December 1214. Before his death, he declared an amnesty for all prisoners, ordering their release. Among the captives emerging into the light of liberty was Olaf Godredsson, known in some sources as 'Olaf the Black'. He was a younger brother of King Rognvald of Man but had spent seven years incarcerated in a Scottish jail, at Rognvald's instigation. What privations Olaf had endured at the hands of his hosts we do not know, but the Manx Chronicle says that he was kept in chains. Upon being released he went to Man but stayed there only a short time before heading off on another, longer journey. His destination was Santiago de Compostela in Spain where the shrine of Saint James the Apostle was one of the main pilgrimage centres of Europe. With him went an entourage of nobles from Man and the Isles. On returning home he was welcomed by his brother King Rognvald, who restored him to his former position as lord of the Isle of Lewis. Rognvald also arranged a dynastic marriage between Olaf and a lady called Lauon, the daughter of a Kintyre nobleman.

Lauon's sister was Rognvald's wife, so the marriage to Olaf strengthened an existing bond of kinship between the two families. All seemed well until a few days after the wedding when the bishop of the Isles, another Rognvald, was met by Olaf while touring the churches of the Hebrides. Bishop Rognvald was Olaf's nephew, his sister's son, and Olaf wanted to celebrate their meeting with a lavish feast. However, the bishop refused to attend, telling his uncle that the marriage to Lauon was illegal under canon law and must be dissolved. At issue was the fact that Olaf had previously kept one of Lauon's cousins as a concubine for many years. Cousins were regarded by the church as close kin, which meant that Olaf was unable to switch his affections from one to the other without transgressing a moral boundary. He therefore had no choice but to accept the annulment of his marriage to Lauon. A new bride was found for him, a Scotswoman called Christina, the daughter of Earl Ferchar of Ross. This was not to the liking of King Rognvald's wife. Enraged that her sister Lauon had been cast aside, she took revenge by rekindling the old antagonism between the two royal brothers. In the words of the Manx Chronicle: 'Angered at her sister's separation and stimulated by bitterness and resentment, Rognvald's wife, Queen of the Isles, sowed the seeds of disharmony between Rognvald and Olaf.'[1] She wrote a letter, bearing the king's seal, to her young son Godred who was at that time the lord of Skye. The letter urged him to arrange for Olaf to be arrested and slain. Godred immediately set off to carry out what he believed to be his father's command. With a band of warriors he sailed to Lewis to capture and kill Olaf, his uncle. Olaf, however, managed to escape in a small boat. He eventually reached the Scottish mainland and came to Ross where his father-in-law Earl Ferchar gave him sanctuary. Godred Rognvaldsson then led his warband on a rampage across Lewis, devastating almost the entire island and slaying a number of the inhabitants. Meanwhile, in Ross, Olaf was joined by Paul Balkisson, the sheriff of Skye, who had not supported the plan to assassinate him. Shortly afterwards, Paul and Olaf sailed in secret to Skye where they hid themselves, biding their time. Within a few days they learned that Godred was on the island accompanied by only a handful of men. Gathering a band of loyal followers, Paul and Olaf launched a surprise attack and captured Godred. Ignoring Olaf's objections, Paul ordered the prisoner to be blinded and castrated.

In the following year, 1224, Olaf asserted his authority over the Hebridean part of his brother's kingdom. Chieftains from various islands swore allegiance to him and sent hostages, most likely from among their own families. Raising an army, he then sailed to Man with a fleet of thirty-two ships. After landing at Ronaldsway he entered into negotiations with his brother. Rognvald agreed to divide the realm, retaining for himself the Isle of Man and the title of king but granting lordship of all his Hebridean territories to Olaf.[2]

The kin strife between the brothers now seemed to be over, but sadly this was not the case. Discontent began to gnaw at Rognvald, who decided that he wanted his Hebridean lands back. He therefore looked for assistance from Alan, the lord of Galloway. In 1225, Rognvald and Alan launched a joint military expedition against Olaf, but it came to nothing when Rognvald's Manx warriors refused to make war upon Olaf's Hebrideans, whom they regarded as friends and fellow Islesmen. This left Rognvald and his Galwegian ally with no option but to call the whole thing off. Manx displeasure with Rognvald then began to grow, especially when, in 1226, he imposed a one-off tax to raise funds for a personal visit to England. No such journey materialised but he kept the money. He instead made a much shorter excursion to Galloway to visit Lord Alan. Rognvald's popularity finally crashed when he betrothed his daughter to Alan's son, a match that the Manx nobles did not want. They deposed Rognvald in favour of Olaf, whom they invited to be their new king. This elevated Olaf to the throne but Rognvald, having held power for 38 years, had no intention of giving up without a fight. Not even Olaf's recognition by King Henry III of England, son of Rognvald's former benefactor John, as the new king of Man and the Isles could persuade Rognvald to back off.[3]

With resentment between the siblings continuing to simmer, King Henry appointed himself as chief mediator. In the spring of 1228, he invited Olaf to England to discuss 'the framing of peace between himself and his brother Rognvald', but no solution was forthcoming. Inevitably, the situation degenerated into violence. The trigger for conflict was Olaf's departure from Man with his nobles and a strong force of warriors. His destination was the Hebrides where he may have intended to reinvigorate his authority among the islands or collect tribute payments. Sensing an opportunity in his absence, his brother Rognvald invaded Man with a large force. Alongside Rognvald was Alan of Galloway and an ally from the Scottish mainland: Thomas, the earl of Atholl. Together these three plundered the southern parts of Man so thoroughly that they left behind what the Manx Chronicle called a 'desert'.[4] Numerous captives were taken and there was much bloodshed. Even the churches were looted. The invaders then sailed back to Galloway, but not before Alan left behind a few followers to collect tax for his treasury. These Galwegians were forced to make a swift exit from Man when Olaf returned from his Hebridean expedition.

Rognvald stayed in Galloway until the winter, gathering there a small force of five ships for a mini invasion of Man. His plan was to burn the main strength of the Manx war fleet while it lay moored beside St Patrick's Isle at Peel. Under cover of darkness, his men set fire to many vessels, no doubt inflicting considerable damage and weakening Olaf's naval power. Rognvald then went on a tour of Man, hoping to negotiate a peace with his brother, before setting up residence at Ronaldsway, a place that is said to be named after him. Over the next month or so, he succeeded in attracting considerable numbers of southern Manx to his cause, a remarkable turnaround considering their tribulations during his previous campaign alongside Alan of Galloway. By contrast, the northern Manx gave allegiance to Olaf. In early 1229, on St Valentine's Day, the brothers with their respective armies clashed in a last, decisive battle near the assembly site of Tynwald Hill. Casualties were very high. Among them was

Rognvald, his death being attributed by the Manx Chronicle to 'ungodly men'.[5] So ended the turbulent life of one of the most colourful characters of the Late Norse period.

Rognvald's body was borne from the battlefield of Tynwald by monks from Rushen who conveyed it to Furness Abbey. His long reign of nearly forty years was not matched by that of his brother, whose comparatively brief tenure ran from 1226 to 1237. Although Olaf may have been relieved to see Rognvald's final, posthumous departure from Man, he would soon discover that their long feud had left an indelible mark on the wider politics of the Irish Sea region. Nor had it passed unnoticed in Norway. There, King Hakon Hakonsson was already drawing up plans for a major expedition into the west. Among his concerns was a lack of respect and loyalty from the MacSorleys who, according to the contemporary Icelandic text *Hákonar saga*, had been 'very unfaithful' to him.[6] Like the kings of Man, the MacSorleys were vassals of the Norwegian crown by virtue of ancestry. An additional anxiety for Hakon was the increasing power of Alan of Galloway whose reputation as a great warlord and prolific pirate had reached Norwegian ears.

King Olaf Godredsson likewise felt anxious about Alan and had not forgotten the part played by Galwegian forces in recent events. What happened next was reported in both the Manx Chronicle and *Hákonar saga*. News reached Olaf that Alan was mustering a huge army for a new assault on Man. The prospect of facing this onslaught so unnerved Olaf that he sailed to Norway to appeal for aid. On arriving at King Hakon's court, he learned that a Norwegian expeditionary force was already being mustered at Bergen for a great expedition 'west across the sea'.[7] He also learned that Hakon had appointed a man called Uspak as commander of the fleet. Uspak was a member of the MacSorley kindred but had been living in Norway for some years. He was loyal to Hakon and, in addition to receiving command of the great expedition, he had been promised the kingship of his family's domains in Argyll and the Isles. He had a legitimate claim on the MacSorley crown, being a grandson of the dynastic founder Somerled. Rather more disconcerting for Olaf of Man was the presence at the Norwegian court of his nephew Godred Don ('the Brown'), one of Rognvald's sons. This Godred is unlikely to be the unfortunate individual who had been blinded and castrated on Skye during the recent feud.[8] He was surely a namesake, a man of health and vigour who had been given a role in the Norwegian venture. It was not unheard of in those times for two brothers to share the same name, their identities being distinguished by an epithet or nickname. Godred Don doubtless had brown hair or a swarthy complexion.

The unlikelihood that he was the man mutilated by Olaf's ally Paul Balkisson is strengthened by the fact that Paul himself was also present at Hakon's court and would be sailing west with the fleet. Nevertheless, Godred Don was still a Rognvaldsson and may have been ill-disposed towards his uncle Olaf.

Olaf himself was assigned a place on one of the Norwegian ships. He used his brief time in Hakon's presence effectively, by trying to land Alan of Galloway in trouble. After informing Hakon about the Galwegian ruler's intention to invade Man, Olaf claimed that Alan had boasted about how easy it would be to raid Norway if he so wished. Olaf added that Alan had also claimed that a sea voyage to Norway required no great effort and that the country had more than enough harbours for his huge fleet.[9] Whether or not Alan actually uttered these boasts is unknown, but Hakon may have been willing to believe that he did, not least to provide extra justification for the expedition. Barely four days after Olaf's arrival in Norway, the great armada sailed out from Bergen.

Its first stop was Orkney where it was joined by local contingents, boosting its numbers to eighty ships. It then sailed south to the narrow strait between Islay and Jura where three leading members of the MacSorley kindred showed their hospitality by laying on a feast. For reasons unknown, one of these men was killed by the Norwegians and another was taken prisoner.[10] The fleet eventually moved on, continuing its southward journey to the Isle of Bute in the Firth of Clyde. Bute's great fortress was Rothesay Castle, which at that time lay under Scottish control. The Norwegians attacked and broke inside, gathering a large amount of loot and taking a Scottish nobleman hostage. Soon after, as a result of being injured in the assault on the castle, Uspak died. His replacement as expedition commander was King Olaf of Man who led the fleet onward to raid Kintyre, a core territory of his MacSorley rivals. However, when news came that Alan of Galloway was approaching with a fleet of 200 ships, the Norwegians decided to avoid a confrontation and instead sailed south to Man. There they spent the winter but, in the spring of 1231, they packed up and departed, turning their prows towards home. Although this might seem a rather inconclusive outcome, the expedition did succeed in its primary objective of reasserting Norwegian overlordship in the two kingdoms of the Isles. Indeed, it marked the beginning of a period in which Norway kept a closer eye on what was happening in this region. Both the Crovan dynasty and the MacSorleys would henceforth be expected to fulfil their obligations as vassals with appropriate diligence.[11]

With their Norwegian friends gone, Olaf and Godred Don partitioned the Crovan kingdom between them, the former retaining Man while the latter took the northern Hebrides. Godred Don soon came into conflict with Olaf's former henchman Paul Balkisson who had presumably returned to his 'sheriffdom' on Skye. Godred instigated the death of Paul on Lewis but was himself slain on the same island. Godred's demise gave Olaf the entire Kingdom of Man and the Isles, which he seems to have ruled trouble-free for the remaining years of his reign. In 1234, he is unlikely to have grieved at news from Galloway reporting the death of his old adversary Alan. In the following year, Olaf sailed over to England for an audience with King Henry III. Despite being a vassal of Norway, Olaf offered homage to Henry, just as his brother Rognvald had offered homage to Henry's father John. In return, Henry pledged to protect Olaf. What the Norwegian king Hakon thought of this relationship we can only guess, but his own amicable relations with Henry may have made it less of an issue. Contemporary English documents refer to Olaf as 'king of Man and the Isles' and describe his responsibilities as guarding at his own expense 'the coast of the sea of England towards Ireland, and towards the Isle of Man, and likewise the coast of the sea of Ireland towards England, and towards the aforesaid Isle of Man, lest injury might befall the aforementioned our lands of England and Ireland'.[12] For this valuable service, Olaf would receive via Henry's underlings in Ireland an annual payment of cash to the value of forty marks, plus large amounts of grain and wine, 'so long as the aforesaid king of Man shall truly and faithfully serve us, by guarding the aforesaid coasts'. Henry III, like his father before him, recognised that no king of England could afford to ignore Man. The island was essentially a pirate lair whose rulers could deploy a large fleet capable of harrying distant shores. Like their Viking ancestors, the Crovan kings could be useful allies or troublesome foes. Henry knew, just as his father John had known, that it was better to have Manx naval power firmly aligned with England's interests.

Harald Olafsson

Olaf Godredsson died on Man, at St Patrick's Isle, in May 1237. He was buried at Rushen Abbey. The Manx Chronicle states that his son Harald, then a youth of fourteen years, succeeded to the throne. Harald left a kinsman called Lochlann in charge of Man while he himself sailed north to the Hebrides 'with all his noblemen'. Why he made such a journey we are not told, but it looks like a royal tour or 'progress' rather than a military expedition. As a new and inexperienced king, Harald was probably seeking to affirm his authority in Skye, Lewis and other places that had been temporarily separated from the rest of the kingdom during the recent conflict between his father, uncle and cousin.[13] That a tense atmosphere nevertheless still lingered is shown by what occurred on Man while he was away. The Chronicle says that during his sojourn in the Isles the young king sent four men – his friend Joseph and three sons of a certain Neil – back to Man, accompanied by their followers. Three days after arriving, they attended an assembly at Tynwald. Harald's kinsman Lochlann was also present, accompanied by his own band of supporters. Bad blood already lay between him and Neil's sons over some past grievance. This boiled over at the gathering, turning the atmosphere hostile. Both sides traded insults until things got out of hand and a fierce battle broke out. When the fighting subsided, two of Neil's sons lay dead. So, too, did King Harald's friend Joseph. Lochlann claimed victory but his triumph was short-lived. In the following spring, he fled from Man with his henchmen as soon as the king returned. The circumstances suggest that Lochlann was not so much deputising in Harald's absence as working against him, perhaps by positioning himself as a rival claimant to the throne.[14] Alternatively, he may have been plotting to install his foster son Godred Olafsson – Harald's brother – as king. Taking Godred with him, Lochlann departed from Man and sailed towards Wales. He never made landfall, for a storm near the Welsh coast completely overwhelmed his ship. Both he and Godred drowned. Yet if Harald hoped that the remaining months of 1238 would be crisis-free, he was soon to be disappointed. Before the year was out, two emissaries arrived on Man with orders from King Hakon of Norway to remove him from power. Their names – Gospatrick and Gilchrist – suggest that they originated in a Gaelic-speaking milieu or among bilingual families in which Gaelic was spoken alongside Norse.[15] The cause of Hakon's displeasure with Harald lay in the Manx king's refusal to go to Norway to pay homage. Whatever Harald's reason for snubbing his Norwegian overlord, it now cost him his throne. Gospatrick and Gilchrist deposed him, took charge of the kingdom and forced him to depart from Man. He made his way to the Hebrides where, after gathering an army, he tried on several occasions to regain his kingship by force. Each attempt was thwarted by an effective shoreline defence organised by Gospatrick and Gilchrist which prevented Harald from disembarking his troops on Manx soil. He eventually gave up and remained in the Hebrides, while Gospatrick and Gilchrist continued to rule on behalf of the Norwegian king. They collected taxes that would normally have been rendered to the Manx royal treasury, diverting them instead to Hakon.[16]

One or more people close to Harald began counselling him to swallow his pride and go to Norway. At some point during 1239 he yielded to this advice and travelled to King Hakon's court. There he remained for the next two years, pledging fealty and eventually coming back into favour. With their relationship now back on track, Hakon confirmed Harald as the rightful king of Man and the Isles. In 1242, Harald left Norway and sailed to the Hebrides where he assembled a large fleet and army. Travelling onward to Man, he landed at St Patrick's Isle to be greeted with joy by the inhabitants. Reassured by this warm welcome, he disbanded his Hebridean forces and settled down to rule in peace.

With no more conflict recorded for the remainder of his reign, Harald Olafsson was able to rule 'quietly and peacefully in Man'.[17] However, wars and feuds were not the only troubles that kings of the Crovan dynasty had to contend with. Even in peacetime they had to weave a careful path among an ever-changing political landscape of alliances and allegiances. In Harald's case, an oath of loyalty sworn to King Hakon in distant Norway did not allow him to ignore other powers whose lands lay closer to his own. Hence, he wisely chose to maintain his family's traditional bond of friendship with England by accepting an invitation to attend the court of King Henry III in 1246. During this visit he was knighted by Henry, an honour that had also been bestowed on his father Olaf. Sometime after his return to Man, laden with English gifts, Harald was summoned to Norway. This time he offered no hesitation but set off on the long journey, shortening it by travelling overland across England. If Hakon's summons was a disgruntled reaction to the friendship between his Manx vassal and the king of England, there is no hint of this in the sources. It seems rather to have simply been an invitation to an important ceremony: Hakon's formal coronation as king, which took place on 29 July 1247.[18] Although Harald arrived too late to attend the main event, he was invited to spend the winter with Hakon at Oslo. There he met the Norwegian king's daughter, Princess Cecilia, and desired to make her his wife. He received her father's blessing and soon the preparations began for a lavish summer wedding at Bergen. Weeks before the great day, a terrible fire reduced much of Bergen to ashes, but the wedding went ahead anyway. Giving his daughter's hand in marriage to a vassal who had recently curried favour with King Henry of England might seem an odd course of action for Hakon to take. It is nevertheless consistent with his policy of strengthening Norway's ancestral bonds with the Isles, a region in which his own chief concern was not so much Henry's ambitions as those of the Scottish king Alexander II. Indeed, from *Hákonar saga* we learn that Alexander had been pestering Hakon for a number of years, urging him to transfer Man and the Hebrides to Scottish overlordship on the grounds that they should never have been answerable to Norway in the first place.[19] Hakon responded by pointing out that Norway's sovereignty over the *Sudreyjar* had been granted by a formal treaty with one of Alexander's predecessors. Alexander then offered a large amount of silver, a payment rejected by Hakon who stated that he was not so short of cash that he needed to sell off his western domains. A second offer of payment was made in 1248, the year of Harald Olafsson's wedding to Cecilia, but was similarly dismissed. Amid the increasing tension, Hakon no doubt saw wisdom in binding one of the two main ruling families of the Isles more closely to his own via a marriage that gave him a firm foothold in a region that the Scots were eyeing hungrily.

If a marriage alliance with the Crovan dynasty was one key element in Hakon's efforts to keep Scottish ambitions at bay, then a positive relationship with the other leading kindred of the Isles – the MacSorleys – was another. A prominent figure among the MacSorleys at this time was a man called Ewen, son of Duncan. A great-grandson of Somerled, Ewen had succeeded his father as king of the MacSorley domains in Argyll and the southern Hebrides. A counterclaim on part of this realm came from Ewen's cousin Dougal, son of Ruairi, sparking a dispute that raised the risk of internecine conflict. In 1248, the two men travelled to Norway to bring their respective cases before King Hakon.[20] They hoped that the Norwegian overlord of the Isles might be able to settle the matter. The result was that Hakon decided in favour of Ewen and instructed him to return home, together with his disappointed cousin. Both Ewen and Dougal were due to travel back to their domains on a ship that was also taking King Harald Olafsson and his Norwegian bride Cecilia back to Man. Before the vessel set forth, the two MacSorley princes decided to extend their stay in Norway, a move that turned out to be fortuitous.[21] The ship left Norway in September, carrying the newlyweds and their entourage, but was caught in a fierce storm near Shetland and everyone aboard perished. Harald's death left the Kingdom of Man and the Isles without a king, a situation of political uncertainty that might swiftly become unstable. Hence, in the following year, Hakon assigned temporary authority over all the Isles to Ewen, ordering him to sail there and take control. Ewen then went to the Hebrides where he remained for a while, consolidating his position as king of the MacSorley domains. On Man, Harald's brother Rognvald Olafsson claimed the vacant throne but was slain within a few weeks by Ivar, a man of unknown origin whom the Manx Chronicle described as a knight (Latin: *miles*). Ivar made no claim on the kingship himself, instead stepping aside to make way for Godred Don's son, another Harald. In the eyes of the Manx chronicler, the new king Harald Godredsson was a villain who 'usurped the title and dignity of king in Man, and banishing practically all of King Harald Olafsson's chieftains and noblemen he introduced his own from exile'.[22]

The Manx Chronicle clearly disapproved of Harald Godredsson's accession to the throne. So, too, did King Hakon. In 1250, the Norwegian king wrote a letter to Harald, ordering him to come to Norway. The Chronicle adds that Hakon was angered by Harald's 'usurpation of the kingdom, to which he had no right'.[23] Harald obeyed his liege lord's command but, after arriving in Norway, he was taken captive. Nothing more is heard of him for the next six years. In the meantime, the MacSorley ruler Ewen had arrived back in the Hebrides in 1249 to learn that King Alexander II of Scotland desired a meeting with him. In fact, the Scottish king had already begun making plans for an invasion of the Isles, intending to wrest them from Norwegian overlordship.[24] Ewen understandably felt wary of such a meeting and, according to *Hákonar saga*, sought a guarantee from Alexander that he would not be harmed. Indeed, while the saga says that the meeting went ahead, the contemporary English chronicler Matthew Paris stated that the negotiations were conducted via letter. Alexander ordered Ewen to give him four castles and a substantial amount of territory, in return for land in Scotland and a promise of protection. What mattered most to Alexander was persuading Ewen to transfer his allegiance from Norway to Scotland. Although Ewen's own henchmen were keen to accept the terms, Ewen himself did not want to break the oaths he had sworn to Hakon. As a compromise, he suggested that he could serve two overlords at the same time, as long as they were not at war with one another. Alexander dismissed this idea, calling Ewen a traitor and deciding that a show of force was required to bring him to heel. According to the saga, Ewen wished to avoid a confrontation with a man whom he still regarded as an ally and patron. So he withdrew northwards, sailing to Lewis. The Scottish king came after him but ultimately ran out of time. In early July 1249, on the Hebridean island of Kerrera, Alexander was struck by illness and died.[25] His army went home, leaving the MacSorley lands in peace. Alexander's successor, his son and namesake Alexander III, was a child of barely eight years who was in no position to oversee a military campaign in the Hebrides. None of this was of much help to Ewen, whose kingship of the MacSorley territories was challenged by his cousin Dougal mac Ruairi.[26] Having previously lost out to Ewen at their audience with King Hakon, Dougal now managed to wrest a large part of the kingdom for himself.

Magnus Olafsson

Dougal's success left Ewen in a weaker position but still capable of pursuing his ambitions. In 1250, Ewen sailed to Man with a fleet of Norwegian and Hebridean ships. Alongside him was Magnus Olafsson, brother of the former king Harald who had tragically drowned off Shetland two years earlier. Magnus was King Hakon's new nominee for the Manx throne, sent as a replacement for the deposed usurper Harald Godredsson who was now a prisoner in Norway. Ewen, however, appears to have decided that *he* was in charge. After landing on Man, at Ronaldsway, he started throwing his weight around. Declaring himself 'King of the Isles' he sent his henchmen out and about to deliver a series of pompous commands to the people. It was not long before the Manx found his presence intolerable. Moreover, they wondered why Ewen of Argyll and not their own prince Magnus was their new king. So they refused to take orders from Ewen, much to his annoyance. Resolving to impose his will by force, he brought his fleet to St Michael's Isle on the south-east coast of Man. There his Norwegian and Hebridean warriors disembarked to take up battle formations, for Ewen expected the Manx to arrive in force. Sure enough, an army of Manxmen approached and likewise formed up in serried ranks. Each side offered peace terms to the other, but these were summarily rejected. What happened next is unclear, but it appears that many of Ewen's soldiers retreated to their ships. Those who remained on St Michael's Isle were attacked by Manxmen under the command of the previously mentioned Lord Ivar. With the battle turning against him, Ewen withdrew his remaining troops and set sail, departing from Manx waters with Magnus Olafsson alongside him.[27]

Ivar's role in this episode is not fully explained in the Manx Chronicle but he may have been acting on behalf of Harald Godredsson, whose usurpation of the throne in the previous year Ivar himself had facilitated. Yet Harald's continuing detention in Norway meant that he was in no position to take advantage of Ivar's victory, so the throne remained vacant after Ewen sailed away. In 1252, Magnus Olafsson made another bid for power, this time without the unpopular Ewen at his side. He was accepted by the Manx as their rightful king. In the following year he travelled to Norway as a guest of King Hakon who formally confirmed him as the new king of Man and the Isles. Magnus sailed home in 1254, secure in the knowledge that he had the full backing of his Norwegian overlord. The Manx Chronicle notes that Magnus still faced opposition from within his kingdom, presumably from Harald Godredsson's supporters, but it also says that any lingering hope of regime change had evaporated.[28] In 1256,

Magnus visited King Henry III of England to pledge his loyalty, receiving in return a knighthood and many gifts. This does not seem to have caused any rift with Hakon, to whom Magnus was similarly bound by oaths. Henry offered protection to Magnus and forbade his own subjects from giving hospitality to the Manx king's enemies, specifically naming Harald Godredsson and Lord Ivar among them.[29] Magnus also secured a useful kinship with the MacSorleys by marrying Mary, a daughter of his former associate Ewen of Argyll. During his reign the main text of *Chronica Regum Manniæ et Insularum*, the Manx Chronicle, was compiled. Another unique document written at this time was a royal charter, now the sole surviving example from the era of the Crovan kings, issued on behalf of Magnus to the monks of Conishead Priory in north-west England.[30]

While Magnus settled down to rule on Man, Ewen and his cousin Dougal seem to have ruled separate parts of the MacSorley realm, the Kingdom of Argyll and the Isles. In 1253, both men were described as kings when they fought alongside their Norwegian overlord Hakon in a war against Denmark.[31] Two years later, Ewen obtained the protection of Henry III of England who at that time was intervening directly in Scottish politics. Possibly with Henry's support and patronage, Ewen was able to enjoy amicable relations with the young Scottish king Alexander III. Some years earlier, Alexander's father and namesake Alexander II had tried to draw Ewen away from Norway's sphere of influence. This had been part of a broader Scottish strategy concerning issues of overlordship in the Isles. When Alexander III acquired the full powers of kingship in 1260, he decided to resurrect the same strategy. In the following year, he sent two envoys to Norway to kickstart negotiations but nothing of substance emerged. Matters then came to a head a year later, in 1262, when news of a shockingly brutal raid on Skye reached the Norwegian court. The raiders were Scots under the command of the earl of Ross. They rampaged across Skye in an orgy of blood and fire, cruelly slaughtering the islanders and destroying churches as well as houses.[32] Skye was one of the Crovan dynasty's Hebridean domains and ultimately lay under Norwegian overlordship. Its ravaging by a Scottish earl whose family were loyal subjects of the Scottish crown implies that the raid was sanctioned by King Alexander III. If provoking Norwegian anger was Alexander's objective then he certainly succeeded. King Hakon responded by assembling a huge force of men and ships during the early months of 1263. According to *Hákonar saga*, he let it be known that 'he meant to sail west across the sea with all that host to Scotland, to avenge that strife which the Scots had made on his realm'.[33] When Alexander heard that the Norwegian king was preparing for war, he did the same. Orders were sent out across Scotland, ordering the chief men of the kingdom to mobilise their warriors. New ships were built, castles were strengthened, and garrisons were reinforced.[34] Meanwhile, in Norway, the armada was ready to depart by mid July. Hakon placed his son Magnus in charge of the kingdom while he himself went aboard his flagship, a large vessel with a gold-plated dragon's head at the prow. The fleet then began its voyage, sailing out from Bergen. It came first to Shetland, remaining there for a fortnight before moving on to Orkney where it stayed for a further couple of weeks. In Orkney the Norwegians learned that Ewen, king of Argyll and the Isles, had switched allegiance and was now on the Scottish side. This news so unsettled King Hakon that he initially refused to believe it. By the second week of August, the armada was on its way again, leaving Orkney behind and sailing first to Lewis and thence to Skye. The latter was part of Magnus Olafsson's kingdom and he had travelled there from Man to meet the Norwegians, bringing his own war fleet with him. Also joining the expedition at this stage was Dougal mac Ruairi who, unlike his kinsman Ewen, was still loyal to Hakon.

Leaving Skye, the Norwegian king's mighty force – now numbering more than 120 vessels – sailed past Mull and came to the small island of Kerrera. Half the fleet, led by Magnus of Man and Dougal mac Ruairi, was sent to raid Kintyre, while a smaller squadron attacked Bute in the Firth of Clyde. The rest remained with King Hakon, berthing on the tiny island of Gigha off the west side of the Kintyre peninsula.[35] Kintyre was at that time ruled by a branch of the MacSorleys led by Angus Mór ('Angus the Great') whose base lay on Islay. The loyalty of Angus was wavering between Norway and Scotland, but his indecision was cured after a severe plundering of Kintyre by Magnus Olafsson and Dougal mac Ruairi. In the wake of the attack, Angus reaffirmed his allegiance to Hakon.

While pausing at Gigha, the Norwegian king received a visit from Ewen, who stated that he had indeed sworn an oath of allegiance to Alexander III. Hakon reminded Ewen that his earlier oath to the Norwegian crown took precedence, but Ewen said that he would have a bigger domain if he stayed true to the Scottish king. This was not what Hakon wanted to hear, so he ordered Ewen to be kept in captivity until such time as he abandoned his pro-Scottish leanings. The island of Bute, meanwhile, fell to Hakon's forces after they captured its great castle at Rothesay. This was an important gain because Bute controlled the Firth of Clyde and was a key stronghold on the western frontier of the Scottish kingdom.[36] Continuing southward, the armada reached the island of Arran and berthed there in Lamlash Bay. It was there that a party of Dominican friars appeared, seeking an audience with King Hakon. They were emissaries sent by Alexander III to conduct negotiations and to strive for an agreement that would avert the need for war. A meeting was duly convened but it failed to bring peace. On the Norwegian side, there was a sense that the Scots were deliberately prolonging the debate with no real intention of seeking a compromise. By then, the summer campaigning season was coming to an end and autumn was approaching. This was a major concern for the Norwegians, who did not relish a long voyage home in unfavourable weather.

A second meeting between the two sides was convened when the Norwegian armada came to Great Cumbrae, another island in the Firth of Clyde. Once again, the talks proved inconclusive. To the Norwegians, it now seemed certain that the Scots were prevaricating to give Alexander more time to muster a big army. Hakon nevertheless tried hard for a breakthrough, even releasing Ewen from captivity on condition that he act as mediator. Kolbein, a trusted henchman of the Norwegian king, made one final effort to broker a truce but nothing came of it. War was now inevitable. It commenced with a foray into Loch Long by a raiding fleet of sixty ships led by five of Hakon's vassals: Magnus Olafsson of Man, Angus Mór of Islay, Dougal mac Ruairi with his brother Alan, and a certain Murchad who was probably from Knapdale in Argyll. The raiders progressed north-eastwards up the entire length of the loch, plundering as they went, before hauling their vessels ashore at Arrochar and dragging them overland via a narrow portage route leading to Loch Lomond. Taking to the water again, the raiders resumed their attacks, targeting the loch's small islands as well as the settlements around its shores. Pillaging, burning and slaying, they behaved much like their Viking ancestors and, in the words of *Hákonar saga*, 'wrought there the greatest mischief'.[37] Yet this successful expedition on the Scottish mainland was overshadowed by a catastrophe that befell the main fleet. On the last night of September, while the armada lay moored in the Cumbraes, a violent storm arose. Many vessels, including the Norwegian king's dragon-prowed flagship, suffered severe damage. Some were cast up on the adjacent mainland near present-day Largs where, over a period of several days, fighting broke out between men sent to retrieve the stricken craft and Scots who waylaid them. These skirmishes constituted what is today commonly known as the 'Battle of Largs', an encounter that was not so much a decisive military victory for the Scots as the last straw for Hakon.[38] Short of supplies and with an eye on the weather, Norway's king decided it was time to go home. Magnus Olafsson then took his leave and sailed back to Man, while other vassals likewise left at various stages of the northward voyage through Hebridean waters. On reaching Orkney in late October, Hakon was advised that the weather was already too rough to contemplate a crossing of the North Sea, so he agreed to pause for the winter. He stayed on Orkney with some twenty ships, giving consent for the rest of his sea captains to sail home if they wished. The weary king, now in his sixtieth year, never saw Norway again. He died on Orkney, at Kirkwall, on 16 December 1263.

The treaty

The Norwegian claim on Man and the Isles did not end with Hakon's death. His son and successor, Magnus Hakonsson, sent envoys to Scotland in the following spring. However, the previous year's Viking-style raids on Scottish territory were too recent to be forgiven or forgotten, so the envoys were sent home empty-handed.[39] Subsequent attempts to establish a dialogue between the two sides were more fruitful and formal peace talks were arranged to take place in Scotland during the summer of 1264. Hostilities nevertheless resumed, with Scottish armies invading Caithness and the Hebrides. In Caithness, the Scots were counter-attacked by Dougal mac Ruairi who deprived them of a large amount of plunder. In the Hebrides, the arrival of hostile Scottish forces was enough to persuade Hakon's erstwhile vassal Angus of Islay to switch allegiance. The same Scots did not deter Dougal mac Ruairi, who fought them in his own domain as vigorously as he had fought their compatriots in Caithness. Dougal remained faithful to Norway throughout this troubled period, even at the cost of being ousted from his lands and forced into exile. Others among the Norse-Gaelic elite who had supported Hakon's expedition were subjected to punitive fines, or saw their kinsfolk borne away to Scotland as hostages. On Man, the imminent threat of a Scottish invasion compelled King Magnus Olafsson to swear an oath of fealty to Alexander III. This was done at a formal ceremony in Dumfries, where Magnus gave hostages as surety against any oath-breaking on his part. Rightly fearing a revenge attack by his Norwegian namesake, Magnus received a guarantee of protection from Alexander, buying this with a contribution of ten ships to the Scottish fleet. These were described at the time as *galeae piraticae*, 'pirate-type galleys', five being twenty-oared vessels and the other five having twelve oars.[40] Alexander then stood down his invasion force and made a promise to the bishop of Sodor and Man that he would not reverse this decision. Magnus Olafsson thereafter reigned for barely one more year until his death in November 1265. He succumbed neither to murder by dynastic rivals nor to wounds sustained in battle, ending his life in a non-violent way at his own abode of Castle Rushen. His grave lay not far distant, at Rushen Abbey, where a carved recumbent slab – now displayed at the Manx Museum in Douglas – is believed by some to be his gravestone.[41]

The Manx Chronicle gives few details about what happened in the immediate aftermath of Magnus Olafsson's death. In its entry for 1266 it merely notes that 'the Kingdom of Man and the Isles was transferred to King Alexander of Scotland'.[42] Eastwards across the Irish Sea, the monks of Furness Abbey in their own chronicle observed that 'kings ceased to reign in Man'. Writing in the next century, the Scottish historian Walter Bower noted the passing of Magnus Olafsson but misplaced it at 1268, adding that Alexander afterwards considered building a fortress on Man 'against the assaults of rebels'.[43]

The long-running dispute between Scotland and Norway over Man and the Hebrides was finally settled by a treaty drawn up at Perth in July 1266. This confirmed the surrender of the Norwegian claim and stated that the Isles would henceforth be subject to the laws of Scotland. In return, Alexander III agreed to give Magnus Hakonsson the princely sum of 4,000 marks (silver coins), payable within four years, plus an additional 100 marks every year.[44] Needless to say, the Northern Isles of Orkney and Shetland were not included in the terms of the treaty and continued to be subject to Norway. The years that followed brought a new era of friendly relations between Norway and Scotland. Both kingdoms also forged connections with England, whose monarch Henry III had watched the events of 1263 to 1266 with a keen eye. To what extent he welcomed the great expansion of Scottish royal authority in the western seaways is difficult to assess. Would he have preferred instead a continuation of distant Norwegian overlordship among the sea-roving elites of Man and the Hebrides? Did the re-directing of their allegiance and military obligations to Scotland cause him more than a little anxiety? In any case, at the time of the treaty he was dealing with a crisis much closer to home: a rebellion by English barons. This serious uprising was not settled until 1267. For Magnus Hakonsson in Norway, the *Sudreyjar* were plainly not worth fighting for. Whereas his father had gone to war to settle the thorny question of overlordship, Magnus seems to have preferred the softer path of diplomacy. He is not, it must be said, remembered by history as a great warrior king.[45] We should also keep in mind that the tale of Norway's influence in the west in the 1260s was not all about loss. There were significant gains, such as securing the allegiance of Iceland and Greenland. For the people of Man, however, the era of their pirate kings was over. Their island's status as the principal royal domain in a powerful sea kingdom was swept aside by the Treaty of Perth. Henceforth, they would be answerable to monarchs in other lands whose authority would be delegated to henchmen and bureaucrats. If there was a single moment when the Manx Viking Age finally came to an end, this was surely it.

11

EPILOGUE AND LEGACY

A 'foolish presumption'

The Treaty of Perth in 1266 marked the end of the Kingdom of Man and the Isles. This, at least, was how the situation looked when viewed from Scotland or Norway. A different view was taken by some among the Manx. These people, as former subjects of the Crovan dynasty, resented the new political order and the imposition of Scottish overlordship. They wanted their own kings back. In 1275, it seemed for a brief time that their wish was answered. In that year, Godred Magnusson arrived on Manx shores with a small fleet of ships. Godred was the son of Magnus Olafsson, the last Manx king before the Scottish takeover, who had died ten years earlier. Where Godred had been living in the intervening years is unknown. When he set foot on Man, he was greeted warmly by some islanders but not by others. Eventually, even the doubters were persuaded to accept him and he was unanimously declared to be the new king.

Our main source here is not the Manx Chronicle, which makes no mention of Godred, but two northern English chronicles written at Furness Abbey and Lanercost Priory respectively. The Furness chronicle describes Godred as 'a son, but not legitimate, of Magnus the former king of Man'. Whether he really was born out of wedlock seems not to have troubled those who rallied to his cause. Enough of them accompanied him in what turned out to be a successful assault on an unidentified fortress, most likely Castle Rushen.[1] This was captured and its commanders, presumably Scottish royal officials, were ejected from Man. Godred's 'reign' thus began with a military victory, but one that was not to be repeated. When tidings reached King Alexander III of Scotland he responded quickly, summoning a force of ships and warriors from his vassals in Galloway and the Hebrides. The restoration of Manx kingship was nothing less than a rebellion against his authority and could not be allowed to endure. An invasion fleet of ninety vessels was duly assembled and five commanders were appointed to lead it. Two were members of the MacSorley kindred, another was a Galwegian while the remaining two were Scottish noblemen of Norman ancestry. The presence of two MacSorleys indicates the extent to which this powerful Hebridean family, long under Norwegian overlordship, had now aligned itself with the Scottish crown. On 7 October 1275, the fleet arrived at Ronaldsway where its commanders sent an offer of peace to the Manx, urging them to put aside 'their most foolish presumption' and pledge allegiance to Alexander. This was dismissed by Godred who ordered his men to prepare for battle.

The next day, at dawn, a fierce contest was fought at St Michael's Isle, not far from where the Scottish fleet lay at anchor. The encounter ended with defeat for Godred and death for many of his warriors. The Furness chronicle depicts the Manx fighting naked and without weapons, a rhetorical description usually reserved for primitive savages. It is reminiscent of ancient Roman accounts of battles against stereotypical barbarians and was intended to make the Manxmen appear hopelessly outmatched by their enemies. Needless to say, the image can be taken with a pinch of salt. On the other hand, we have no reason to doubt that Godred's soldiers were comprehensively routed. Many of them were cut down by a deadly hail of slingshot, arrows and crossbow bolts. Their total losses were 537, a figure given by the Manx Chronicle not only in its brief report of the battle but also in two lines of verse that may be from a contemporary poem or song.[2] The Scots followed up their victory by plundering Rushen Abbey and harassing its monks before rampaging across the entire island, leaving a trail of destruction in their wake. Godred managed to escape, taking his wife and a few retainers with him to seek refuge in Wales. Whether he thereafter dwelt among the Welsh as a royal exile, plotting another attempt to regain his father's throne, we do not know.[3] The sources give no hint of what became of him.

Lord of Man

At some point between 1266 and 1282, the Scottish king Alexander III bestowed the title 'Lord of Man' on his eldest son, also called Alexander. This seems to have been an honorary position created to boost the status of the king's heir, not least because of his youth (he was born in 1264).[4] The practical duties of government on the island were handled by officials appointed by the Scottish king to represent his interests. One of these was Godred MacMaras whose name is suggestive of a Norse-Gaelic background in the Hebrides, Galloway or Man. Prince Alexander's untimely death in 1284, shortly after his twentieth birthday, deprived the king of his only surviving son. The title 'Lord of Man' nevertheless continued to be used, although not by Scottish princes. Its future bearers would be English aristocrats whose rule over the island was often undertaken in pursuit of their own ambitions.

The later medieval history of Man

King Alexander III of Scotland died in 1286. Having outlived his children, he had selected his granddaughter Margaret as his heir, but Margaret's death in 1290 at the tender age of seven triggered a succession crisis. A number of powerful factions emerged, each putting forward a claim on the vacant throne before eventually coalescing into two opposing blocs. On one side stood the Bruces, a Scottish noble family of Norman origin, together with their allies who included some of the leading kindreds of the Isles; on the other stood the Comyns and Balliols, both also with Norman roots and likewise with their own supporters among the Islesmen.[5] The contest proved to be the catalyst for a complete collapse of peaceful relations between the kingdoms of England and Scotland. Edward I, who had succeeded his father Henry III as king of England in 1272, saw the new phase of dynastic strife north of the Border as an opportunity. Disunity among the Scots would make them more vulnerable to English conquest. In 1290, the Isle of Man became the first Scottish territory to fall under Edward's sway when its leaders submitted to him. This happened after a period of uncertainty following the death of King Alexander III in 1286. At some point in the ensuing years, control of Man was seized by Richard de

Burgh, the earl of Ulster. Richard was a vassal of Edward I but, like many of the Anglo-Norman elite in Ireland, he frequently pursued his own interests. The motives behind Richard's takeover of Man are unknown but it was not necessarily done on Edward's behalf. Richard's friends included the Bruce family of Scotland, and he may have moved against Man to stop the Comyns and their allies from seizing it.[6] He nevertheless yielded up the island to King Edward in 1290, sometime before the fourth day of June. On that date, Edward formally granted his protection to the Manx people after acknowledging the aforementioned submission of their leaders. The latter had convened at Rushen Abbey to draw up a document in which they offered allegiance to England's king, seeking his protection because their island had been 'abandoned and afflicted by many woes' and had become 'desolate and full of wretchedness'.[7] Disregarding the fact that Man was part of the kingdom of Scotland, Edward appointed an English knight, Walter de Huntercombe, to govern it. However, the change of ownership was not welcomed by everyone on the island and a pro-Scottish faction took shape, possibly encouraged by the bishop of Sodor and Man.[8] Meanwhile, Edward succeeded in imposing his overlordship on Scotland, not by defeating the Scots in war but as his price for agreeing to mediate in their succession crisis. As both overlord and mediator he was asked by an assembly of Scottish nobles to supervise discussions on who should be their next king. The outcome was that a man called John Balliol ascended the throne of Scotland in November 1292. The succession crisis thus ended favourably for the Comyns and Balliols but left their main rivals, the Bruces, on the sidelines. Four weeks after his coronation, John Balliol swore an oath of allegiance to Edward.

Early in the following year, Edward acknowledged Scotland's right to govern Man by yielding up the island to Balliol. He did, however, retain overall sovereignty over the Manx by virtue of being Balliol's liege lord. Prior to the handover, Edward collected what he regarded as overdue payments owed by Scotland to Norway under the terms of the treaty of Perth, sending these monies across the North Sea.[9] Somewhat later in 1293, Balliol undertook a reorganisation of his Hebridean territories by creating three new sheriffdoms out of what had once been the great sea kingdom of the Isles. One of these was centred on the mainland territory of Lorn in Argyll. Its first sheriff was Alexander, a son of the ambitious Ewen whose eventful career we charted in Chapter 10. Ewen had been a king, ruling part of the MacSorley realm in the southern Hebrides. His son Alexander held no such title, for the era of independent kingship in the Isles was over. The various branches of the MacSorley kindred had once enjoyed considerable autonomy from both Scotland and Norway. As the thirteenth century drew to a close, they had given up their royal status to become noble families serving the interests of the Scottish crown.

In 1296, John Balliol rejected Edward's overlordship. He was immediately punished with a full-scale invasion from England. Edward's forces defeated the Scots in a battle at Dunbar and Balliol was deposed soon afterwards. This was the start of a sixty-year period of hostilities known as the Wars of Scottish Independence.[10] It was a time of upheaval and uncertainty for the people of Man, who saw control of their island switch back and forth between Scotland and England. For a time during the late 1290s Man was in the hands of Antony Bek, bishop of Durham in northern England. As well as holding high ecclesiastical rank, Bek was a military commander in Edward's Scottish campaigns. He may have had possession of Man from the dethroning of Balliol in 1296 to a revival of Scottish fortunes under William Wallace (1297–8). The island then reverted to Scottish authority for a couple of years until its capture by Simon Montacute (Montagu), another of Edward's warlords. By June 1301, Antony Bek was back in charge, styling himself *dominus terre Manniae*, 'Lord of the land of Man'. He is said to have acquired the island and its revenues on a seven-year mortgage arranged with Simon Montacute.[11] The latter had tried to self-fund his military activities in the Anglo-Scottish war but had run up a large debt in the process and needed the kind of financial bailout that a wealthy individual like Bek could offer. Bek thus regained control of Man as a private enterprise rather than under the auspices of Edward I. The king allowed this situation to continue for a number of years until, in June 1307, he asked Bek to explain why Man was not a possession of the English crown. Edward had even considered confiscating Man for himself, but his death in July allowed Bek to remain as lord of the island. The next king of England was Edward's son and namesake Edward II, who formally confirmed Bek as ruler of Man for life.[12]

It was during the turmoil of the 1290s and early 1300s that claimants for the defunct Manx throne stepped forward. One was a noblewoman called Affrica of Connacht who claimed to be a cousin of Magnus Olafsson, the king whose death in 1265 had paved the way for the treaty of Perth. Who this lady actually was and where she fitted into the Crovan dynasty's genealogy is unclear, but she bore a name that the Manx royal family had certainly used before. In 1293, Affrica brought her claim to the Scottish king John Balliol and also to Edward I of England. Balliol was initially disinterested but was urged by Edward to give the lady a proper response.[13] What eventually transpired is unknown, but Affrica's claim made no further progress and she slipped into the background for the next ten years. In 1305, she transferred her claim to Simon Montacute to whom she may have been married at that time. By 1307, Simon and his son William were undertaking naval patrols in the seaways between Scotland and Ireland, leading a fleet of 15 ships. They operated on behalf of both Edward I and his successor Edward II against Scottish foes, especially the Bruces who now represented Scotland's main opposition to English domination. By 1310, the Montacute fleet was using Man as a base, not only because of the island's strategic location but also, perhaps, to promote the claim of rulership that Simon Montacute had acquired from Affrica. The claim finally expired in 1311 when, following the death of Antony Bek, Simon Montacute was imprisoned at Windsor Castle on a charge of attempting to seize control of Man.[14] Another claimant to the Manx throne was Mary, a daughter of King Rognvald Olafsson who had reigned for less than a month in 1249. Mary's case was later pursued by her grandson John Waldeboef who brought it to Edward I in 1304. However, Waldeboef's petition made no progress in England, so Edward suggested that he try his luck in Scotland. With an Anglo-Scottish war still raging at that time, it is little surprise that we hear no more on this matter.[15]

Queen Mary of Man

Magnus Olafsson, the last king of Man from the Crovan dynasty, had been married to the MacSorley princess Mary, a daughter of the renowned Ewen of Argyll. Magnus died in 1265 and the Kingdom of Man and the Isles was extinguished in the following year. His widow Mary subsequently remarried, possibly in 1268, her second husband being the Scottish earl Malise of Strathearn. Malise died in 1271 and Mary went on to marry Hugh, the lord of Abernethy in Fife, with whom she had several children. Hugh's death widowed her again, but she later married William FitzWarin, a leading English soldier who is perhaps best known for surrendering Stirling Castle to William Wallace in 1297. FitzWarin, too, was outlived by Mary. Her own passing eventually came in 1302, in London. There she was laid to rest beside her fourth husband at the monastery of Greyfriars. Interestingly, although contemporary documents sometimes referred to her as the Countess of Strathearn, she evidently preferred the title that she had borne during her first marriage. Soon after her passing, thirty-seven years after Magnus Olafsson's death widowed her for the first time, an English document guaranteeing safe travel for her relatives referred to her as 'Mary, Queen of Man'.[16]

Robert Bruce, the earl of Carrick, seized the Scottish throne in 1306. Four years later, news that he was planning to conquer Man reached the court of Edward II via Antony Bek's steward on the island. The steward, Gilbert MacAskil, was most likely a native Manxman.[17] Edward II ordered MacAskil to gather men and ships from north-west England for the defence of Man. MacAskil's personal correspondence suggests that some among the Manx were actively supporting Robert Bruce by sending supplies to his fleet. However, the Scottish invasion did not happen immediately and, during the next couple of years, Bruce turned his energies to consolidating his position as king of Scotland. In 1311, Anthony Bek died. One contemporary English text described him as *rex Mannorum* ('king of the Manx'), which looks at first glance like an anachronism harking back to the Norse era. Encountering such a title in the fourteenth century is not, in fact, as unusual as it might seem. It simply reflects the continuing use of the term 'Kingdom of Man' in official documents issued from the English royal court.[18] In the meantime, Bek's death left Man in need of a new lord. Edward II appointed two men in quick succession, the one a court favourite and the other a second cousin.

In 1312, Scotland and Norway renewed the Treaty of Perth. The Norwegians also acknowledged the authority of Robert Bruce in northern and western Scotland.[19] The following year saw the arrival of Bruce's fleet at Ramsey to begin the long-awaited Scottish invasion of Man. After besieging and capturing Castle Rushen, Bruce ordered that it be demolished. Almost exactly twelve months later, he decisively routed the forces of Edward II on the battlefield of Bannockburn. A fleet loyal to Edward, led by Ewen MacDougall of Argyll, recaptured Man in 1315. A scion of the MacSorley kindred, Ewen was a grandson of his namesake from the previous century. He had been appointed by Edward II as admiral of the Irish Sea, tasked with foiling Bruce's naval campaigns. Man reverted back to Scottish control when the earl of Moray, an ally of Bruce, invaded in 1317. This time the island remained in Scottish hands for more than fifteen years until 1333 when it was recaptured by Edward's forces. William Montacute, a military commander of renown like his grandfather Simon, became the new English lord of Man. There would be no more reversions to Scottish rule, except during a thirty-year period in the eighteenth century when the dukes of Atholl held the lordship. Memories of Scottish connections were nevertheless slow to fade, not least because English royal officials still regarded Man as geographically part of Scotland long after the fourteenth century.

Medieval to modern

The Montacute family ruled the Isle of Man for some sixty years before selling it to Sir William Scrope, the earl of Wiltshire, in 1392. Fourteen years later, Sir John Stanley was granted the lordship of Man by King Henry IV.[20] Sir John, who never actually set foot on the island, was the first in a long line of Stanley rulers whose authority would endure for more than 300 years. The title borne by Sir John and his immediate descendants was 'King of Man', but this was changed to 'Lord of Man' in 1504. From a Manx perspective the Stanley kings and lords were despots, some more benevolent than others. They received rents and taxes, most of which were paid in kind via agricultural produce, livestock or labour services. A portion of these renders supported soldiers who garrisoned the great castles of Rushen and Peel as well as smaller fortifications around the island. The castle garrisons were backed up by a militia comprising all Manxmen between the ages of 20 and 60.[21] With most Stanley rulers being absentees, the day-to-day business of government was delegated to a governor supported by various officials. A parliament known as the House of Keys dispensed justice and enacted laws, but its representatives were elected among themselves rather than by the wider populace. This body convened at the traditional Manx assembly site of Tynwald.[22]

Stanley rulership of Man ended in 1736 when the lordship passed to James Murray, the duke of Atholl, who was a kinsman of the Stanleys. Murray's daughter and her husband later sold the island's sovereignty to the English government in 1765 for the princely sum of £70,000.[23] The deal was formalised in the English parliament by the Revestment Act, essentially an act of union that designated Man as a territory of the English crown. Many islanders were not happy to see their ancient autonomy bartered away by Scottish landowners and English bureaucrats. Their simmering discontent aroused so much concern in Britain that an infantry regiment, the famed Black Watch, was despatched to keep an eye on them. The Revestment Act led to the disbanding of the Manx militia and the locally recruited castle garrisons. Although the Tynwald Court was allowed to retain its legislative powers, its proceedings were now carried out under the gaze of a governor answerable to England's monarch. This is the political and administrative situation that persists on the Isle of Man today.[24]

The Three Legs of Man

Present-day visitors to Man encounter the island's famous triple-legged emblem in a variety of contexts. It appears on the official Manx flag and on the ferryboats of the Steam Packet Company, to name two familiar instances. Much uncertainty surrounds the origin of its association with Man, but the symbolic representation of three legs is known to be very ancient indeed. It is called a triskeles and can be seen on coins minted in the fourth century BC in the Greek colony of Syracuse in Sicily. The earliest reference to the triskeles as an emblem of Man is in a document of the late 1200s in which the arms of the *Roy de Men* ('King of Man') are described in heraldic terms.[25] Although this raises the possibility that the emblem was used by monarchs of the Crovan dynasty, their surviving seals show a galley of the type that comprised their war fleets. Perhaps one or more of these kings used both emblems simultaneously? On the island itself the earliest instances of the Three Legs can be dated to the fourteenth century, namely the churchyard cross at Kirk Maughold and the seal of Sir William Scrope, Lord of Man.[26]

The lost records of ancient Man

Joseph Train, writing in the nineteenth century, referred to old traditions about two princesses of the Crovan dynasty who supposedly denuded Man of its oldest documents. The first was Mary, daughter of King Rognvald Olafsson. This is the Mary whose claim on the defunct Manx throne was raised by her grandson John Waldeboef in 1304. According to one tradition, Mary sailed to England 'with all the public deeds and charters of the Island'.[27] This may preserve a kernel of truth, for it is likely that she would have needed official documents from her father's kingdom to substantiate her claim. Another tradition, reported by James Johnson in the early nineteenth century, claimed that a princess called Matilda or Maud took 'the most ancient records' of Man to Trondheim in Norway in 1292. There they were afterwards destroyed in a fire. I can find no additional information on Matilda, nor have I located Johnson's source for this story.[28] Train also cites a traditional belief that the remaining ancient documents on Man were taken away by Charlotte, countess of Derby, wife of one of the Stanley lords of Man in the seventeenth century. Train was sceptical about this and wondered if there might not have been many documents left on the island for Charlotte to remove. He also noted another tradition that the records of the Kingdom of Man and the Isles had been kept in the monastic library of Iona before being transferred to Aberdeen where the Scottish historian Hector Boece (died 1536) allegedly saw them.[29] The fate of these records, if indeed they survived into Boece's time, is unknown.

King Orry

Laxey, a village on the east coast of Man, is one of the most popular 'must see' destinations for present-day tourists. The village is famous for its gigantic waterwheel, the largest still in operation anywhere in the world. Laxey also has the Isle of Man's largest Megalithic tomb, dating from more than 4,000 years ago. This structure, commonly known as King Orry's Grave, lies beside Ballaragh Road on the north side of the village.[30] Although in a ruinous state, partly due to nearby house construction in the modern era, it is known to have comprised several burial chambers, each formed of huge slabs. A cairn once covered the chambers, but all that now survives is a number of broken standing stones. On the other side of the road stands a tall monolith known as King Orry's Stone, marking the entrance to another multi-chambered tomb, similarly ruinous. Both tombs were built in the Neolithic period and are presented to modern visitors as the 'eastern' and 'western' parts of King Orry's Grave. Whether their prehistoric builders regarded them in this way, as separate elements of a single monument, is an open question.[31]

King Orry is a familiar figure in Manx legend. He is said to have been the island's greatest king, credited with introducing the first set of Manx laws, the Tynwald Court and the House of Keys. He is associated with a number of sites, including another 'tomb' at the Giant's Grave behind Tynwald Hill. Orry's supposed gigantic stature – a common attribute of pagan gods – might be due to conflation of his legend with that of Manannán mac Lir. A large stone in Bulgham Bay in Lonan parish, known as Creg Vanannan, 'Manannán's Rock', is reputed to have been hurled from the summit of North Barrule by Orry rather than by Manannán himself. Other tales of Orry include one in which he is said to be sleeping in the Devil's Den, a hollow cave at the foot of South Barrule, awaiting there a summons from the Manx people to resume his rule over them. This is clearly a borrowing from the legend of King Arthur, who is said to sleep alongside his knights in a subterranean chamber, awaiting a call to protect Britain from invaders.

Orry, otherwise known as Gorree, is none other than the eleventh-century Manx king Godred Crovan in legendary guise. The name Gorree derives from Godred but lost its initial G through direct speech after being combined with the English word 'king', hence 'King Gorree' became 'King Orry'. Like his historical alter ego, Orry is said to have sailed to Man with an army. Both figures arrived on the island as foreigners whose origins lay elsewhere. One tradition says that Orry came with a fleet to the mouth of the Lhen River on the northern edge of Jurby parish, while another has him making landfall a few miles further south. He supposedly arrived in 938, more than a hundred years before Godred Crovan. When local people came down to the shore to ask Orry where he had come from, he pointed to the night sky and said that he came from the Milky Way. Since then, this great band of stars has been known in Manx Gaelic as *Raad Mooar Ree Gorree*, 'The Great Road of King Gorree'. After setting himself up as ruler of Man, Orry reorganised the island into six districts known as 'sheadings', a tier of administration that still exists today. His story ends with his murder at Laxey in 947. It hardly needs stating that the entire legend is fiction, adding nothing to our knowledge of the historical Godred Crovan. It nevertheless shows how Godred's favourable literary treatment in the Manx Chronicle has been mirrored in local storytelling tradition in which he has been elevated to the status of supernatural hero. The historical monarch and dynastic founder, depicted in the Chronicle as ambitious yet merciful, has become the island's very own 'once and future king'. Orry is essentially a Manx Arthur who will protect his kingdom in perpetuity. The main difference between the two is that Orry can be traced back to an individual who definitely existed, whereas Arthur cannot. Despite their fame as figures of legend rather than of history, both Orry and Arthur have sometimes been seen as 'real'. In Arthur's case this is still happening, with plenty of books and websites still insisting that he played an important role in fifth- or sixth-century Britain. By contrast, depictions of Orry as a historical king are rarely encountered today and belong rather to the Victorian imaginations of Joseph Train and his contemporaries. Hence we see Train portraying Orry as the forefather of the Norse kings of Man, not only those of the Crovan dynasty but their tenth-century predecessors. Train assigned Orry to the early 900s, more than a hundred years before Godred Crovan came to Man, and believed that Orry and Godred were separate historical figures.[32]

Heritage: conservation and display

Visitors seeking traces of the early medieval and Late Norse periods in Man will not be disappointed. The needs of heritage tourism relating to all eras of Manx history are well served by a number of governmental and non-governmental organisations on the island, the most prominent being Manx National Heritage. The latter operates the Manx Museum in Douglas which, for the heritage tourist, is always a good place to start. Visitors desiring to see ancient and medieval artefacts at the Museum encounter objects from a range of sites, such as early Christian sculptured stones and Viking-Age weaponry. The Viking assemblage is especially rich, with archaeological finds from excavated sites such as the ship burials at Balladoole and Knock y Doonee, respectively in the south and north of the island. Particularly noteworthy are the artefacts discovered in the grave of the so-called 'Pagan Lady', a middle-aged woman interred in an ancient cemetery on St Patrick's Isle at Peel.[33] She was buried wearing a fabulous necklace of more than seventy coloured beads. The museum's presentation and interpretation of archaeological material of this sort attains a very high standard, with scale models and miniature dioramas enabling visitors to see artefacts in their original contexts. A particularly striking exhibit is a life-size tableau depicting a Viking settler with his horse.[34]

Everyone who visits the Manx Museum is indebted to Philip Kermode (1855–1932), its founder and first director. Those who enjoy seeing early medieval carved stones at close quarters can be especially thankful to him. This is because the preservation and conservation of these monuments can be credited in large part to Kermode's eagerness to protect them. In 1884, he made an impassioned plea for the Manx government to assume overall responsibility for this unique corpus of sculpture.[35] Indeed, he himself spent more than twenty years gathering information on the stones by making notes and sketches and taking photographs. He ensured that many were relocated inside churches instead of being exposed to damage by adverse weather or human activity. Several monuments had been used as gateposts on farmland, a role to which rectangular slabs and cross shafts unfortunately lend themselves all too easily.

The displays in the Manx Museum contain some original early medieval stones alongside replicas of others. While the replicas are meticulous copies, reproducing the carvings in fine detail, the visitor may wish to see a particular monument in – or close to – its original location. Guidebooks indicating the current whereabouts of each stone are useful resources in this regard and can be purchased on the island or remotely via the internet. There are also booklets and leaflets giving information on specific sites, such as the various churches where local sculptural collections have been assembled. Aside from the Manx Museum, the island's premier location for ancient sculpture is Kirk Maughold where, in a picturesque setting, a small church now stands on the site of what was once an important monastery. On one side of the churchyard stands a purpose-built 'cross house', a sturdy timber structure housing an impressive collection of carved stones. Information on the Maughold collection is presented in both the cross house and the church. A smaller cross house can be seen at the old church of Lonan. Here, one of the most impressive ancient monuments on Man currently stands in the churchyard, exposed to the elements.[36]

The largest relics of Man's medieval history are the great castles at Rushen and Peel, both of which were founded in the time of the Crovan dynasty. At Peel, the castle's perimeter walls are still standing but the interior buildings are mostly in ruins. Within the enclosed area lie the remains of St German's Cathedral and a round tower erected c.1100. Castle Rushen, by contrast, is remarkably well preserved. Both castles are in the care of Manx National Heritage and offer the visitor a rewarding experience with plenty of accessible, well-presented information. The same can be said of Rushen Abbey where the ruins of the principal ecclesiastical centre of the Manx kings are a major heritage attraction.[37]

A different kind of experience can be found at the House of Manannan in Peel where the entire history of Man is told in chronological sequence as the visitor moves through a series of rooms. A guided tour is provided by the voice of the sea god himself, here taking the role of heritage narrator. The tour includes reconstructions of an Iron Age roundhouse and a Norse longhouse, together with audio examples of Viking speech. The venue's most impressive feature relating to the period covered in this book is Odin's Raven, a modern replica of the famous Viking ship from Gokstad in Norway. The Gokstad vessel, dating from the ninth century, was unearthed by archaeologists in 1880 and has since been restored. It now resides at the Viking Ship Museum in Oslo. Odin's Raven, built to a scale of two-thirds of the original, was made in Norway to commemorate the millennium of Tynwald in 1979. It sailed across the North Sea to Peel with a Manx and Norwegian crew, completing the 1,500-mile voyage in just over a month. Its route was essentially the one taken by Norse raiding fleets a thousand years earlier, passing via Shetland, Orkney and the Hebrides to enter the North Channel and the Irish Sea.[38] Today the vessel's human occupants are static models in Viking-Age garb, one of whom is a bound female captive whose presence starkly reminds us that gold and silver were not the only portable loot acquired by Viking raiders. A particularly eye-catching cameo in the Odin's Raven display is a group of life-size figures, clad in warrior attire and hauling the ship with ropes. They stand partly inside and partly outside the House of Manannan, heedless of the large external window that one warrior is striding purposefully through as if it was nothing more than a veil of falling water.[39]

Legacies

Physical relics of the early medieval and Late Norse periods in Manx history include sculptured stones, grave goods and the remains of settlements. Other relics are less tangible, such as elements of present-day Manx society and culture that originated, or are believed to have originated, in those eras. The bishopric of Sodor and Man is one example, having been founded in the time of the Crovan kings. Another is the annual ceremony at Tynwald, a site with a long tradition of law-making and justice. Although we lack written evidence for the use of Tynwald Hill for these purposes before the early 1400s, the name's derivation from Norse *þingvollr*, 'field of the assembly' is highly suggestive. There is broad agreement among historians that the site was probably used for assemblies in the Viking Age and that its legislative and judicial functions continued thereafter through the medieval and early modern periods.[40] Some administrative divisions on Man are likewise assumed to have ancient roots, despite a dearth of early records. Which divisions – if any – can be traced back to the Viking Age or earlier is a question that continues to be discussed. One suggestion is that the traditional division of the island into Northside and Southside may have originated as far back as prehistory.[41] Beneath this binary divide, the next tier of administration is represented by the sheadings, three in the north and three in the south. The term 'sheading' has been interpreted as deriving from a Norse term meaning 'ship district' (from *skeid*, 'galley') or 'sixth part' (from *settungr*) or from a medieval English word meaning simply 'a division' (*scheding*). Although certainty remains elusive, the fact that there are six sheadings appears to support a derivation from *settungr*.[42] Five of the sheadings contain three parishes each, the sixth containing only two. While there is no doubt that parishes were created after the Viking period, much uncertainty surrounds the origin of the treen, the administrative unit below the parish. The most likely derivation of 'treen' is from *tir-unga* (Gaelic: 'land ounce'), a term with the same meaning as *urisland* in Orkney (Norse: 'ounceland'). Both terms were used in assessing the value of land for taxation purposes. There is thus a strong case for seeing the treen, with its four subdivisions or 'quarterlands', as a territorial unit of considerable antiquity, most likely originating in the Viking Age.[43] A theory that each treen was required to send four warriors to serve in the army of the Crovan kings cannot, however, be proved or disproved.

The Manx language seems, at first glance, to be another legacy from the ancient past. Being a form of Gaelic, it appears to connect its present-day speakers with people of Irish ancestry who lived on Man before the first Norse settlers arrived. However, doubts remain over the extent to which this language has evolved from the Gaelic spoken on the island in pre-Norse times. No consensus on the topic has yet emerged, despite much debate by specialist scholars.[44] With persuasive philological arguments being voiced on both sides, the non-specialist is hard pressed to choose one over the other. At present, I incline towards the view that post-medieval Manx does incorporate something of the language spoken by Gaelic-speaking islanders before c.900. The alternative, which I do not support, is to see no continuity of Gaelic speech and to envisage instead its total disappearance prior to or during the upheavals of the Viking Age. In this stark scenario, the ancestral form of today's Manx language arrived with or even after the Vikings, as Gaelic speech brought from Ireland by Hiberno-Norse settlers in the late ninth and early tenth centuries or as a later import from mainland Scotland and the Hebrides following the end of Norse rule in the thirteenth. The only real certainty in the debate is that Manx is definitely a Gaelic language and that its beginnings must lie somewhere in the medieval period.[45]

Conclusions

My original objective in writing this book was to present a narrative political history of the Isle of Man in the early medieval and Late Norse periods. Readers who have followed the main chronological sequence from Chapters 3 to 10 will have seen that the narrative contains many gaps, some wider than others. Wherever possible, I have tried to bridge these with informed speculation, usually based on theories devised by other writers. The absence of contemporary information has frequently made this task extremely difficult, especially when a gap is so wide that any attempt to bridge it seems futile. This problem is felt most acutely in the early chapters covering the pre-Norse era of the fifth to ninth centuries. In these chapters I have presented what I currently regard as the most plausible version of events. Here I use the word 'currently' as a kind of disclaimer, for my opinions might change or evolve, especially if a new theory – or even an old theory repackaged in a new way – offers a different interpretation that I subsequently find persuasive.

In summary, I envisage the political history of Man in the period c.400 to 1265 as comprising three phases, each determined by the cultural affiliations of the island's ruling elite. The first phase, spanning the fifth century and most of the sixth, I see as a mixture of Irish and British, with Gaelic-speaking and Brittonic-speaking elites competing for control. To this era belong the ogham inscriptions, the stories of Irish missionaries and the military activities of Irish kings. Concealed behind the fragments of textual and archaeological data I envisage a lengthy period of immigration from Ireland, beginning in the early fifth century (if not before) and continuing over many decades, during which Gaelic-speaking people settled on Man for the first time. These settlers would have encountered a pre-existing population of Britons with whom they may have engaged in hostilities before reaching a position of largely peaceful co-existence. Around this time, until the late sixth century, some or all of Man lay under the sovereignty of ambitious Irish kings from Ulster.

The political situation then shifted in the final quarter of the sixth century when Britons, most likely from Gwynedd, wrested control of Man out of Irish hands. What I envisage thereafter is a phase in which the Brittonic- and Gaelic-speaking communities on Man were ruled by a royal family of Britons who had a close connection with the First Dynasty of Gwynedd. This situation, I propose, continued unbroken for nearly 300 years, despite a brief period of some fifty years in the seventh century when Man fell under the overlordship of English kings from Northumbria. We know from Bede that Gwynedd, including its island domain of Anglesey, lived under this Northumbrian yoke. If Man, like Anglesey, was in some sense an offshore territory of Gwynedd's kings then it, too, may have fallen to the English simply because Gwynedd had fallen. This scenario draws support from Bede who apparently regarded Man and Anglesey as comprising a single archipelago when he referred to them as the 'Mevanian' islands. Moving forward into the 700s we encounter a blank page in Manx history until we reach the 800s and the emergence of Merfyn Frych. To him is credited the founding of the Second Dynasty of Gwynedd amid the growing uncertainty of the Viking Age. I incline towards the view that Merfyn's family, a kin group with strong Manx connections, lost control of Man in the 870s. This is when Vikings – probably from Dublin – took control of the island.[46] So began the third phase of Manx history, in which Old Norse became the dominant language. The Brittonic language all but disappeared while Gaelic probably survived in some form. If the incoming Norse-speaking settlers came from Ireland, as seems likely, they would already have been exposed to Gaelic-speaking Irish neighbours for a couple of generations. Some among the 'Hiberno-Norse' immigrants were no doubt bilingual in Gaelic and Norse before they arrived on Man. They may have interacted with Gaelic-speaking Manx people more easily, perhaps more amicably, than with Manx Britons. Whether the latter were slaughtered, forced to leave or decided to emigrate of their own accord is unknown, but we quickly lose sight of them. Moving through the tenth and eleventh centuries, we see Manx political history becoming entangled in the affairs of the Uí Ímair dynasty of Dublin. From a branch of this famous Hiberno-Norse family came Godred Crovan who seized the kingship of the Isles – these being the *Sudreyjar* or 'Southern Isles', comprising Man and the Hebrides – in 1079. Godred's descendants, the Crovan dynasty, primarily spoke Norse. They shared with other Hiberno-Norse elites around the coasts of northern Britain an ancestral allegiance to Norway. This relationship became a thorny issue for the Crovan kings on a number of occasions and remained so until the last of them, Magnus Olafsson, died in 1265. With the death of Magnus, the Norse phase of Manx history came to an end. So, too, did the dominance of the Norse language. Authority over Man then passed to the kings of Scotland and, later, to their counterparts in England. At that point, the chronological narrative of this book draws to a close.

One aspect of early Manx history that I have highlighted is the part played by the Britons. The presence of this people on the island in pre-Norse times has often been overlooked or given only a brief mention.[47] Yet their importance is attested by stone monuments inscribed with Brittonic names. Contemporary texts likewise refer to high-status Britons with Manx connections, such as Merfyn Frych and his son Rhodri Mawr in the ninth century, as well as Merfyn's earlier namesake 'Muirmin' in the seventh. Bede, writing in the eighth century, regarded Man as a territory of the Britons and would not have done so without good reason. I believe that we should distinguish Brittonic speakers from Gaelic speakers when discussing Manx history in the period 400 to 900, rather than applying the vague label 'Celtic' to the pre-Norse population as a whole. This population was surely bicultural, comprising two separate communities who nevertheless managed to co-exist. Making a distinction between Manx Britons and Manx Gaels is particularly important when discussing the

Norse colonisation, a process in which the fates of the two groups seemingly embarked on different trajectories. As noted above, the Norse colonists may have interacted negatively with the Manx Britons, perceiving them as speakers of a language spoken by the island's pre-Norse rulers. By contrast, Norse colonists and Manx Gaels may have developed areas of common ground based on the former's prior contact with Gaelic speakers in Ireland and the Hebrides. If this kind of commonality existed, it might have a bearing on key philological questions, such as how many Gaelic place-names on Man really are genuine survivals from the pre-Norse period and whether any of them had formerly existed in Brittonic as well as in Gaelic forms. This kind of musing is possible only when the island's two language/culture groups in pre-Norse times are not subsumed under an imprecise label such as 'Celtic'.

Throughout the period covered by this book it is clear that the Isle of Man played a significant role in the history of the Irish Sea region, exerting an influence out of all proportion to its size.[48] In the second half of the period, Man was the principal centre of power in a powerful political entity: the Kingdom of the Isles. Created in the Viking Age, this kingdom continued to flourish until the mid-thirteenth century, even after its partition between the Crovan kings and the family of Somerled. The survival of the Crovan dynasty ensured that Man was one of the last of the Norse colonies in Britain and Ireland to give up an ancestral allegiance to the kings of Norway.[49] The original Viking settlers had taken control of Man because it was economically valuable and strategically useful. Its nodal position in the seaways made it eminently suited as a base for maritime trade passing east–west or north–south. It was also an ideal haven for pirate fleets, not only those originating in other lands but one that could be mustered by the Manx themselves. When modern historians speak of medieval Man as a great sea power, they are referring to this home-grown fleet, a prized naval asset that was available to whoever held sovereignty over the island.[50] In the twelfth and thirteenth centuries, the Crovan kings made good use of Manx ships, combining them with Hebridean vessels to form a mighty fleet that was much feared by enemies and much welcomed by allies. Of course, the maritime advantages of the Isle of Man had been recognised long before the era of Godred Crovan and his heirs. Even before the Viking Age, ambitious kings from Ireland and Britain had coveted Man as far back as the sixth century. Attacks on the island by outsiders seeking conquest or plunder – or both – were an inevitable consequence of its position amid a busy sea. Such actions were surely counterbalanced by what must have been the frequent involvement of Manx ships in raids on other lands during every phase of the island's medieval history. Indeed, seaborne raiding is so entwined with the story of medieval Man that one historian has described the island as 'a haunt of the freebooter or pirate'.[51] This was no doubt an apt description in the late tenth century, when predatory Viking warlords such as Maccus Haraldsson and his brother Godred almost certainly had their headquarters on Man, but we can probably apply it across a much broader span of years. A chronicler referred to Maccus as *archipirata*, 'chief of pirates'. I suggest that this would have been an appropriate description for many more among the kings, princes and sea lords who held power on Man during the period covered by this book.

NOTES

Abbreviations

AC *Annales Cambriae* (Welsh Annals)
ASC *Anglo-Saxon Chronicle*
AT *Annals of Tigernach*
AU *Annals of Ulster*
ByT *Brut y Tywysogyon*
FAI *Fragmentary Annals of Ireland*
HE *Historia Ecclesiastica Gentis Anglorum* (Bede)

Chapter 1

1. Defining the sub-divisions of the medieval period is not an exact science. Compare, for example, the chronological spans I have defined here with those of other authors, such as Rob Collins, *Early Medieval Europe, 300–900* (New York, 1999) and David Power, *The Central Middle Ages: 950–1300* (Oxford, 2006).
2. The concept of a Late Norse period is explained succinctly by R. Andrew McDonald (2019a, 7).
3. On the idea that *Scotti* meant 'Gaelic speakers', see Duffy 2005, 698.
4. *Godred/Guthfrith*: In this book I include both of these anglicised forms of the original Norse name, using 'Godred' in the context of the Crovan dynasty of Man and 'Guthfrith' for namesakes elsewhere. *Rognvald*: Some modern authors adhere more closely to the Old Norse nominative form of this name by adding a terminal 'r' (*Rognvaldr*).
5. The reliability of the various Irish chronicles is discussed in Evans 2010.
6. Chronicle of Melrose: an accessible English version is the 1991 reprint of Joseph Stevenson's edition/translation of 1856 (Stevenson 1991). John of Fordun, *Chronica Gentis Scottorum*: English translation in Skene 1872. Walter Bower, *Scotichronicon*: English translation in MacQueen and MacQueen 1989–95.
7. For a useful discussion of *AC*, see Charles-Edwards 2013, 346–56.
8. See Swanton 1996 on the various manuscripts of *ASC*.
9. The English chroniclers referred to here include John of Worcester (died c.1140),

William of Malmesbury (died c.1143), Roger of Hoveden (died 1202), Roger of Wendover (died 1236) and Ranulf Higden (died 1364).

10. An essential companion for readers of Bede's *Historia Ecclesiastica* is Wallace-Hadrill 1988.
11. On the hagiography attached to Patrick, see the papers in Dumville 1993. Hagiography as a genre is discussed in Heffernan 1992 and MacQuarrie 1997, 1–14.
12. The historical value of the Norse sagas is examined in Woolf 2007, 277–85.
13. *Orkneyinga saga*: English translation in Pálsson and Edwards 1981. *Hákonar saga*: English translation (by G. Dasent) in Vigfusson 1894.
14. Crawford 1987, 9; Woolf 2007, 277–85.
15. Manx Chronicle: I have used George Broderick's 1973 edition and translation throughout this book, employing his chapter numbering system to cite specific passages.
16. Williams 2015, 310.
17. McDonald 2019a, 33.
18. Broderick 1973, ix-x.
19. British Library, Harley Charters MS 43A70, dated May 1256: King Magnus Olafsson to the priory of Conishead in north-west England, exempting its ships from tolls. See McDonald 2019a, 47.
20. McDonald 2019a, 39.
21. Broderick 1973, vii–ix. On the Chronicle of Melrose, see Oram 2011, 160–1.
22. McDonald 2019a, 11.
23. P.A. Munch (ed.) *Chronica Regum Manniae et Insularum. The Chronicle of Man and the Sudreys* (Christiania, 1860). Revised with an English translation by A. Goss (Douglas, 1874). Online version at http://isle-of-man.com/manxnotebook/manxsoc/msvol22/index.htm [accessed 1 July 2022]. G. Broderick (ed.) *Chronicle of the Kings of Mann and the Isles* (Edinburgh, 1973).
24. Verse 23. English translation by Robert L. Thomson (1961, 544).
25. McDonald 2019a, 6, 9.
26. Moore 1900, I, 80.
27. Hill 2012. On the life and career of Joseph Train see Patterson 1857.
28. Train 1845, i, 63–5.
29. Airne 1949, 32.
30. Kinvig 1975, 53.
31. Volume 1: Chiverrell and Thomas 2006; Volume 3: Duffy and Mytum 2015; Volume 5: Belchem 2001. The as-yet unpublished titles in the series are Volume 2 (*Prehistory*) by Peter Davey and Volume 4 (*Derby and Atholl Periods, 1405–1830*) by J.R. Dickinson and John Belchem.
32. Mytum 2015, vii.
33. Kerrison 2016.
34. Wilson 2018.
35. Goodwins 2020; Clague 2021 (I am grateful to Mike Clague for drawing my attention to his book when I visited Kirk Andreas in September 2021); Steinforth 2021a. See also the concise overview of the Viking-Age sculpture of Man by Heidi Stoner and Aya van Renterghem (2014).

Chapter 2

1. Moffat 2002, 44–5.
2. On the geology of Man, see Chiverrell 2002 and Chiverrell and Thomas 2006.
3. Davey 2002, 87.
4. Davey 2002, 99.
5. On the beginnings of human settlement on Man, see Kinvig 1975, 21–3.
6. Goodwins 2017, 12.
7. Freke 2002, 438. For a comprehensive study of the Ronaldsway culture, see Burrow 1997.
8. Goodwins 2017, 15.
9. Goodwins 2017, 18.
10. On the Bronze Age in Man, see Crellin 2019.
11. Davey 2002, 93.
12. On the Iron Age in Britain, see Cunliffe 2005.
13. Goodwins 2017.
14. Kinvig 1975, 33.
15. Kinvig 1975, 36.
16. The older view is discussed in James 1999.
17. For modern approaches to the spread of Celtic culture in Iron Age Europe see, for example, Fitzpatrick 1996, James 1999 and Cunliffe 2003.
18. Roman assaults on Anglesey: Tacitus, *Annals*, 60; Tacitus, *Agricola*, 18.
19. Caesar: *Gallic Wars*, v, 13.
20. Ptolemy, *Geographia*, II, 2, 10.
21. Ó Corráin 2017, 124.
22. Broderick 2008, 167.
23. Wilson 2018, 3.
24. Manannán: Welsh traditions, see Davies 2007; Irish traditions, see Spaan 1965 and MacQuarrie 2015. On the idea that Welsh *Manawydan* probably derives from Irish *Manannán*, see Sims-Williams 2010, 12.
25. Moore 1891, 6. See also Morrison 1911.
26. Moore 1895, 43.
27. Tacitus, *Annals*, bk 14, Chapter 30.
28. Goodwins 2017, 26.
29. Clarkson 2016, 78–83.
30. Ammianus Marcellinus, *Res Gestae*, xxvii, 8, 1.

Chapter 3

1. On the end of Roman Britain see Esmonde-Cleary 1989.
2. The Anglo-Saxon settlement of Britain is discussed in Hills 2003. Less recent but still useful are the papers in Bassett 1989.
3. For an overview of Pictish history, see Clarkson 2010a.

4. The foundation legend of the Scots appears in the eleventh-century Gaelic poem *Duan Albanach* ('Song of the Scots'). An alternative form of the legend was given by Bede (*HE*, I, i).
5. Campbell 2001. For a critique of this theory, see McSparron and Williams 2011.
6. Charles-Edwards 2013, 174.
7. Dugdale 1998, 25.
8. Broun 2001.
9. Duffy 2005, 698.
10. Freeman 2001, 93.
11. Thomas 1981, 197.
12. Dugdale 1998, 165.
13. Dugdale 1998, 47.
14. Dugdale 1998, 114.
15. Crawford 2016.
16. On Cronk y Dooney keeill, see Kermode 1930, 84–5. For Manx *dooney* = 'Sunday' see Kneen 1925, 13, 30.
17. Dugdale 1998, 133.
18. On the Manx traditions of St Sanctan, see Cotter 1977. On the likelihood that the cult came to Man in the Viking Age, see Edmonds 2019, 139–40.
19. Trench-Jellicoe 2002.
20. Hemer 2014, 242; Wilson 2018, 12–13.
21. Wilson 2008, 129; Wilson 2018, 17–18.
22. Charles-Edwards 2013, 181.
23. Charles-Edwards 2013, 175.
24. Wilson 2018, 15.
25. Cubbon 1982, 259.
26. On the name Ambicatus/Ammecatus, see Jackson 1953, 173. On the date of the inscription, see Trench-Jellicoe 2002, 13.
27. Muhr 2002, 44.
28. Wilson 2018, 17.
29. Trench-Jellicoe 2002, 13, 15.
30. Byrne 1973, 109–10; Ó Cróinín 1995, 50; Mac Niocaill 1972, 77.
31. *Berchan's Prophecy*: see Hudson 1996 for an English translation.
32. Anderson 1922, I, 88.
33. Byrne 1973, 110.
34. *AU* 577: *Primum periculum Uloth in Eufania. AU* 578: *Reversio Uloth de Eumania.*
35. O'Rahilly 1946, 503–5; Bannerman 1974, 83–4.
36. Miller 1980, 306. The poem, *Clann Ollaman Uaisle Emna*, is preserved in several manuscripts, the oldest written in the fourteenth century.
37. *AT* 582: *Cath Manonn in quo victor erat Áedán mac Gabráin.*
38. *Historia Brittonum*, Chapter 8 (on the three large islands around the coast of Britain): *secunda sita est in umbilico maris inter Hiberniam et Britanniam, et vocatur nomen eius Eubonia, id est Manau* ('... the second is situated in the

middle of the sea between Ireland and Britain, and is named Eubonia, that is Man').

39. On the kingdom of Gododdin, see Jackson 1969. On the location of Manau see Watson 1926, 103.
40. I discuss the Miathi/Maeatae in Clarkson 2010b, 46.
41. Muhr 2002, 39; Fraser 2009, 133.
42. Anderson 1922, I, 90.
43. Charles-Edwards 2013, 151.
44. Hughes 1973.
45. On the case for locating Rheged in Galloway, see Toolis and Bowles 2017.
46. Koch 1997, xcvii, n2.
47. On the value of Taliesin's poetry as a source of sixth-century history, see Williams 1975.
48. One of Urien's battles was fought in *Manau* but this is presumed to be the place in northern Britain (Clarkson 2010b, 77).
49. *HE*, ii, 9.
50. Hughes 1981; Davies 1992; Corning 2006.

Chapter 4

1. *HB* 61 (Ida) and *HB* 62 (Outigirn).
2. On the likelihood that Bede was deliberately portraying the Northumbrian overkingship of the seventh century as more extensive than the Mercian overkingship of the eighth, see Higham 1995, 66. I am grateful to Hugh Andrew for discussion of this topic.
3. Higham 1995, 83.
4. *HE* ii, 9.
5. Edmonds 2019, 31.
6. Edmonds 2019, 36.
7. On the identification of Dun Guaire as Bamburgh (Din Guaryoi), see Watson 1926, 132.
8. Breeze 2008, 93–4.
9. *AC* 629. Priestholm is nowadays more commonly known as Puffin Island.
10. Higham 2015, 62; Edmonds 2019, 35.
11. *HE* ii, 9.
12. *Tribal Hidage*: see Dumville 1989 for an introduction to the text.
13. Higham 1995, 97–99.
14. Higham 1995, 84 and 137.
15. Higham 1995, 84–5. For discussion of Bede's sources of information on hidage figures, see Shaw 2016.
16. Adomnán, *Life of St Columba*, i, 1.
17. *AU* 638: *obsesio Etin*.
18. Higham 2015, 233.
19. Miller 1980, 306.

20. Clarkson 2010b, 144.
21. *Bellum Ratha More Maighi Line contra Britones ubi cecidit Cathusach m. Maele Duin, ri Cruithne, & Ultán filius Diccolla.*
22. Watson 1926, 193; Fraser 2005, 108; Higham 2015, 204.
23. Smyth 1984, 25–6. I argue against the Rheged theory in Clarkson 2010b, 151.
24. Mac Niocaill 1972, 112–14; Miller 1980, 310–11; Charles-Edwards 2000, 433 n75; Charles-Edwards 2006, 164 n3; Wilson 2018, 6; Edmonds 2019, 42.
25. Mac Airt and Mac Niocaill 1983.
26. Edmonds 2019, 42; Charles-Edwards 2000, 433, n75.
27. Radford 1949; Dugdale 1998, 58.
28. *HE* iv, 26; *AU/AT* 684. On the idea that the attack on Brega was Ecgfrith's challenge to Finsnechta see Higham 2015, 206.
29. Edmonds 2019, 42. Another event of 684, not included in the main narrative of this chapter, was reported in the Welsh Annals as *terrae motus in Eubonia factus est magnus* ('a great earthquake on Man'). Nothing more is known about it.
30. Higham 2015, 236.
31. Britones & Ulaidh uastauerunt Campum Muirteimhne.
32. *Irgalach nepos Conaing a Britonibus iugulatus i n-Insi Mac Nesan ('Írgalach grandson of Conaing was killed by Britons in Inis Mac Nesáin').*
33. *Bellum Campi Culind i n-Airdd Nepotum n-Echdaigh inter Ultu & Britones, ubi filius Radhgainn cecidit, aduersarius eclesiarum Dei. Ulaith uictores erant* ('The battle of Mag Cuilinn in Ard Ua nEchdach between the Ulaid and the Britons, in which Radgann's son, an enemy of God's churches, fell. The Ulaid were victors.').
34. *Bellum Selgge h-i Fortuathaibh Laigen contra Nepotes Cennselaig, in quo ceciderunt .ii. filii Ceallaigh Cualann,Fiachra & Fiannamhail, & Luirgg cum Britonibus Ceallaigh; & post paululum Coirpri m. Con Coluinn iugulatus est.* ('The battle of Selg in Fortuatha Laigen against the Uí Cheinnselaig, in which fell two sons of Cellach of Cuala, Fiachra and Fiannamail, and Luirg with Cellach's Britons; and shortly afterwards Cairpre, son of Cú Cholainn, was killed.').
35. Smyth 1984, 25.
36. Having previously (Clarkson 2010b, 151) taken the view that Alt Clut was where the British military forces originated, I am now inclined to favour the Isle of Man.
37. The main source for Osred's brief reign, Manx exile and failed comeback is *Historia Regum Anglorum et Dacorum* ('History of the Kings of the English and Danes'), a twelfth-century chronicle attributed to Symeon of Durham. In this sequence of events, the chronicler refers to Man as *Eufania*.

Chapter 5

1. See Chapter 3 above.
2. Wilson 2018, 23.
3. Trench-Jellicoe 2002, 30; Edmonds 2019, 146.

4. Wilson 2018, 24, figure 7.
5. Wilson 2018, 25.
6. Trench-Jellicoe 1980, 202.
7. Cubbon 1977, 6–7.
8. On the uncial lettering, see Cubbon 1982, 262. On Branhui as a Brittonic name, see Cubbon 1982, 257; Chadwick 1963, 227. Megaw 1950, 169 saw the name as Gaelic.
9. Cubbon 1982, 257. The bishop's name was formerly read as *Itspli* but this is now seen as incorrect. A plausible alternative reading is *Arneit*: Trench-Jellicoe 2002, 15.
10. Cubbon 1977, 6–7. On similarities with the Suffolk bishop's seal, see Wilson 2018, 31–2.
11. Wilson 2018, 35.
12. Wilson 2018, 35.
13. Freke 1995, 11; Hemer 2014, 243, 247. On the round tower, see Dugdale 1998, 109–10.
14. Kermode 1897, 51; Rhys 1897; Jones 1990; Sims-Williams 2003, 148–9, 366.
15. Charles-Edwards 2013, 37–9.
16. Chadwick 1949, 146; Shaw 1964, 31.
17. Charles-Edwards 2013, 470 (pedigree of Rhodri Mawr). On the idea that Merfyn Frych was a descendant of the Merfyn ('Muirmin') slain on Man in 682, see Sims-Williams 1994–45, 11–20.
18. Sims-Williams 2010, 12. On the identification of Gwriad who died in 878 as a son of Merfyn Frych, see Downham 2007, 218, n105. For a suggestion that Guriat's Cross might commemorate a cleric, see Wilson, 2009, 313.
19. *AU* 878 – the accompanying poem, in an English translation:

    Rhodri of Manu, splendid here,
    Áed from the lands of Cenn Tíre,
    Donnchad, lustrous stuff of sovereignty,
    Gairíth, diadem of smooth Macha –
    Whenever I bring it to mind
    It inflames the limits of my heart,
    Cold flags over temples of the buried,
    Barrfhinn of Bile is distraught.
20. Charles-Edwards 2013, 468.
21. For the view that pre-Norse Man had a mainly Gaelic-speaking elite, see Megaw 1976 and Broderick 2010. For the opposing view (a Brittonic-speaking elite) see Dumville 1997, 23; Downham 2007, 180, 218 n107; Charles-Edwards 2000, 589.
22. Kinvig 1975, 52.
23. Charles-Edwards 2013, 478.
24. Interestingly, one version of the Welsh text *Brut y Tywysogyon* calls Hywel ap Caradog 'king of Man' (*Manaw*) at his death in 825. Whatever this alleged Manx connection means, Welsh sources usually associate Hywel with Anglesey (Charles-Edwards 2013, 475).

25. Thornton 1997, 94–5; Kirby 1978, 97.
26. As proposed by Thomson 2015.
27. Miller 1980, 306; Fellows-Jensen 2015, 260; Muhr 2002, 45.
28. Fiona Edmonds (2019, 9) has suggested that Gwriad ab Elidir 'may have ruled over a mixed population of Britons and Gaels, as was appropriate to an island located in the middle of the Irish Sea.'
29. Lindisfarne: *ASC* 793; Iona: *AU* 795. For discussion of these early raids, see Woolf 2007, 45–7.
30. For an overview of the Viking Age in Britain, see Williams 2017. On the meaning of the term 'viking', see Downham 2007, xv. Common misconceptions about Vikings are discussed in McMahon 2014.
31. Downham 2007, 180; Graham-Campbell and Batey 1998, 11. One of the writers who thought the raid of 798 targeted the Manx site was Moore (1900, I, 75, 85). For a recent discussion, see Steinforth 2021b.
32. Charles-Edwards 2013, 471.
33. On the political fallout from Áed's death, see Charles-Edwards 2013, 471.
34. Charles-Edwards 2013, 475.
35. Thornton 2006, 92–3.
36. *AU* 856: 'Orm, chief of the Dark Foreigners, was killed by Rhodri son of Merfyn, king of Wales'. On the 'Dark Foreigners', see Chapter 6, note 1.
37. Charles-Edwards 2013, 479.

Chapter 6

1. The terms 'Fair Foreigners' and 'Dark Foreigners' are discussed in Downham 2007, 14. See also Dumville 2004.
2. On the composition of the Great Heathen Army, see Hadley and Richards 2021.
3. For discussion of Ivar, see Downham 2007, 15–16.
4, Dumville 2004; Downham 2007, 23.
5. *AU* 870; *AC* 870.
6. Clarkson 2014.
7. On assigning the Viking takeover of Man to the late ninth century, see Steinforth 2015; Steinforth 2018; McDonald 2019a, 19–20 and Wilson 2008, 51–3. On the case for the early tenth century, see Graham-Campbell 1998, 117–18.
8. For an edition, analysis and English translation of *FAI* see Radner 1978.
9. On Tomrar, see Downham 2008.
10. For example: Gregory 1881, 4.
11. Hudson 2015, 188.
12. *AU* 877; *AC* 876 (=877); Charles-Edwards 2013, 487, n94.
13. Woolf 2007, 141; Steinforth 2018.
14. On the Viking graves of Man, see Wilson 2008, Chapter 2 and, for an older study, Shetelig 1945.
15. Dumville 1997, 23–4.

16. On the possibility that the 'Pagan Lady' was a sorceress, see Gardeła 2014, 33. See Symonds et al (2014) for discussion of the skeletal data.
17. See Bersu and Wilson 1966 and Gardeła 2014 on the Viking graves of Man and Weale 2019 on the osteoarchaeology of the human remains.
18. Wilson 2008, 38–46.
19. Megaw 1976.
20. Wilson 2008, 38.
21. David Dumville (1997, 23) suggested that the Hebrides had a mixed Gaelic-Norse population in the Viking Age.
22. Gelling 1970–1; Gelling 1978; Gelling 1991. See also Fellows-Jensen 1983.
23. Crawford 1987, 102. The definitive survey of Manx place-names was formerly John Kneen's *The Place-Names of the Isle of Man with their Origins and History*, published in 6 volumes (Douglas, 1925–28). This has been superseded by George Broderick's *Placenames of the Isle of Man*, in seven volumes (Tübingen 1994–2005).
24. Wilson 2018, 57. See also Gelling 1977, 80–1.
25. Megaw 1976; Thomson 1983; Broderick 2008; McDonald 2021.
26. Gelling 1977, 80. Braddan may be another pre-Norse name (Wilson 2018, 57). A possible Brittonic placename survival is the now-lost *Hentre*, attested c.1280, which might represent *hendref*, 'old farm' (Broderick 2008, 167).
27. Crawford 1987, 101.
28. Crawford 1987, 102.
29. Fellows-Jensen 2001, 45.
30. Wilson 2008, 103; Fellows-Jensen 2015, 277.
31. Downham 2009, 140.
32. Downham 2009.
33. Downham 2007, xvi–xviii. On trade and other connections between Norse Dublin and the Great Army, see Horne 2021.
34. *AU* 853: Amhlaim m[ac] righ Laithlinde.
35. Ó Corráin 1998. See also Dirk Steinforth's recent suggestion that Laithlind may have been 'a Viking realm of unknown size in Scotland' (Steinforth 2020, 28).
36. Downham 2007, 15.
37. Kinvig 1975, 77; Wilson 2008, 57–8.
38. Wilson 2008, 59.
39. Gelling 1977, 80.
40. On Gaut (Gautr), see Wilson 2018, 130–1. On the mythological aspects of Manx Norse sculpture, see Margeson 1983 and Bourns 2014. On the runic inscriptions see Page 1983 and (for an older study) Cumming 1857.
41. Wilson 2018, 64 (Onchan 85).
42. Wilson 2018, 47 (Lonan 71).
43. Wilson 2018, 63 (Lonan 73). A photograph of this 'wheel-headed' monument can be seen in the plate section.
44. Wilson 2018, 72.
45. Wilson 2018, 73.
46. *AU* 878: *Ruaidhri m. Muirminn, rex Brittonum a Saxonibus interemptus.*

47. Asser, *Life of Alfred*, Chapter 80; Charles-Edwards 2013, 489–94.
48. *AU* 902.
49. Downham 2007, 28.
50. Downham 2007, 207. On Ingimund see Clarkson 2018, 88–91.
51. Wilson 2008, 55.
52. Downham 2007, 181. *AU* 914: A naval battle at *Manu* between Bardr son of Ottar and Rognvald grandson of Ivar, in which Bardr and almost all his army were destroyed.
53. Downham 2007, 181.
54. Downham 2007, 31–2.
55. Clarkson 2014, 59–60.
56. Davidson 2001.
57. Downham 2007, 36.
58. On these events, see Downham 2007, 34–42.
59. John of Worcester, s.a. 937; Etchingham 2001, 167. Battle of Brunanburh: see the papers in Livingston 2011. My own views on the battle (and on the question of its location) can be found in Clarkson 2014.
60. Wilson 2008, 119.
61. On Olaf Cuarán's career, see Downham 2007, 43–54, 107–15, 190.
62. See Cubbon 1983 and Broderick 2003 for discussions of the history and antiquity of Tynwald.
63. Wilson 2018, 109–11.

Chapter 7

1. Etchingham 2001, 167–71; Downham 2007, 219.
2. *AC* 969. The epithet *archipirata* appears in *Gesta Regum Anglorum* by William of Malmesbury: Mascusius archipirata (Charles-Edwards 2013, 543).
3. Etchingham 2001, 180.
4. Downham 2007, 194.
5. *ASC* 973; John of Worcester, s.a. 973; William of Malmesbury, *Gesta Regum*. One source renders the name *Siferth* as *Giferth*. If the latter is a more correct form, this attendee might be Godred Haraldsson, brother of Maccus (Edmonds 2019, 64 n138).
6. Downham 2007, 221; Wilson 2008, 23.
7. Thornton 2001; Barrow 2001.
8. *AFM* 972; *AI* 974.
9. Thornton 1997. The idea that Maccus represents the Norse name Magnus was suggested by Benjamin Hudson (2005, 65–74).
10. *AU* 987.
11. Downham 2007, 195.
12. Thomson 2008, 60–1.
13. Crawford 1987, 66.
14. Woolf 2007, 219, 298.

15. Downham 2007, 196.
16. McDonald 2019a, 25.
17. The source is the 'C' manuscript of *ASC*: '. . . so it plundered the Isle of Man' (*þa geherergodon hi Monige*).
18. On the meanings of *Cumbria* and *Cumberlande* in this period, see Clarkson 2014. On Æthelred the Unready, see Williams 2003.
19. Henry of Huntingdon, iv, 35.
20. Downham 2007, 131 n151.
21. Williams 2003, 52
22. *AU* 1005; *AI* 1005; see also Etchingham 2001, 180.
23. *Njáls saga*, chapters 154–55.
24. Brodir's alleged link with York is briefly discussed by Fiona Edmonds (2019, 67).
25. Duffy 2013.
26. Hudson 2002.
27. Hudson 2005, 75–6; Duffy 2013, 149–50.
28. Edmonds 2019, 67. For more on Cnut, see the papers in Rumble 1994.
29. Downham 2007, 133.
30. *ASC* 1031.
31. *AT* 1061.
32. Edmonds 2019, 68; Ditchburn and Hudson 2015, 396. On Manx coins of the eleventh century, see Bornholdt Collins 2015, 423–31.
33. Woolf 2007, 246.
34. Hudson 1992.
35. Edmonds, 2019, 68.
36. Clarkson 2014, 143.
37. Etchingham 2001, 182–3.
38. Crawford 1987, 76.
39. Woolf 2007, 244.
40. *AU* 1052.
41. McDonald 2019a, 29.
42. *AT* 1061.
43. *AT* 1064.
44. Etchingham 2001, 182; Duffy 2015, 15.
45. Downham 2007, 178.
46. Crawford 1987, 26.
47. Crawford 1987, 48.
48. Downham 2007, 178.
49. Downham 2007, 183.
50. Crawford 1987, 50.
51. Crawford 2015, 212.
52. Manx Chronicle, §21: *Eodem anno obit Godredus filius Sytric rex Manniae. Cui successit filius eius Fingal.*
53. Wilson 2008, 23: Maccus 'may be identified as a king of Man'.
54. Kinvig 1975, 78.
55. Forte, Oram and Pedersen 2005, 93–8.

56. Clarkson 2014, 148–9.
57. Wilson 2018, 121.

Chapter 8

1. On the battles of Fulford and Stamford Bridge, see DeVries 1999. On the Battle of Hastings, see Higham 2000.
2. *ASC* 1066.
3. *AU* 1073.
4. Duffy 2015, 16.
5. Manx Chronicle, §22.
6. Duffy 2002, 55–6; Hudson 2005, 170.
7. McDonald 2019a, 82–3.
8. *AU* 1087; Oram 2011, 32.
9. McDonald 2019a, 81.
10. Duffy 2015, 21.
11. McDonald 2019a, 82.
12. McDonald 2019a, 80.
13. Watt 1994, 109–10; Woolf 2015, 333 notes that either scenario is possible.
14. Crawford 1987, 82.
15. Kinvig 1975, 77.
16. Woolf 2015, 333.
17. Manx Chronicle: English translation in Broderick's edition of 1973, p. 48.
18. Woolf 2015, 333–4.
19. On the epithet 'Barelegs' (or 'Barefoot'), see Power 1986, 122.
20. This reconstruction of events was proposed by Sean Duffy (2015, 23–4).
21. Manx Chronicle, §26A.
22. *Morkinskinna*: English translation in Andersson and Gade 2000.
23. Manx Chronicle, §26.
24. McDonald 2019a, 89.
25. Power 2015, 33.
26. See McDonald 2019a, 91–4, for discussion.
27. Callow 1899, Chapter 5; Hudson 2015, 198. See also Parsons 2019, 277–8, for discussion.
28. *AU* 1115.
29. On the extent of the lordship of Galloway in this period, see Oram 2000.
30. On royal concubinage in Man and the Isles, see McDonald 2019, 239–42.
31. The source for Olaf's relationship with Ingibjorg Hakonardottir is the thirteenth-century Icelandic saga *Fagrskinna*. For a modern English translation of this text see Finlay 2003.
32. Manx Chronicle, §28.
33. Clarkson 2014, 153–4.
34. McDonald 2019a, 125. For a detailed study of the reasons behind Godred's journey to Norway, see Beuermann 2002.

35. Manx Chronicle, §39.
36. Davey 2015, 357.
37. Davey 2015, 356. In 1147, the Savignac Order was absorbed into the Cistercian Order. The Savignac monasteries, including Rushen Abbey, became daughter-houses of the Cistercian headquarters at Citeaux and were expected to abide by its rules. Not all Savignac monks welcomed the takeover and, at Furness, there was open dissent bordering on disobedience.
38. McDonald 2019a, 272–3.
39. Woolf 2015, 335.
40. Hudson 2015, 189.
41. Oram 2008, 182–5.
42. Woolf 2015, 335.
43. *Scotichronicon*, iii,154; Hudson 2015, 190.

Chapter 9

1. Manx Chronicle, §40.
2. McDonald 2019a, 125.
3. Oram 2011, 111–12.
4. McDonald 2015, 67–8. On Somerled's origins, see Woolf 2005. For a modern biography of Somerled, see Marsden 2008. A useful recent study is Ellis 2020.
5. On the identity of the 'sons of Máel Coluim', see Oram 2011, 112.
6. Manx Chronicle, §28; *Orkneyinga saga*, Chapter 100.
7. Manx Chronicle, §41; McDonald 2019a, 105.
8. Manx Chronicle, §44.
9. McDonald 2019a, 109.
10. In the year of his death, Somerled had tried to persuade Flaithbertach, abbot of Derry, to become abbot of Iona (*AU* 1164).
11. Manx Chronicle, §43.
12. Sellar 2000.
13. Martin 1987.
14. McDonald 2019a, 127.
15. Duffy 1992, 132.
16. Costain-Russell 2015, 82.
17. Martin 1987.
18. On John de Courcy, see Flanders 2015.
19. McDonald 2019a, 129.
20. Manx Chronicle, §48.
21. Davey 2015, 351.
22. Costain-Russell 2015, 88.
23. MacQuarrie 2015, 297–300.
24. McDonald 2019a, 133.
25. McDonald 2007b, 55.
26. Costain-Russell 2015, 90.

27. Manx Chronicle, §65A.
28. For the broader context of the conflict between de Courcy and the de Lacys, see Duffy 1995 and MacNeill 1996.
29. McDonald 2019a, 136.
30. Costain-Russell 2015, 91.
31. Oram 2011, 169.
32. *Boglunga sogur*: Anderson 1922, II, 381 for an English translation.
33. McDonald 2019a, 139; Beuermann 2008.
34. McDonald 2019a, 139–40.
35. McDonald 2019a, 140–1.
36. McDonald 2007a, 139–40 (gift of Carlingford); McDonald 2019a, 140 (release of captives).
37. McDonald 2019a, 142.

Chapter 10

1. Manx Chronicle, §67.
2. Manx Chronicle, §69.
3. McDonald 2019a, 146.
4. Manx Chronicle, §73: *et redacta est australis pars Manniae fere in solitudinem.*
5. Manx Chronicle, §74: *viri impii.*
6. McDonald 2019a, 149.
7. *Hákonar saga*, §166; Oram 2011, 192.
8. McDonald 2019a, 149–50.
9. *Hákonar saga*, §166.
10. Cowan 2015, 99.
11. McDonald 2019a, 151.
12. McDonald 2019a, 152.
13. Manx Chronicle, §77.
14. Cowan 2015, 101.
15. McDonald 2019a, 157.
16. Cowan 2015, 101.
17. Manx Chronicle, §83.
18. McDonald 2019a, 159.
19. Brown 2004, 80.
20. Johnsen 1969.
21. Cowan 2015, 103.
22. Manx Chronicle, §90.
23. Manx Chronicle, §92.
24. McDonald 2019a, 165.
25. Manx Chronicle, §85.
26. McDonald 2019a, 168.
27. Manx Chronicle, §94.
28. Manx Chronicle, §97.

29. McDonald 2019a, 163.
30. McDonald 2019a, 284.
31. McDonald 2019a, 169.
32. *Hákonar saga*, §314.
33. *Hákonar saga*, §317.
34. Cowan 1990, 118.
35. McDonald 2019a, 173.
36. McDonald 2019a, 175.
37. *Hákonar saga*, §354–5.
38. On the Battle of Largs see Alexander, Neighbour and Oram 2002.
39. McDonald 2019a, 181.
40. Cowan 2015, 111.
41. McDonald 2019a, 182.
42. McDonald 2019a, 182.
43. McDonald 2019a, 183.
44. Lustig 1979.
45. McDonald 2019a, 184.

Chapter 11

1. McNamee 2015, 122; McDonald 2019a, 296. The Furness chronicle mentioned here is actually a continuation, written by a monk of Furness Abbey, of *Historia Rerum Anglicarum* ('History of English Affairs') by the twelfth-century historian William of Newburgh.
2. McDonald 2019a, 297.
3. McDonald 2019b, 37.
4. Barrow 1990, 122.
5. Brown 2004, 165.
6. McNamee 2015, 125.
7. Brown 2004, 257; McDonald 2019a, 199.
8. McNamee 2015, 126.
9. McNamee 2015, 126.
10. On the Scottish Wars of Independence, see Brown 2004.
11. Camden's *Britannia* (1806, IV, 516) is the only source for Bek's mortgaging of Man from Simon Montacute, but the information may be authentic (McNamee 2015, 127–8). For Bek's career in general, see Fraser 1957.
12. McNamee 2015, 128.
13. McNamee 2015, 124–6.
14. McNamee 2015, 133; Simon Montacute was given a royal pardon in 1313.
15. McDonald 2019a, 301–2.
16. McDonald 2019a, 301.
17. McNamee 2015, 131.
18. McNamee 2015, 132.
19. McNamee 2015, 135.

20. Manx history from the end of the fourteenth century to the beginning of the fifteenth is discussed in Bennett 2015.
21. Moore 1901, 57.
22. Moore,1901, 62.
23. Kinvig 1975, 115.
24. On the Manx government of the twenty-first century and its relations with the United Kingdom, see Sharpe 2002.
25. Broderick 2004.
26. Kinvig 1975, 91.
27. Train 1845, I, iii.
28. Johnson 1811, 5.
29. Train 1845, I, iv.
30. The name 'King Orry's Grave' was apparently coined as a joke c.1840.
31. See Burrow 1997 on the archaeology.
32. Train 1845, I, 63–5.
33. Gardeła 2014, 33, 35–6.
34. Seen during a visit to the Manx Museum in September 2021.
35. Kermode 1884.
36. The Lonan churchyard cross is shown in the plate section of this book.
37. On the castles and abbey, see Davey and Johnson 2015.
38. Crawford 1987, 19.
39. Seen during a visit to the House of Manannan in September 2021. The venue is included in an informal and very useful 'Isle of Man Viking Trail' described in van Renterghem and Stoner 2014.
40. On the current relationship between Tynwald and the UK government, see Sharpe 2002. The 'millennium' year 1979 was chosen arbitrarily.
41. Davey 2002, 99.
42. Kinvig 1975, 12 n1.
43. Treens: Kinvig 1975, 14; Andersen 1983. On ouncelands, see Crawford 1987, 86–7. On the antiquity of Manx quarterlands, see Fletcher and Reilly 1988. The antiquity of the Isle of Man's territorial divisions is discussed by Gareth Williams (2015). Key aspects of the topic are concisely summarised by David Griffiths (2010, 61).
44. See the references cited in Chapter 6.
45. See also Thornton 2015, 549. On the modern revival of the Manx language, see Gawne 2002.
46. Steinforth 2018.
47. See also Lewis 2016, 235–6 on this point.
48. Hudson 2015, 206.
49. Hudson 2015, 197.
50. On the naval resources of the Crovan dynasty, see McDonald 2007b.
51. The words quoted here are from Hudson 2015, 190.

BIBLIOGRAPHY

Primary sources: editions and translations

AC *Annales Cambriae* (Welsh Annals). J. Morris (ed. and trans.) *Nennius: British History and the Welsh Annals* (Chichester, 1980)

ASC *Anglo Saxon Chronicle.* M.J. Swanton (ed.) *The Anglo-Saxon Chronicle* (London, 1996)

AT *Annals of Tigernach.* Online edition at CELT: the Corpus of Electronic Texts http://celt.ucc.ie/published/G100002/

AU *Annals of Ulster.* S. Mac Airt and Gearóid Mac Niocaill (eds and trans) *The Annals of Ulster* (Dublin, 1983)

Berchan's Prophecy B.T. Hudson (ed.) *The Prophecy of Berchan: Irish and Scottish High-Kings of the Early Middle Ages* (Westport, 1996)

Brut y Tywysogyon J. Williams ab Ithel (ed. and trans.) *Brut y Tywysogyon or the Chronicle of the Princes* (London, 1860). Selected English translations in A.O. Anderson (ed.) *Early Sources of Scottish History, AD 500 to 1286*, 2 vols (Edinburgh, 1922)

FAI *Fragmentary Annals of Ireland.* J. Radner (ed. and trans.) *The Fragmentary Annals of Ireland* (Dublin, 1978)

Hákonar saga Hákonarsonar G. Vigfusson (ed.) *Icelandic Sagas and Other Historical Documents Relating to the Settlements and Descents of the Northmen on the British Isles*. Vol. 4b – English translation by G.W. Dasent (London, 1894)

HE Bede, *Historia Ecclesiastica Gentis Anglorum*. J. McClure and R. Collins (eds) *Bede: The Ecclesiastical History of the English People* (Oxford, 1994)

Manx Chronicle. G. Broderick (ed. and trans.) *Chronicle of the Kings of Mann and the Isles.* Part 1 (Edinburgh, 1973)

Morkinskinna T.M. Andersson (ed.) and K.E. Gade (trans.) *Morkinskinna: The Earliest Icelandic Chronicle of the Norwegian Kings (1030–1157)* (New York, 2000)

Modern scholarship

Airne, C.W. (1949) *The Story of the Isle of Man.* Vol. 1 *The Earliest Time to 1406* (Southport)

Alexander, D., Neighbour, T. and Oram, R.D. (2002) 'Glorious Victory? The Battle of Largs, 2 October 1263', *History Scotland* 2 (2): 17–22

Anderson, A.O. (ed.) (1922) *Early Sources of Scottish History, AD 500 to 1286*, 2 vols (Edinburgh)

Andersen, P.S. (1983) 'To What Extent Did the Balley/Balla (Baile) Names in the Isle of Man Supplant Place-Names of Norse Origin?', pp. 147–68 in C. Fell et al. (eds) *The Viking Age in the Isle of Man* (London)

Andersson, T.M. (ed.) and K.E. Gade (trans.) (2000) *Morkinskinna: The Earliest Icelandic Chronicle of the Norwegian Kings (1030–1157)* (New York)

Bannerman, J. (1974) *Studies in the History of Dalriada* (Edinburgh)

Barrow, G.W.S. (1990) 'A Kingdom in Crisis: Scotland and the Maid of Norway', *Scottish Historical Review* 69: 120–41

Barrow, J. (2001) 'Chester's Earliest Regatta? Edgar's Dee-Rowing Revisited', *Early Medieval Europe* 10: 81–93

Bassett, S. (ed.) (1989) *The Origins of Anglo-Saxon Kingdoms* (Leicester)

Belchem, J. (ed.) (2001) *A New History of the Isle of Man.* Vol 5: *The Modern Period* (Liverpool)

Bennett, M.J. (2015) 'English Rule Confirmed: The Isle of Man, 1389–1406', pp. 170–84 in S. Duffy and H. Mytum (eds) *A New History of the Isle of Man.* Vol. 3: *The Medieval Period, 1000–1406* (Liverpool)

Bersu, G. and Wilson, D.M. (1966) *Three Viking Graves in the Isle of Man* (London)

Beuermann, I. (2002) *Man Amongst Kings and Bishops: What Was the Reason for Godred Olafsson's Journey to Norway in 1152/53?* (Oslo)

Beuermann, I (2008) 'King John's Attack on Man in 1210', *Northern Studies* 40: 23–50

Bornholdt Collins, K. (2015) 'Coinage', pp. 411–65 in S. Duffy and H. Mytum (eds) *A New History of the Isle of Man.* Vol. 3: *The Medieval Period, 1000–1406* (Liverpool)

Bourns, T.J.S. (2014) 'Mythological and Heroic Motifs in Manx Stone Sculpture', pp. 22–29 in L. Gardeła and C. Larrington (eds) *Viking Myths and Rituals on the Isle of Man* (Nottingham)

Breeze, A. (2008) 'Scéla Cano Meic Gartnáin, Fiachna son of Báitán and Bamburgh', *Scottish Studies* 24: 87–95

Broderick, G. (1973) *Chronicle of the Kings of Mann and the Isles.* Part 1 (Edinburgh)

Broderick, G. (2003) 'Tynwald: A Manx Cult-Site and Institution of Pre-Viking Origin?', *Cambrian Medieval Celtic Studies* 46: 55–94

Broderick, G. (2004) 'Under the "Three-Legged Swastika": Celtic Studies and the Celtic Revival in the Isle of Man in the Context of the National Socialist Idea', pp. 39–50 in J. Fischer, P. Ó Dochartaigh and H. Kelley-Holmes (eds) *Irish-German Studies: Yearbook of the Centre for Irish-German Studies, 2001/2002* (Trier)

Broderick, G. (2008) 'Pre-Scandinavian Place-Names in the Isle of Man', pp. 165–84 in O.J. Padel and D.N. Parsons (eds) *A Commodity of Good Names: Essays in Honour of Margaret Gelling* (Donington)

Broderick, G. (2010) 'A Grammar of Manx Place-Names', *Journal of Scottish Name Studies* 4: 1–42

Brøndsted, J. (1965) *The Vikings* (London)

Broun, D. (2001) 'Dál Riata', pp. 161–2 in M. Lynch (ed.) *The Oxford Companion to Scottish History* (Oxford)

Brown, M. (2004) *The Wars of Scotland, 1214–1371* (Edinburgh)

Burrow, S. (1997) *The Neolithic Culture of the Isle of Man: A Study of Sites and Pottery*. BAR British Series 263 (Oxford)

Byrne, F.J. (1973) *Irish Kings and High-Kings* (London)

Callow, E. (1899) *From King Orry to Queen Victoria: A Short and Concise History of the Isle of Man* (London)

Campbell, E. (2001) 'Were the Scots Irish?', *Antiquity* 75: 285–91

Chadwick, H.M. (1949) *Early Scotland* (Cambridge)

Chadwick, N.K. (1963) *Celtic Britain* (London)

Charles-Edwards, T.M. (2000) *Early Christian Ireland* (Cambridge)

Charles-Edwards, T.M. (ed.) (2006) *The Chronicle of Ireland* (Liverpool)

Charles-Edwards, T.M. (2013) *Wales and the Britons, 350–1064* (Oxford)

Chiverrell, R. (2002) 'The Changing Landscape of the Isle of Man', pp. 1–9 in P. Davey and D. Finlayson (eds) *Mannin Revisited: Twelve Essays on Manx Culture and Environment* (Edinburgh)

Chiverrell, R. and Thomas, G. (eds) (2006) *A New History of the Isle of Man. Vol 1: The Evolution of the Natural Landscape* (Liverpool)

Clague, M. (2021) *The Michael Crosses* (Kirk Michael)

Clarkson, T. (2010a) *The Picts: A History* (Edinburgh)

Clarkson, T. (2010b) *The Men of the North: The Britons of Southern Scotland* (Edinburgh)

Clarkson, T. (2012) *Columba: Pilgrim, Priest and Patron Saint* (Edinburgh)

Clarkson, T. (2014) *Strathclyde and the Anglo-Saxons in the Viking Age* (Edinburgh)

Clarkson, T. (2016) *Scotland's Merlin: A Medieval Legend and its Dark Age Origins* (Edinburgh)

Clarkson, T. (2018) *Æthelflæd: The Lady of the Mercians* (Edinburgh)

Corning, C. (2006) *The Celtic and Roman Traditions: Conflict and Consensus in the Early Medieval Church* (London)

Costain-Russell, R. (2015) 'The reigns of Guðröðr and Rögnvaldr, 1153–1229', pp. 79–96 in S. Duffy and H. Mytum (eds) *A New History of the Isle of Man.* Vol. 3: *The Medieval Period, 1000–1406* (Liverpool)

Cotter, J.M. (1977) *A Short History of St Sanctain's Church* (Santon)

Cowan, E.J. (1990) 'Norwegian Sunset – Scottish Dawn: Hakon IV and Alexander III', pp. 103–31 in N. Reid (ed.) *Scotland in the Reign of Alexander III, 1249–1286* (Edinburgh)

Cowan, E.J. (2015) 'The Last Kings of Man, 1229–1265', pp. 97–117 in S. Duffy and H. Mytum (eds) *A New History of the Isle of Man.* Vol. 3: *The Medieval Period, 1000–1406* (Liverpool)

Crawford, B.E. (1987) *Scandinavian Scotland* (Leicester)

Crawford, B.E. (2015) 'Man in the Norse World', pp 210–40 in S. Duffy and H. Mytum (eds) *A New History of the Isle of Man.* Vol. 3: *The Medieval Period, 1000–1406* (Liverpool)

Crawford, D.K.E. (2016) 'St Patrick and St Maughold: Saints' Dedications in the Isle of Man', *e-Keltoi: Journal of Interdisciplinary Celtic Studies* 8, Article 4. https://dc.uwm.edu/ekeltoi/vol8/iss1/4

Crellin, R. (2019) 'The Emergence of a Bronze Age on the Isle of Man', pp. 13–34 in D. Brandherm (ed.) *Aspects of the Bronze Age in the Atlantic Archipelago and Beyond: Proceedings from the Belfast Bronze Age Forum, 9–10 November 2013* (Hagen)

Cubbon, A.M. (1977) *The Art of the Manx Crosses*, 2nd edn (Douglas)

Cubbon, A.M. (1982) 'The Early Church in the Isle of Man', pp. 257–82 in S.M. Pearce (ed.) *The Early Church in Western Britain and Ireland.* BAR British Series 102 (Oxford)

Cubbon, A.M. (1983) 'The Archaeology of the Vikings in the Isle of Man', pp. 13–26 in C. Fell et al. (eds) *The Viking Age in the Isle of Man* (London)

Cumming, J.G. (1857) *The Runic and Other Monumental Remnants of the Isle of Man* (London)

Cunliffe, B. (2003) *The Celts: A Very Short Introduction* (Oxford)

Cunliffe, B. (2005) *Iron Age Communities in Britain* (London)

Davey, P. (ed.) (1978) *Man and Environment in the Isle of Man,* 2 vols. BAR British Series 54 (Oxford)

Davey, P. (2002) 'At the Crossroads of Power and Cultural Influence: Manx Archaeology in the High Middle Ages', pp. 81–105 in P. Davey and D. Finlayson (eds) *Mannin Revisited: Twelve Essays on Manx Culture and Environment* (Edinburgh)

Davey, P. (2015) 'Medieval Monasticism and the Isle of Man, c. 1130–1540', pp. 349–76 in S. Duffy and H. Mytum (eds) *A New History of the Isle of Man.* Vol. 3: *The Medieval Period, 1000–1406* (Liverpool)

Davey, P. and Johnson, A.C.C. (2015) 'Medieval Archaeology and Architecture', pp. 484–545 in S. Duffy and H. Mytum (eds) *A New History of the Isle of Man.* Vol. 3: *The Medieval Period, 1000–1406* (Liverpool)

Davidson, M.R. (2001) 'The (Non-)Submission of the Northern Kings in 920', pp. 200–11 in N.J. Higham and D.H. Hill (eds) *Edward the Elder, 899–924* (London)

Davies, S. (2007) *The Mabinogion* (Oxford)

Davies, W. (1992) 'The Myth of the Celtic Church', pp. 12–21 in N. Edwards and A. Lane (eds) *The Early Church in Wales and the West: Recent Work in Early Christian Archaeology, History and Place-Names* (Oxford)

DeVries, K. (1999) *The Norwegian Invasion of England in 1066* (Woodbridge)

Ditchburn, D. and Hudson, B.T. (2015) 'Economy and Trade in Medieval Man', pp. 377–410 in S. Duffy and H. Mytum (eds) *A New History of the Isle of Man.* Vol. 3: *The Medieval Period, 1000–1406* (Liverpool)

Downham, C. (2007) *Viking Kings of Britain and Ireland: The Dynasty of Ivarr to AD 1014* (Edinburgh)

Downham, C. (2008) 'Tomrar's Death at Port Manonn and a Possible Longphort Site in Ireland', *Ainm* 9: 57–64

Downham, C. (2009) '"Hiberno-Norwegians" and "Anglo-Danes": Anachronistic Ethnicities in Viking Age England', *Medieval Scandinavia* 19: 139–69

Duffy, S. (1992) 'Irishmen and Islesmen in the Kingdoms of Dublin and Man 1052–1171', *Ériu* 43: 92–133

Duffy, S. (1995) 'The First Ulster Plantation: John de Courcy and the Men of Cumbria', pp. 1–28 in T.B. Barry, R. Frame and K. Simms (eds) *Colony and Frontier in Medieval Ireland: Essays Presented to J.F. Lydon* (London)

Duffy, S. (2002) 'Emerging from the Mist: Ireland and Man in the Eleventh Century', pp. 53–83 in P. Davey and D. Finlayson (eds) *Mannin Revisited: Twelve Essays on Manx Culture and Environment* (Edinburgh)

Duffy, S. (2005) *Medieval Ireland: An Encyclopedia* (London)

Duffy, S. (2013) *Brian Boru and the Battle of Clontarf* (Dublin)

Duffy, S. (2015) 'Man and the Irish Sea World in the Eleventh Century', pp. 9–26 in S. Duffy and H. Mytum (eds) *A New History of the Isle of Man. Vol. 3: The Medieval Period, 1000–1406* (Liverpool)

Dugdale, D.S. (1998) *Manx Church Origins* (Felinfach)

Dumville, D.N. (1989) 'The Tribal Hidage: An Introduction to its Texts and their History', pp. 225–30 in S. Bassett (ed.) *The Origins of Anglo-Saxon Kingdoms* (Leicester)

Dumville, D.N. et al. (eds) (1993) *St Patrick, AD 493–1993* (Woodbridge)

Dumville, D.N. (1997) *The Churches of North Britain in the First Viking Age* (Whithorn)

Dumville, D.N. (2004) 'Old Dubliners and New Dubliners in Ireland and Britain: A Viking-Age Story', *Medieval Dublin* 6: 78–93

Edmonds, F. (2019) *Gaelic Influence in the Northumbrian Kingdom: The Golden Age and the Viking Age* (Woodbridge)

Ellis, C. (2020) 'Impressions of a Twelfth-Century Maritime Ruler – Somerled: Viking Warrior, Clan Chieftain or Traitor to the Scottish King?', *Northern Studies* 51: 1–14

Esmonde-Cleary, S. (1989) *The Ending of Roman Britain* (London)

Etchingham, C. (2001) 'North Wales, Ireland and the Isles: The Insular Viking Zone', *Peritia* 15: 145–87

Evans, N. (2010) *The Present and the Past in Medieval Irish Chronicles* (Woodbridge)

Fell, C., Foote, P., Graham-Campbell, J. and Thomson, R. (eds) (1983) *The Viking Age in the Isle of Man* (London)

Fellows-Jensen, G. (1983) 'Scandinavian Settlement in the Isle of Man and Northwest England: The Place-Name Evidence', pp. 37–52 in C. Fell et al. (eds) *The Viking Age in the Isle of Man* (London)

Fellows-Jensen, G. (2001) 'The Mystery of the *by*-names in Man', *Nomina* 24: 33–46

Fellows-Jensen, G. (2015) 'The Manx Place-Name Evidence', pp. 257–80 in S. Duffy and H. Mytum (eds) *A New History of the Isle of Man. Vol. 3: The Medieval Period, 1000–1406* (Liverpool)

Finlay, A. (2003) *Fagrskinna: A Catalogue of the Kings of Norway* (Leiden)

Fitzpatrick, A.P. (1996) 'Celtic Iron Age Europe: The Theoretical Basis', pp. 238–55 in P. Graves-Brown, S. Jones and C. Gamble (eds) *Cultural Identity and Archaeology* (London)

Flanders, S. (2015) *John de Courcy, Prince of Ulster* (Newtownards)

Fletcher, M. and Reilly, P. (1988) 'Viking Settlers in the Isle of Man: Some Simulation Experiments', pp. 95–117 in C.N.L. Ruggles and S.P.Q. Rahtz (eds) *Computers and Quantitative Methods in Archaeology, 1987*. BAR International Series 393 (Oxford)

Forte, A., Oram, R.D. and Pedersen, F. (2005) *Viking Empires* (Cambridge)

Fraser, C.M. (1957) *A History of Antony Bek, Bishop of Durham 1283–1311* (Oxford)

Fraser, J.E. (2005) 'Strangers on the Clyde: Cenél Comgaill, Clyde Rock and the Bishops of Kingarth', *Innes Review* 56: 102–20

Fraser, J.E. (2009) *From Caledonia to Pictland: Scotland to 795* (Edinburgh)

Freeman, P. (2001) *Ireland in the Classical World* (Austin)

Freke, D. (1995) *The Peel Castle Dig* (Douglas)

Freke, D. (ed.) (2002) *Excavations on St Patrick's Isle, Peel, Isle of Man, 1982–88: Prehistoric, Viking, Medieval and Later* (Liverpool)

Gardeła, L. (2014) 'Viking Death Rituals on the Isle of Man', pp. 30–7 in L. Gardeła and C. Larrington (eds) *Viking Myths and Rituals on the Isle of Man* (Nottingham)

Gawne, P. (2002) 'Securing the Future for Manx Gaelic', pp. 173–83 in P. Davey and D. Finlayson (eds) *Mannin Revisited: Twelve Essays on Manx Culture and Environment* (Edinburgh)

Gelling, M. (1970–1) 'The Place-Names of the Isle of Man', *Journal of the Manx Museum* 7: 130–9, 168–75.

Gelling, M. (1978) 'Norse and Gaelic in Medieval Man', pp. 251–64 in P. Davey (ed.) *Man and Environment in the Isle of Man*. Vol. 2. BAR British Series 54 (Oxford)

Gelling, M. (1991) 'The Place-Names of the Isle of Man', pp. 141–55 in P.S. Ureland and G. Broderick (eds) *Language Contact in the British Isles* (Tübingen)

Gelling, P. (1977) 'Celtic Continuity in the Isle of Man', pp. 77–82 in L. Laing (ed.) *Studies in Celtic Survival*. BAR British Series 37 (Oxford)

Goodwins, S. (2017) *A Brief History of the Isle of Man*. 2nd edn (Maughold)

Goodwins, S. (2020) *Cross Purposes: An Introduction to Mediaeval Manx Crosses* (Maughold)

Graham-Campbell, J. (1998) 'The Early Viking Age in the Irish Sea Area', pp. 104–30 in H.B. Clarke et al. (eds) *Ireland and Scandinavia in the Early Viking Age* (Dublin)

Graham-Campbell, J. and Batey, C.E. (1998) *Vikings in Scotland: An Archaeological Survey* (Edinburgh)

Gregory, D. (1881) *The History of the Western Highlands and Isles of Scotland, 1493–1625* (London)

Griffiths, D. (2010) *Vikings of the Irish Sea: Conflict and Assimilation, AD 790–1050* (Stroud)

Hadley, D. and Richards, J. (2021) *The Viking Great Army and the Making of England* (London)

Heffernan, T.J. (1992) *Sacred Biography: Saints and Their Biographers in the Middle Ages* (Oxford)

Hemer, K. et al. (2014) 'No Man is an Island: Evidence of Pre-Viking Age Migration to the Isle of Man', *Journal of Archaeological Science* 52: 242–9

Higham, N.J. (1995) *An English Empire: Bede and the Early Anglo-Saxon Kings* (Manchester)

Higham, N.J. (2000) *The Death of Anglo-Saxon England* (Stroud)

Higham, N.J. (2015) *Ecgfrith: King of the Northumbrians, High-King of Britain* (Donington)

Hill, I. (2012) 'Joseph Train, Antiquarianism and the Statistical Accounts of Scotland and Man', *Transactions of the Dumfriesshire and Galloway Natural History and Antiquarian Society* 86: 175–96

Hills, C. (2003) *Origins of the English* (Bristol)

Horne, T. (2021) *A Viking Market Kingdom in Ireland and Britain: Trade Networks and the Importation of a Southern Scandinavian Silver Bullion Economy* (London)

Hudson, B.T. (1992) 'Cnut and the Scottish Kings', *English Historical Review* 107: 350–360

Hudson, B.T. (ed.) (1996) *The Prophecy of Berchan: Irish and Scottish High-Kings of the Early Middle Ages* (Westport)

Hudson, B.T. (2002) 'Brjáns Saga', *Medium Aevum* 71: 241–68

Hudson, B.T. (2005) *Viking Pirates and Christian Princes: Dynasty, Religion, and Empire in the North Atlantic* (Oxford)

Hudson, B.T. (2015) 'The Isle of Man in a European Context', pp. 187–209 in S. Duffy and H. Mytum (eds) *A New History of the Isle of Man*. Vol. 3: *The Medieval Period, 1000–1406* (Liverpool)

Hughes, K. (1973) 'The Welsh Latin Chronicles: *Annales Cambriae* and Related Texts', *Proceedings of the British Academy* 59: 233–58

Hughes, K. (1981) 'The Celtic Church: Is This a Valid Concept?', *Cambridge Medieval Celtic Studies* 1: 1–20

Jackson, K.H. (1953) *Language and History in Early Britain: A Chronological Survey of the Brittonic Languages, First to Twelfth Century AD* (Edinburgh)

Jackson, K.H. (ed.) (1969) *The Gododdin: The Oldest Scottish Poem* (Edinburgh)

James, S. (1999) *The Atlantic Celts: Ancient People or Invention?* (London)

Johnsen, A.O. (1969) 'The Payments from the Hebrides and Isle of Man to the Crown of Norway, 1153–1263: Annual Ferme or Feudal Casualty?', *Scottish Historical Review* 48: 18–34

Johnson, J.A. (1811) *A View of the Jurisprudence of the Isle of Man* (London)

Jones, B.L. (1990) 'Gwriad's Heritage: Links between Wales and the Isle of Man in the Early Middle Ages', *Transactions of the Honourable Society of Cymmrodorian* 39: 29–44

Kermode, P.M.C. (1884) 'The Monumental Crosses of Mann, with Suggestions as to Means to be Adopted for their Better Preservation', *The Manx Sun*, 16 December

Kermode, P.M.C. (1897) 'A Welsh Inscription on the Isle of Man', *Zeitschrift für Celtische Philologie* 1: 48–51

Kermode, P.M.C. (1930) 'Ship-burial in the Isle of Man', *Antiquaries Journal* 10: 126–33

Kermode, P.M.C. (1994) *Manx Crosses*, 2nd edn (Balgavies)

Kerrison, S. (2016) *Jurby and the Vikings* (Jurby)

Kinvig, R.H. (1975) *The Isle of Man: A Social, Cultural and Political History* (Liverpool)

Kirby, D.P. (1978) 'British Dynastic History in the Pre-Viking Period', *Bulletin of the Board of Celtic Studies* 27: 81–115

Kneen, J.J. (1927) *The Place Names of the Isle of Man* (Douglas)

Koch, J.T. (ed.) (1997) *The Gododdin of Aneirin: Text and Context from Dark-Age North Britain* (Cardiff)

Lewis, B.J. (2016) 'A New Synthesis of Early Medieval Brittonic History (Review of *Wales and the Britons 350–1064* by Thomas M. Charles-Edwards)', *Celtica* 28: 217–237

Livingston, M (ed.) (2011) *The Battle of Brunanburh: A Casebook* (Exeter)

Lustig, R.I. (1979) 'The Treaty of Perth: A Re-examination', *Scottish Historical Review* 58: 35–57

Mac Airt, S. and Mac Niocaill, G. (eds) (1983) *The Annals of Ulster* (Dublin)

McDonald, R. (2021) 'The Problem of Manx: Norse Linguistic Evidence for the Survival of Manx Gaelic in the Scandinavian Period', pp. 87–104 in D.H. Steinforth and C.C. Rozier (eds) *Britain and its Neighbours: Cultural Contacts and Exchanges in Medieval and Early Modern Europe* (London)

McDonald, R.A. (2007a) *Manx Kingship in its Irish Sea Setting* (Dublin)

McDonald, R.A. (2007b) 'Dealing Death from Man: Manx Sea Power in and around the Irish Sea, 1079–1265', pp. 45–76 in S. Duffy (ed.) *The World of the Galloglass* (Dublin)

McDonald, R.A. (2012) 'The Manx Sea-Kings and the Western Ocean: The Late Norse Isle of Man in its North Atlantic Context 1079–1265', pp.143–83 in B.T. Hudson (ed.) *Studies in the Medieval Atlantic* (London)

McDonald, R.A. (2015) 'Man, Somerled, and the Isles: The Rise of a New Dynasty, c.1100–64', pp. 58–78 in S. Duffy and H. Mytum (eds) *A New History of the Isle of Man.* Vol. 3*: The Medieval Period, 1000–1406* (Liverpool)

McDonald, R.A. (2019a) *The Sea Kings: The Late Norse Kingdoms of Man and the Isles c.1066–1275* (Edinburgh)

McDonald, R.A. (2019b) *Kings, Usurpers and Concubines in the Chronicles of the Kings of Man and the Isles* (London)

McMahon, B. (2014) 'The Vikings: Myths and Misconceptions', pp. 12–15 in L. Gardeła and C. Larrington (eds) *Viking Myths and Rituals on the Isle of Man* (Nottingham)

McNamee, C. (2015) 'The Isle of Man Under Scottish Rule, 1266–1333', pp.118–50 in S. Duffy and H. Mytum (eds) *A New History of the Isle of Man.* Vol. 3: *The Medieval Period, 1000–1406* (Liverpool)

MacNeill, T.E. (1996) *Anglo-Norman Ulster: The History and Archaeology of an Irish Barony 1177–1400* (Edinburgh)

Mac Niocaill, G. (1972) *Ireland Before the Vikings* (Dublin)

Macquarrie, A. (1997) *The Saints of Scotland: Essays in Scottish Church History, AD 450–1093* (Edinburgh)

MacQuarrie, C.W. (2015) 'The Isle of Man in Medieval Gaelic Literature', pp. 281–304 in S. Duffy and H. Mytum (eds) *A New History of the Isle of Man.* Vol. 3: *The Medieval Period, 1000–1406* (Liverpool)

MacQueen, J. and MacQueen, W. (eds) (1989) *Scotichronicon* (Aberdeen)

McSparron, C. and Williams, B. (2011) '… And They Won Land Among the Picts by Friendly Treaty or the Sword', *Proceedings of the Society of Antiquaries of Scotland,* 141: 145–58

Margeson, S. (1983) 'On the Iconography of the Manx Crosses', pp. 95–106 in C. Fell et al. (eds) *The Viking Age in the Isle of Man* (London)

Marsden, J. (2008) *Somerled and the Emergence of Gaelic Scotland* (Edinburgh)

Martin, F.X. (1987) 'Diarmait mac Murchada and the Coming of the Anglo-Normans', pp. 43–66 in A, Cosgrove (ed.) *Medieval Ireland, 1169–1534* (Oxford)

Megaw, B. (1950) 'The Monastery of St. Maughold', *Proceedings of the Isle of Man Natural History and Antiquarian Society* 5: 169–80

Megaw, B. (1976) 'Norseman and Native in the Kingdom of the Isles', *Scottish Studies* 20: 19–20

Miller, M. (1980) 'Hiberni Reversuri', *Proceedings of the Society of Antiquaries of Scotland* 110: 305–27

Moffat, A. (2002) *The Sea Kingdoms: The History of Celtic Britain and Ireland* (Edinburgh)

Moore. A.W. (1891) *Folk-Lore of the Isle of Man* (Douglas)

Moore, A.W. (1895) 'Further Notes on Manx Folklore', *The Antiquary* 31: 38–43

Moore, A.W. (1900) *History of the Isle of Man*, 2 vols. (London)

Moore, A.W. (1901) *The Story of the Isle of Man: An Historical Reader for Manx Schools* (London)

Morrison, S. (1911) *Manx Fairy Tales* (London)

Muhr, K. (2002) 'Manx Place-Names: An Ulster View', pp. 37–52 in P. Davey and D. Finlayson (eds) *Mannin Revisited: Twelve Essays on Manx Culture and Environment* (Edinburgh)

Mytum, H. (2015) 'Preface', p.vii in S. Duffy and H. Mytum (eds) *A New History of the Isle of Man. Vol. 3: The Medieval Period, 1000–1406* (Liverpool)

Ó Corráin, D. (1998) 'The Vikings in Scotland and Ireland in the Ninth Century', *Peritia* 12: 296–339

Ó Corráin, D. (2017) 'Orosius, Ireland and Christianity', *Peritia* 28: 113–34

Ó Cróinín, D. (1995) *Early Medieval Ireland, 400–1200* (London)

O'Rahilly, T.F. (1946) *Early Irish History and Mythology* (Dublin)

Oram, R.D. (2000) *The Lordship of Galloway* (Edinburgh)

Oram, R.D. (2008) *David I: The King Who Made Scotland* (Stroud)

Oram, R.D. (2011) *Domination and Lordship: Scotland, 1070–1230* (Edinburgh)

Page, R.I. (1983) 'The Manx Rune-Stones', pp. 133–46 in C. Fell et al. (eds) *The Viking Age in the Isle of Man* (London)

Pálsson, H. and Edwards, P. (1981) *Orkneyinga Saga: The History of the Earls of Orkney* (London)

Parsons, S.T. (2019) 'The Inhabitants of the British Isles on the First Crusade: Medieval Perceptions and the Invention of a Pan-Angevin Crusading Heritage', *English Historical Review* 134: 273–301

Patterson, J. (1857) *Memoir of Joseph Train, the Antiquarian Correspondent of Sir Walter Scott* (Glasgow)

Power, R. (1985) 'Magnus Barelegs' Expedition to the West', *Scottish Historical Review* 73: 107–32

Power, R. (2015) 'The Isle of Man and the Kings of Norway: Magnus Barelegs and After', pp. 27–57 in S. Duffy and H. Mytum (eds) *A New History of the Isle of Man. Vol. 3: The Medieval Period, 1000–1406* (Liverpool)

Radford, C.A.R. (1949) 'Excavations at Whithorn', *Transactions of the Dumfriesshire and Galloway Natural History and Antiquarian Society* 27: 87–126

Radner, J.N. (ed. and trans.) (1978) *The Fragmentary Annals of Ireland* (Dublin)

Rhys, J. (1897) 'A Note on Guriat', *Zeitschrift für Celtische Philologie* 1: 52–3

Rumble, A. (ed.) (1994) *The Reign of Cnut: King of England, Denmark and Norway* (London)

Sellar, W.D.H. (2000) 'Hebridean Sea-Kings: The Successors of Somerled', pp. 187–218 in E.J. Cowan and R.A. McDonald (eds) *Alba: Celtic Scotland in the Medieval Era* (East Linton)

Sharpe, S. (2002) 'The Isle of Man – In the British Isles but Not Ruled by Britain', pp. 161–72 in P. Davey and D. Finlayson (eds) *Mannin Revisited: Twelve Essays on Manx Culture and Environment* (Edinburgh)

Shaw, R. (2016) 'Bede's Sources for his References to "Hides" in the *Ecclesiastical History and the History of the Abbots*', *Historical Research* 89: 412–34

Shaw, R.C. (1964) *Post-Roman Carlisle and the Kingdoms of the North West* (Preston)

Shetelig, H. (1945) 'The Viking Graves in Great Britain and Northern Ireland', *Acta Archaeologica* 16: 1–55

Sims-Williams, P. (1994–95) 'Historical Need and Literary Narrative: A Caveat from Ninth-Century Wales', *Welsh History Review* 17: 1–40

Sims-Williams, P. (2003) *The Celtic Inscriptions of Britain: Phonology and Chronology, c.400–1200* (Oxford)

Sims-Williams, P. (2010) *Irish Influence on Medieval Welsh Literature* (Oxford)

Skene, W.F. (ed.) (1872) *John of Fordun's Chronicle of the Scottish Nation*, 2 vols (Edinburgh)

Smyth, A.P. (1984) *Warlords and Holy Men: Scotland, AD 80–1000* (London)

Spaan, D.B. (1965) 'The Place of Manannan mac Lir in Irish Mythology', *Folklore* 76: 176–95

Steinforth, D. (2015) 'Early Vikings in the Isle of Man: Old Paradigms and New Perspectives', *Viking and Medieval Scandinavia* 11: 203–29

Steinforth, D. (2018) 'That Stepping-Stone in the Middle of the Irish Sea: The Dublin Vikings and the Isle of Man in the Late Ninth Century', *Journal of Irish Archaeology* 27: 81–97

Steinforth, D. (2020) 'Whence and Whither, Óláfr? A Short Conjecture about the Location of Laithlind', *Northern Studies* 51: 15–33

Steinforth, D. (2021a) *Thorvald's Cross: The Viking-Age Cross-Slab Kirk Andreas MM 128 and its Iconography* (Oxford)

Steinforth, D. (2021b) 'Inis Phátraic, Dochonna, and the 798 Incident', *Peritia* 32: 241–59

Stevenson, J. (ed.) (1991) *A Medieval Chronicle of Scotland: The Chronicle of Melrose* (Felinfach) [reprint of 1856 edition]

Stoner, H. and Van Renterghem, A. (2014) 'Viking-Age Stones and Crosses', pp. 16–21 in L. Gardeła and C. Larrington (eds) *Viking Myths and Rituals on the Isle of Man* (Nottingham)

Swanton, M. (1996) *The Anglo-Saxon Chronicle* (New York)

Symonds, L. (2014) 'Medieval Migrations: Isotope Analysis of Early Medieval Skeletons on the Isle of Man', *Medieval Archaeology* 58: 1–20

Thomas, A.C. (1981) *Christianity in Roman Britain to AD 500* (London)

Thompson, W.P.L. (2008) *The New History of Orkney* (Edinburgh)

Thomson, R.L. (1961) 'The Manx Traditionary Ballad', *Études Celtiques* 9: 521–48

Thomson, R.L. (1983) 'The Continuity of Manx', pp. 169–74 in C. Fell et al. (eds) *The Viking Age in the Isle of Man* (London)

Thomson, R.L. (2015) 'Language in Man: Prehistory to Literacy', pp. 241–56 in S. Duffy and H. Mytum (eds) *A New History of the Isle of Man. Vol. 3: The Medieval Period, 1000–1406* (Liverpool)

Thomson, W.P.L. (2008) *The New History of Orkney* (Edinburgh)

Thornton, D. E. (1997) 'Hey, Macc! The Name Maccus, Tenth to Fifteenth Centuries', *Nomina* 20: 67–94

Thornton, D.E. (2001) 'Edgar and the Eight Kings, AD 973', *Early Medieval Europe* 10: 49–80

Thornton, D.E. (2006) *Kings, Chronologies and Genealogies: Studies in the Political History of Early Medieval Ireland and Wales* (Oxford)

Thornton, T. (2015) 'Conclusion – Man: The Medieval Legacy', pp. 546–53 in S. Duffy and H. Mytum (eds) *A New History of the Isle of Man. Vol. 3: The Medieval Period, 1000–1406* (Liverpool)

Toolis, R. and Bowles, C. (2016) *The Lost Dark Age Kingdom of Rheged: The Discovery of a Royal Stronghold at Trusty's Hill, Galloway* (Oxford)

Train, J. (1845) *An Historical and Statistical Account of the Isle of Man, from the Earliest Times to the Present Date*. 2 vols (Douglas)

Trench-Jellicoe, R. (1980) 'A New Chi-Rho from Maughold, Isle of Man', *Medieval Archaeology* 24: 202–3

Trench-Jellicoe, R. (2002) 'Manx Sculptured Monuments and the Early Viking Age', pp. 11–33 in P. Davey and D. Finlayson (eds) *Mannin Revisited: Twelve Essays on Manx Culture and Environment* (Edinburgh)

Van Renterghem, A. and Stoner, H. (2014) 'The Isle of Man Viking Trail', pp. 5–11 in L. Gardeła and C. Larrington (eds) *Viking Myths and Rituals on the Isle of Man* (Nottingham)

Wallace-Hadrill. J.M. (1988) *Bede's Ecclesiastical History of the English People: a Historical Commentary* (Oxford)

Watson, W.J. (1926) *The History of the Celtic Place Names of Scotland* (Edinburgh)

Watt, D.E.R. (1994) 'Bishops in the Isles Before 1203: Bibliography and Biographical Lists', *Innes Review* 45: 99–119

Weale, M.C. (2019) 'An Osteoarchaeological Assessment of Viking Burial on the Isle of Man', *Isle of Man Studies* 16: 1–9

Williams, A. (2003) *Æthelred the Unready: The Ill-Counselled King* (London)

Williams, I. (ed) (1975) *The Poems of Taliesin* (Dublin)

Williams, B. (2015) 'The Chronicles of the Kings of Man and the Isles', pp. 305–28 in S. Duffy and H. Mytum (eds) *A New History of the Isle of Man.* Vol 3: *The Medieval Period, 1000–1406* (Liverpool)

Williams, G. (2015) 'The System of Land Division and Assessment', pp. 466–83 in S. Duffy and H. Mytum (eds) *A New History of the Isle of Man.* Vol. 3: *The Medieval Period, 1000–1406* (Liverpool)

Williams, T. (2017) *Viking Britain: An Exploration* (London)

Wilson, D.M. (2008) *The Vikings in the Isle of Man* (Oxford)

Wilson, D.M. (2009) 'Stylistic Influences in Early Manx Sculpture', pp. 310–28 in J. Graham-Campbell and M. Ryan (eds) *Anglo-Saxon/Irish Relations Before the Vikings* (London)

Wilson, D.M. (2018) *Manx Crosses: A Handbook of Stone Sculpture 500–1040 in the Isle of Man* (Oxford)

Woolf, A. (2005) 'The Origins and Ancestry of Somerled: Gofraid Mac Fergusa and the Annals of the Four Masters', *Medieval Scandinavia* 15: 199–213

Woolf, A. (2007) *From Pictland to Alba 789–1070* (Edinburgh)

Woolf, A. (2015) 'The Early History of the Diocese of Sodor', pp. 329–48 in S. Duffy and H. Mytum (eds) *A New History of the Isle of Man.* Vol. 3: *The Medieval Period, 1000–1406* (Liverpool)

INDEX